BUILDING BRAND TRUST

BUILDING BRAND TRUST

Discovering the Advertising Insights Behind Great Brands

Josh McQueen
Mill Valley, California

Edited by Caroline M. Smith

Library of Congress Control Number:		2012907696
ISBN:	Hardcover	978-1-4771-0501-6
	Softcover	978-1-4771-0500-9
	Ebook	978-1-4771-0502-3

This book was printed in the United States of America.

Xlibris Corporation
1-888-795-4274
www.Xlibris.com
Orders@Xlibris.com
111253

CONTENTS

Contributors

I was and am a student of advertising. My BS and MS from the University of Illinois were in advertising. I maintained close relationships with professors throughout my career and would like to especially acknowledge Richard Nielsen, Simon Broadbent, Ken Miller, John Deighton, and Patrick Vargas. I continue to read professional peer-reviewed journals where advances in understanding continue to be shared.

I cannot begin to list the many clients who challenged the agency to produce ever-better advertising, who worked side by side in brand teams, and who funded the brand research that revealed so many insights.

I'm thankful for the long, late hours at creative review meetings, which gave voice to the most articulate in the agency about why some ideas and campaigns were superior and why the hundreds, which never went to the client, were not.

Research and planning are team processes. I worked in teams at the agency, with clients, with research suppliers, and with professional associations. My R&D partner was Carol Foley, who inspired and authored innovation.

My ability to focus on ideas at work flowed from the love I felt at home from Chris, Cary, Carl, and Jon.

This book is shared with Caroline Smith, who has edited every revision. The cover design is by Jim Hanon—screenwriter, filmmaker, art director, and friend.

About the Author

Josh McQueen

Josh McQueen resides in Mill Valley, California.

During his twenty-eight years with the Leo Burnett Company, Josh was research director in London, regional research director of Australia-Asia, and then worldwide head of research and planning until December 31, 2002.

Josh served on the privately held Leo Burnett Worldwide board. He was a member of the investment and technology committees of the board.

Josh received his BS magna cum laude and MS in communication from the University of Illinois at Urbana-Champaign.

Josh and his wife, Chris, have three children: Cary, Carl, and Jon. He enjoys hiking and exploring. Currently, Josh consults with nonprofits via Chay McQueen LLC.

Foreword

Building Lasting, Trusted Relationships through Brand Communication

Brands must meet internal and external mandates if they aspire to longevity and greatness. Internally, their commitment must be to quality and to a focused aspiration mission. Externally, their reputation for integrity must be communicated through a set of values and consistency in delivering the promises they make. If both of these exist, then the brand is worthy of the trust that underpins all great brands.

Your unconscious is able to instantly detect, skip, and disbelieve boring, unbelievable, irrelevant, and unfocused brand communication. You use this skill hundreds of times daily to filter the ads you choose to not consciously notice. Some manage to be relevant enough to notice: recognizing a brand you know, an issue that is of active concern, or communication that is enjoyable and rewarding to consume.

Those who advertise are focusing on a possible future. They want to reinforce your current behavior if you are using and buying their products. They would like you to try a brand again if you have lapsed or try it for the first time if you have never bought it before. They are seeking to build brand trust.

Brand trust is the storehouse of feelings about the brand's integrity and reputation, judgments about the brand's values, and whether it can be reliably trusted. Work by academic researchers in the past few years, which is reviewed in the "Notes to Chapter One," has demonstrated that building trust precedes changes in behavior. Trust, though, is never stable. It is constantly updated by our experience with a brand, our familiarity with its promises, and how our social networks recommend it—either through their actions or words.

This book is about the crucial role that advertising insights play in the ongoing relationship between people and brands.

Advertising

Most people seem to hold two seemingly conflicting views about advertising. On the one hand, many believe advertising is capable of hidden persuasion, but on the other hand, many also feel advertising "doesn't influence me." Both are true to a limited extent. Because you make decisions about advertising instantaneously, it feels hidden. This book slows down and surfaces the process and lets you see how it works.

The moment you are exposed to advertising, it ceases to be separate from your experience with other ads, your previous category and brand experience, your life experiences, and your unique persona. Advertising alone does not build trust; your ongoing interaction with the advertising and the brand is what builds and maintains trust.

This book shares a lifetime of advertising experience—over two thousand individual insights that either helped create, justify, sustain, change, or cast doubt on the advertising of a hundred different brands in several different countries. Reading it will help you be even more of an expert on advertising and help you appreciate the insights that fuel its effectiveness.

Advertising provides a sense that this brand shares my core values or not. It provides a sense of the brand's integrity: Is it making honest statements? Will it keep the promise that it is making in the ad? Advertising enhances the reputation you have of a brand, either counterarguing against the negative impression you might have or reaffirming the positive impression you have tentatively held. Importantly, advertising seeks to assure you that the brand's promise is supported by a good reason to believe. These four capabilities either support or undermine your trust in the brand, depending on its personal relevance to you.

Advertising insights are at the center of this process of building brand trust.

What Is an Insight Anyway?

An insight is an elucidating glimpse of the true nature of a situation. It is obvious and intuitive when brought to light although, until expressed, is assumed more than known. A creative once said, "It reminds you of something you didn't know you knew." Insights are important in advertising because they create the link between you and the brand—the relevance quota so vital to effective advertising. They tap into the human condition of your own life—the personal relevance that helps to create empathy and identification with a brand.

Advertising Insights

Advertising insights help close the gap between the brand and its intended buyer. Some find insights while shifting through information about people who buy the brand. Others watch the brand being used naturally in the home. Others observe, listen, and doodle, letting their unconscious guide their search. Most advertising insights come to light in what Leo Burnett called "a moment of fortunate lucidity." Once they emerge, the job of advertising is to dramatize, demonstrate, personify, and ultimately communicate those insights to current and potential users of the brand.

Caution in Applying Insights

The action of a hand reaching out to pull one brand off the shelf instead of another is remarkably alike around the world. These choices are made in huge supermarkets and small London shops, on frantic Hong Kong corners, and in the interactive dynamic world of Amazon.com. These choices have many more similarities than differences, yet those differences matter *a lot*. You may be surprised, but no successful worldwide campaign runs exactly the same ads everywhere, including famous ones like Kellogg's and McDonald's. Insights matter, but differences matter more; using insights requires dynamically applying them to specific situations with incredibly different contexts.

The Theory: Building Brand Trust

Chapter 1 will share insights about how insights are discovered. Chapter 2 will discuss how successful advertising works.

The Practice: In the context of Donald Gunn's "Master Formats of Advertising"

The next twelve chapters will separate advertising into highly recognizable formats that advertisers have used for decades and will continue to be used because they work. Donald Gunn, a creative at Leo Burnett and now a brilliant commentator on advertising, developed this typology of formats to help creative escape the tyranny of the usual: the repetitive use of stereotypical, category-bound advertising formats. He wanted to help the agency, and then the industry, escape having to have every car ad showing the new model hugging a curve in the glinting sunlight or having all hair-care ads showing newly shampooed hair bouncing off a turtleneck.

Advertising insights build brand trust only in the context of viewing the total ad. This book examines advertising insights in the context of each format and why some ads in each format worked brilliantly and why some failed.

Firsthand Knowledge of Examples, Examples, Examples

I was involved in the advertising process that created most of the examples in this book. This book examines these insights in the context of actual advertising campaigns that had actual results, good and bad. Many are captured in storyboards that show key frames and reproduce the words spoken in the ad.

All these examples were captured from available YouTube videos, and links are provided that will allow you to find and view the original ads for yourself. For those of you on smartphones and tablets reading this book, a swipe that gets you to the Internet will allow you to receive "a word from our sponsors."

Summary: Case History of Volkswagen Advertising Over Time

Most serious students of advertising are very aware of Volkswagen advertising. Ad Age awarded the "Think Small" Volkswagen ad, created by Doyle Dane Bernbach in 1959, as the number one campaign of all time. Number two was the Coca-Cola work on "The Pause That Refreshes" from D'Arcy in 1929; number three was "The Marlboro Man" from Leo Burnett in 1955.

Over the years, Volkswagen has been consistently awarded with more Cannes Gold Lions than any other company. During these fifty years, Volkswagen has grown from a niche carmaker to vie for the number one carmaker in the world, competing on equal footing with GM and Toyota.

As a maker of high-quality innovative cars for the masses, Volkswagen has also enabled its agencies to produce consistently fresh, insightful advertising.

To summarize the role of advertising insights in building brand trust, I have taken the themes developed in this book and used award-winning ads from Volkswagen over time and across international borders.

Chapter One

Identifying Advertising Insights That Build Brand Trust: Five Different Goals and Seven Fertile Areas to Examine

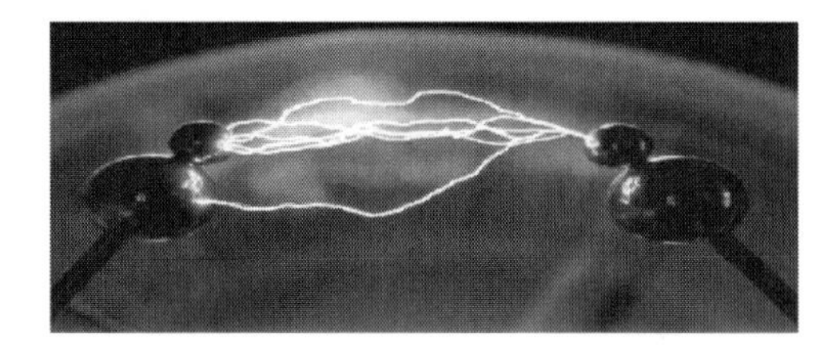

Brand Trust

In a talk to his Pure Oil client in 1956, Leo Burnett said, "Public confidence in a name becomes the margin between leadership and indifferent success" (*Communications of an Advertising Man*, 1961, p.111). The academic understanding of trust and brand trust is extensive and is summarized in the note that follows this chapter. Our thesis is that trust is at the root of the relationship that advertisers are attempting to build with people who might buy and use their brand. Implicit in trust is that the promises a brand makes in its communications need to be met. Advertising insights are, again in Leo's words, "simply a case of knowing the customer before you make the advertising."

Purposeful Insights: Connecting a Brand to Potential and Current Consumers

Advertising insights are like the yeast in bread making, the magic that transforms the ingredients of advertising: the words and visuals, the strategy and execution, the investment and media choices. Insights don't just happen; they are earnestly sought to underpin brand trust, and that brand trust enables a brand to achieve five different goals. Examination of hundreds of campaigns and brands across three different continents over thirty years reveals that insights can be found in seven fertile areas. This chapter shares those goals and areas, and this book will give you a behind-the-scenes appreciation of the purpose and power of advertising insights.

Like the electric arc, advertising insights connect a brand to a consumer. Like a proverb, they reflect the truth; they don't create the truth. Advertising insights do not surprise anyone; they make instant sense. The wonder is not that you identified the insight; the wonder is that no one ever revealed that connection. Great advertising builds brand trust by resting on truths, dramatizing the truth's essence, linking the brand to the truth, and cementing its connection through repetition.

Insights: Sometimes Unwelcome and Sometimes Cherished

Sometimes the insight is unwelcome. In 1976, a brand insight popped out of extensive analysis of sales data. Despite a decade of uninterrupted growth, Schlitz beer lacked a core franchise. Schlitz had achieved its growth only because it had become an acceptable brand that most people only purchased when it was on sale. Schlitz was almost never the most trusted beer in any single city. In Denver, Coors created the mystique of Rocky Mountain Water—Schlitz was second. In upstate New York, Schaefer Beer was the beer to have when you were having more than one—Schlitz was fourth. In St.

Louis, Budweiser established the depth and breadth of a brand leader as the king of beers—Schlitz was third. In Chicago and Milwaukee, its homeland as "the beer that made Milwaukee famous," Schlitz was number two to Old Style. As Schlitz produced its beer faster, it could sell it cheaper and sales grew. However, Schlitz insisted on constantly changing its advertising just as it constantly changed its beer-making process in the pursuit of more and more efficient production. Without having built on a foundation of brand trust through consistent quality and imagery, twenty years of building a billion-dollar franchise disappeared.

Sometimes an insight transforms a brand. In the midnineties, the agency discovered a huge group of Disney World lovers who trusted Disney to give them a truly magical, valued vacation experience. However, those with babies were waiting until their children could walk. Parents assumed their teens would not want to visit and delayed going themselves. Those with married children were waiting for their grandkids to get old enough. Up until then, the advertising had been about building the Disney World reputation or the next exciting ride. Disney World created a series of ads that laid out the magic of visiting the park for the different reasons Disney World lovers had in their current life stage and urged them to indulge now. Their trust in having a great experience now was rewarded; sales, which had been declining, reversed. A simple insight had been leveraged.

Advertising insights can help a brand build brand trust in five ways. Brands today pursue a mixture of these goals, but each goal dominates different eras of advertising.

1. Madison Avenue and the Fifties: Trusting the Brand to Satisfy "New" Needs

As *Gunsmoke*, *The Lawrence Welk Show*, and *The Honeymooners* premiered on TV, advertising was attempting to sell whole new categories of products to a generation back from the war, birthing a booming generation of kids, and moving into track houses in the suburbs. Unionized good-paying jobs were offered by companies that could hardly keep up with demand; transistor radios, detergents for modern washing machines, kitchen garbage bags, store-bought cookies, children's cereals, and mass airline travel were suddenly and widely available.

Advertising insights looked to the core benefits of the category. Who was going to take a radio with them? Kids who wanted to listen to AM pop stations. What was the torture test for clothes? White socks and white shirts. How do you sell a two-ply plastic bag that costs 50 percent more than one-ply when no bag had ever been needed before? You show the cheaper brand breaking on the kitchen floor. What do kids willingly eat fast in the morning? Sugar-frosted flakes. What would make flying less fearful? "The friendly skies." Why do cats go off their food and stop eating what you spoon out to them in the morning? Nature has taught them to seek a more nutritious variety, so they have evolved finicky tastes. In each case, any brand could have owned these category insights, but Sony, Tide, Glad, Kellogg's Frosted Flakes, United Airlines, and Morris the Finicky Cat for 9Lives successfully branded these insights as their own.

2. The Rise of Brand Management in the Sixties: Trusting What Made the Brand Different Would Make the Brand Better "for You"

Procter & Gamble found that they grew their total corporate share by having Tide willing to compete with Cheer. Other companies followed by launching multiple brands within a category. At the same time, GM found they could grow their corporate profitability by standardizing technology across a range of brands. Chevrolet, Pontiac, Oldsmobile, Buick, and Cadillac showrooms started unwrapping their new "outer coats" each September, and for the first time, GM passed Ford for leadership in US auto sales. Consumers felt good enough about brands to brag about nuances that advertising needed to describe; companies felt good enough about brands to invest millions, differentiating products that fulfilled the same overall set of category needs.

Advertising insights looked to find brand "differentials" that best suited each brand. They dug into their product features to discover those that were merely ingredients and those that could truly be perceived as benefits. They visualized intangible benefits, helped people see how they would benefit over time with their brand, and gave the brand the charisma of a consistent persona.

The image of sailors finding their Schlitz beer in harbors around the world gave beer-drinking laborers a reason to reach for the Gusto. Meanwhile, a suburban family man painted the bottom of his pool with the Budweiser label. Budweiser drinkers typically didn't own pools, but they appreciated the effort. Old Style drinkers didn't exactly know what the kräusening process did to beer, but it served as a great reason to defend their choice of tap beer at the local pub.

3. Expanding the Brand's Horizon: Trusting the Brand to Offer Appealing Varieties within the Category

As dominant brands emerged by owning the central category benefit ("The Friendly Skies") or through owning the best reason to believe ("The King of Beers"), brands sought to extend their reach by adding to their brand's stable all the other potential reasons to buy a brand within a category. A common set of magic words dominated advertising: new, now, finally, announcing, all-for-one low price! In fact, you could almost make the typical "bad" ad by combining all the magic words in one headline.

Crest no longer was just endorsed by the American Dental Association (because it had preempted the virtue of fluoride for children) but offered distinct versions that whitened teeth, prevented gum disease, gave you better breath, and a version that did all this in one toothpaste. Advertising insights came from figuring out how to combine two different benefits that seemed on the surface mutually exclusive: Miller Lite could be less filling and taste great because two ex-jocks representing those extremes memorably told you so. Southwest Airlines could be friendly and cheap because they flew one airplane, offered one class of airfare, effectively connected their regional cities through short hops, and hired only sociable attendants who laughed along with you as they handed out peanuts. Walmart could afford to offer the best prices not only because they mastered the logistics of the supply chain, but also because they could let the popular brand they carried fund the advertising that made them a great value at the price Walmart could charge.

4. Clarify the Source of Trust: The Essence of the Brand

Megabrands destroyed the host of little brands that surrounded them in their category. Box and discount stores replaced little shops on Main Street—the record store, the book nooks, and the corner cafés. Franchise specialty restaurants replaced the ubiquitous luncheonettes and diners of previous eras. Advertising insights could no longer simply highlight the single most powerful benefit of the brand.

Instead, the search was on for identifying a brand message and image that embraced both the breadth and depth of a brand. Instead of looking for the essence of the category, advertisers sought the essence of the brand. Instead of calculating current brand sales, they tried to estimate the future value of brand equity.

Failure to identify an essence of a brand led to confusion—GM found itself advertising Mr. Goodwrench and GM Visa cards (which gave you a discount on any GM car), sponsoring events as GM or Buick or Oldsmobile, and advertising the physically identical Regal and Cutlass, all with different ads from different ad agencies at the same time. Car buyers voted for a global brand image when they paid more for a Toyota Corolla FX16 than a Chevrolet Nova, even though the same workers made them on the same assembly line. Ford, Toyota, BMW, and Lexus meanwhile focused more advertising insights on their brand and thrived.

5. Trusting a Brand as It Expanded into New Categories

Technology brands earned their stripes in one area and then quickly asked their agencies to help them jump into new domains. Microsoft expanded from the operating system to the integrated software Office. Hewlett-Packard moved from great printers to average-priced computers, absorbing Compaq along the way. Apple progressed from computers to music to telephones.

Starbucks wanted to challenge McDonald's and vice versa, but both got healthier when they made sure they did not abandon the core of what had made them so successful. When offering diverse products on their site, online merchants and brands now express advertising insights by the nature of their landing page, the style of copy and visuals on the web, and the types of events corporations sponsor.

Five Different Goals: All Relevant to the Integrated Media Efforts of Today

The brands that communicate in all their various forms are all pursuing either one or a mix of these five goals: branding the central category benefit, differentiating each brand's reason to believe, expanding the brand into diverse subbranded products, sharing a single brand essence across all forms of the brand, and helping the brand expand across categories.

With these goals in mind, let's turn to where companies can look for advertising insights that will permit their brand to connect with potential customers.

Identify and Integrate Consumer Insights Up Front

The search for the insight to leverage must begin early in the process. The goal is to identify the electric arc between people and the brand and make it available to the creative team before they create the ad, to the brand team before they plan the marketing expenditures, to the media team before they fit together the media jigsaw puzzle, and before the entire budget is spent. Advertising needs to connect to the human condition, creating a sense of empathy and identification for the viewer, which helps them have confidence that the brand knows them and what they need and want, not just how people can help the brand.

Advertising agencies and brand teams use lots of different planning and research tools to unleash new insights. They examine how the product fits within different lifestyles. They separate people into different groups that buy brands in quite different ways: from those who loyally bought one brand or are loyal to a small subset of the brand, to those who will buy almost any recognizable brand if it is discounted, to those who always find the lowest price, whether it is a brand on sale or a generic brand. Advertisers talk in depth to one person, to pairs of friends, groups of neighbors, groups of people who had common brands in their repertoire, and/or groups of strangers who were always the first one in their circle to try new brands. They try to become naturalistic observers, visiting homes and retailers with open eyes, not preformed questions. They look at brands as if the brands are people; they try to describe the brand's emotions, their personalities, and their charisma. Agencies divide up people based on their behavior, whether they could be individually reached by different choices of media or by the benefits they seek in the category.

Often, after describing what they have learned, someone in the room doodling on a pad or musing overnight comes up with a way to describe what they've heard. It is usually this almost unconscious connection that becomes the insight.

These tools can be used in the seven areas to find insights, so deciding where to look provides the potential for vastly different kinds of insights. Pursuing a different one than a main competitor or examining several areas will increase the chances of reaching what Leo Burnett himself described as "one of those hot, unreachable stars."

If the insights that are revealed are true, they are never surprising but obvious when brought to light. In fact, when everyone is surprised by a newly revealed insight, after the meeting, each person should triple-check the facts or their guts to see if a mistake has been made. Great insights, like proverbs, make sense on their own, without "defense," without proof, when offered with a dose of humility and common sense.

Seven Fertile Areas for Finding Advertising Insights

1. Motivational Cues about the Category

Why do you do what you do? If only we were self-aware enough to be able to answer this question, the job of insight providers would be so much simpler. The problem is that the reasons most often cited are exactly the same for the users of every brand available, in almost the same rank order among the same percent of the users, suggesting either that brand choice is random, which it seldom is, or that there are additional reasons not immediately voiced.

There are two dynamic tensions to buy a brand that are tied to broad motivation. The first is the tension between the desire to change and to grow as a person versus the desire to preserve continuity and feel safe and secure. The second dynamic tension is whether to focus on my own needs and wants versus the alternative, which would be to focus on the needs and wants of others. Promises of achievement, adventure, and freedom speak to growth and personal pleasure. Promises of inspiration, good judgment, taste, and altruism speak to growth and an "other focus." Promises of increased responsibility, safety, and dependability speak to "other focus" and stability. Promises of indulgence, influence, or acceptance are about the self and stability.

Greeting cards have to recognize both sides of the self-selfless dynamic, even though it is tempting to focus on the selfless ones. Beer-drinking ads seem to run on a continuum; after a surfeit of ads showing cheery people drinking, ads featuring personal taste, satisfaction, and confidence become comparatively more effective. We buy reading material for personal growth, and yet we are attracted to the classic genres that feel comfortable (i.e., "the types of books I prefer to read"). At any one time, the resourceful professional has to make a call of where on the motivation continuum a brand should be positioned and focus insights that best match up people and the advertising they will see.

2. Current Brand Assets

Like a share's stock price, there are certain consumer measures of brand health that reveal not only a brand's current strength but also future potential. In 1976, Schlitz beer was the nation's second-leading beer. Schlitz sales looked good to investors; it had grown to the second-largest beer and had never had a three-month period in which sales had fallen. However, brand volatility revealed underlying weaknesses. Sales varied week to week more than competing brands within each outlet in which it was sold. Even in bars where it was the featured tap beer, it rarely sold more than other brands. It had grown because of geographic expansion into new markets, not because a core group of drinkers were becoming passionate about the brand. Schlitz invested in salesmen who sold into each of the different types of sales outlets: packaged liquor stores, bars, supermarkets, and restaurants. Most individuals who came into these outlets bought Schlitz only when it was on sale. The small regional breweries could not match those sales force investments and discounts offered to each different channel of distribution.

Detailed analysis of every brand in every market reveals strengths and weaknesses, risks and opportunities. Some brands depend on only a few core users who have quite different likes and dislikes than the average user. Talking to the average user without understanding their relative importance can mislead as easily as inform. Some brands are propped up by the way they are featured in particular stores. Shorn of those "out of the control of the brand" strengths, they are particularly vulnerable. Some brands appeal to their base for historical reasons and find few new users from those who are entering the category for the first time.

These types of insights fundamentally alter the message, tone, and frequency of exposure that an advertising campaign must have to succeed. Negative news is ugly, rarely desired by those internal to the company, and usually goes undetected in the sheer chaos of a typical brand's marketing.

3. Understand the Brand in Context

Nothing happens in a vacuum; we choose one brand instead of another, we use one category instead of another, and how we occupy our very limited time precludes us doing something else. Apple introduced its new computer in a famous ad called "1984." A lone blond figure dashes through the gray crowd and hurls a hammer through a "Big Brother" screen being watched by the mesmerized dull audience. Much of this ad was about the context of what was going to happen to the computer industry. Apple was correctly anticipating how personal computers would fundamentally change the world of not only business but also people and their interactions with their lives. Apple ran this ad only once and leveraged the buzz of that once-only showing for years. They projected their persona onto plastic and metal, whirling electrons, and preset software. They didn't focus on how the change would happen; it was enough at this moment to simply state the obvious well: "Big Brother" (either IBM then or Microsoft to come) was no longer in charge.

Ethnographic research developed in anthropology was applied to brands to understand context. It was similar to the Japanese corporate mandate to get out of their offices and into the homes and shops of their users. This mandate extended from the factory floor, to the product design team, to the chairman.

Naturalistic research was implemented by researchers who asked to be invited into the homes of people using the products under focus. They would silently observe their brand without telling the people beforehand which category was of interest, and certainly not which brand was sponsoring their visits. Unlike previous self-reported surveys, cereal was used throughout the day, not just in recipes, but also as snacks, midmorning cravings, and late-night raids. Chocolate was played with in the mouth; thicker chocolate was much more involving and fun and therefore satisfying. A detergent's ability to perform was found to be more a function of the materials that were used to apply them than the quantities listed on the bottle. Advertising became more real and insightful because the number of unanticipated context effects was understood.

I once explored the introduction of waffles into the UK market. When the product was placed into homes without any suggestion of its use, it was used with enthusiasm and truly liked. In the UK, an entirely different context caused more enthusiasm than an American marketer would have suspected. Mums bought waffles for immediate use, kept them in the refrigerator (not the freezer), popped them under the grill (not the toaster), and served baked beans on top to their hungry after-school children. They and their children loved them; crisper than crumpets, the dimples in the waffle captured sauce from the beans and made little mess. Despite these findings, the product was launched with pictures of syrup and breakfast morning products into the tiny freezer cases in the supermarket. They failed miserably. As I suggested earlier, some insights are cherished, and some are unwelcome.

4. User Imagery

When we see people using a brand in an ad, it can prompt two different questions from the viewer: Are these people like me? Are they someone I'd like to be? If the answer to the first is yes, then the advertising is held to a higher standard of believability, and if it passes, it can be a powerful mirror. If the characters are aspirational, then the role the product plays in their lives is internalized. Most advertising characters are neither; the actors become spokespeople, or characters in a story, or the audience for the brand.

Insights can be about what makes one group of people unique. Some differences are physical, like the obvious difference of gender that worked so well for Luvs Diapers. Luvs Diapers introduced diapers for girls and boys and grew from 2 percent of the market to 15 percent of the market in three months.

Some differences are psychological. Harley-Davidson transformed itself by being willing to take a clear niche of rebellion, ultra-masculinity, and freedom and thrive in a narrow space instead of trying to appeal to safety, quality, and mass appeal like Honda. Both are productive areas of the motorcycling world but are mutually exclusive.

Many other differences are sociological—subgroups that we can choose to identify with, either wholeheartedly or just when we put on a brand. Teenage culture is famous for brands that define the user as preppy or goth or cool, and the same teenager can be in different groups by moving from look to look.

The advertising insight is how, or even whether, to acknowledge each difference, to try to reach the commonalities that overlap between different groups, or to be a unique and inspirational difference between the groups. Lee and Levi's dominance as large brands of jeans were eroded by all the specific niches occupied by brands like Calvin Klein, Lucky, True Religion, Diesel, DC, and Rich & Skinny. Ultimately, they had to dive into the many different pools of potential buyers with subbrands that offered different looks, different images, and different advertising.

5. Brand Persona

When asked to describe a brand they particularly like, it is not long before people refer to these inanimate products as if they were people they know, using the same language they might use to describe the personality of a friend, a boss, or a famous celebrity. This insight is so well entrenched that almost all brand managers brief their agencies about the personality they want their brand to reflect.

The more difficult question for a brand is, should the brand adopt a common, attainable, easily recognized personality? Should it attempt to be iconic, aspirational, and complex? Or should it simply be an extroverted personality that is fun to be with for the moment? During the eighties, Budweiser did a fabulous job of capturing the persona of the average Joe. Michelob tried to be the upscale weekend "treat" by depicting aspirational men and women in suit coats and turtlenecks. Miller Lite, on the other hand, with its fun use of former sports professionals, tried neither to mirror their drinkers or inspire them but merely to entertain them with lighthearted banter in the mythical “fun bar.”

6. Brand Stretch

Whether a brand can stretch to include more varieties within a category into close-fit neighboring categories or into completely new-to-the-corporation categories is a critical insight before advertising for these brands is conceived.

A successful “within the category” example is Altoids. Altoids became a huge success behind a powerful advertising idea and print executions: “Curiously strong mints.” Without a huge television campaign imbuing the brand with many different qualities simultaneously, the earnest question of whether and how to expand was fraught with risk. At first, the insight used was simple: expand the original (1780) peppermint flavor to Wintergreen and Spearmint, still packed in tins, still using the same advertising format, letting the point-of-purchase appeal propel the brand. The next step was Cinnamon, not strictly a mint but easy to reproduce a “curiously intense” popular flavor. Next were the timeless flavors Ginger and Crème de Menthe, and the future is bright for more. Having established a breadth of product line, the stretch into minitins, heart-shaped tins, round tins, and family-sized tins were lower in risk and seemed to be successful.

Of course, eager companies try to define the category in the most expansive terms possible; the insight of what is too much is ultimately left to the consumer. Starbucks has expanded in every way possible. They see themselves as coffee, so they launch instant “you pour in the hot water” Via in grocery stores. They see themselves as a morning restaurant and so launch handheld grilled breakfast products to go with the drive-through express. Ultimately, Howard Schultz, on his return to Starbucks as chairman (replacing the grocery executive who served in between his tenure as CEO), once again turned the focus to the coffee-shop cachet that powered its successful growth.

Secret Deodorant explored jumping into other bathroom products for women but continued their success by expanding the form and potency of various new lines and scents of women's deodorants. Crayola successfully jumped into categories beyond crayons by keeping their focus on the art, creativity, age-safe, and appropriate products that their brand promised. Meanwhile, Nivea boldly took its brand of trusted and accessible skin crème from one core product to over three hundred, across fourteen different product categories from body care, to hair care, to sun care, to products for men and babies. The advertising insight involved visualizing fresh wellness and thus had an attractive core feature to promote.

Failures to stretch a brand abound. Bic unsuccessfully tried taking their small lighter shape and French heritage into a range of French spray perfumes. The advertising translation of "real French perfume" seems in retrospect to try too hard to stretch a point. Redhead Matches tried to expand into fireplace firelighters, but the image of an instant flash never translated to the steady flame needed in the line extension. Several beers have tried to market a women's beer—all, including Swan Gold in Australia, failed terribly. Women drink beer, but the need for a brand of their own exists only in the minds of brand managers.

The risks to the core brand are that current customers feel abandoned. Retailers are resistant to yet another "me too" product with no heritage in a new category. One line extension can succeed, and perhaps the next, and the maybe the third, but each weakens the parent brand, and they may all collapse if each does not strengthen the other.

Pillsbury introduced new dough product after new product but failed to get expanded refrigerated shelf space. Since each required the same refrigeration, retailers simply subdivided the space. Each new brand could meet its sales goals, yet all the other unsupported brands would slip back, and little new revenue would flow into corporate headquarters.

The advertising insight needed for each of these requires always using binoculars and not telescopes to peer into the brand's future. Only thinking about the success of the line extension limits the field of vision and invites failure. Keeping the vision wide enough to look for insights for the new brand form *and* evolving the insights for the core brand are both paramount.

7. Anticipating Change

Most brands are not content to listen to Doris Day's advice: "Que sera, sera, whatever will be, will be. The future's not ours to see, Que sera, sera."

The pace of change has been accelerating for a long time. Alvin Toffler celebrated this in his seminal book, *Future Shock* (1970). Kodak made photography a mass-market product one hundred years after its first use. The telephone took fifty years to get 70 percent market penetration. Radio took thirty-five years to do the same. After only six years, the transistor radio was a mass-market product thanks to Sony. Today, a new chip from Intel is lucky to have two years before the next chip does more for half the price. Advertising insights have to have some modicum of future vision, or in twenty-twenty hindsight, they will appear foolish.

The biggest challenge is to decide the appropriate length of time we are trying to forecast. Five-year plans can anticipate the size of the first grade classroom because the babies have already been born. But ten-year plans developed in 1980 did not predict the One-Child Policy of China, declining populations in Europe, the rapid decline of marriages among those under thirty, or the disappearance from the "actively seeking employment" of over thirty million Americans under the age of sixty-five.

Apple's success lies as much in their detailed anticipation of the future as with their innovative design. Sometimes their anticipation of change preceded public desire. Remember the Lisa or the Newton? However, more often, their commitment to the change ushered in the change (iTunes, iPod, and iPhone) that was multiplied as they were imitated by lower-priced products around the world in countries where they weren't even available.

The speed of change can make a good insight very bad. Oldsmobile had a steady stream of truly innovative new models ready to roll out across their six-car lineup over a six-year period. Starting with the top-end Aurora, they planned to introduce a new European BMW beater every year for the next six years. But GM wanted an image prepared to attract the young urban professionals who were buying BMW and Japanese car brands. GM officials had experience with how long they thought it took to change a brand's image, so they started as soon as the first model appeared. The agency was briefed and created the "Not Your Father's Oldsmobile" campaign. It succeeded, but too fast. People who otherwise preferred the imports streamed into showrooms in record numbers to look at the new cars, expecting to find a brand with a full range of import-beating alternatives but found the Trofeo next to the Oldsmobile '88 and tired Cutlass Supremes. They walked away, never to return. Meanwhile, the over-seventy market, which wanted to buy their comfortable garage filler, was sure Oldsmobile had abandoned them, so they stayed away. The result of the image change was dramatic—abysmal sales and a brand that was discontinued two years short of its hundredth anniversary.

Future's work is not to be confused with trend watching and trend following. Reading the pulse of New York and LA helps those in the flyover Midwest get ready for the next phase of music, clothes, and popular slang. Going to Milan and Paris helps the popular mass brands anticipate the next wave of color, length, and cut. Figuring out which celebrities are being followed by the paparazzi will help advertisers seem current when the voice-over behind their ads is recognized. However, these are not seeking future insights but merely trying to ride the top of a wave. Of course, most waves crash abruptly, as do most trends.

Identifying Advertising Insights

Clarity about the goal of the advertising will enhance the process of developing advertising insights. Clarifying the need the category can fulfill, or what the brand can best fulfill within the category, usually calls for different insights and quite different advertising. Building a dominant brand whose many variants cover the category, or cross category boundaries, needs clear intent, or the brand will lack substance and distinctiveness.

Advertising is best nurtured by having the insights available early. "Early" can be as the advertising is about to be created. "Earlier and better" would be as the brand was developed by the company and before launching brand extensions. Early is good; consistent tending and nurturing is vital.

Of course, where to seek the insights determines which ones will be found. The brand's health gives the earliest clues. Insights are the connective tissue between the brand and the consumer, so insights that flow from the essence of the brand and the nature of the target consumer are commonly sought.

Left unanswered is the bigger general question: how do advertising insights work to sell products? I'll turn to that question in the next chapter.

Notes to Chapter 1: The Academic Background of Brand Trust

Trust is a concept that spans many different disciplines of academic inquiry and thus is well researched. In psychology, trust is viewed as the essential need in therapeutic relationships that can help develop wellness (Laughton-Brown, 2010). Erickson saw that the development of trust in others, and ultimately in the self, comes from the infant-mother relationship and is the first social product of infancy (Erickson, 1950, p. 247). Those children who experienced predictable social contacts developed a sense of basic trust, whereas those who did not developed a sense of basic mistrust. The first group was far more likely to be optimists in adulthood while the second were more likely to be pessimists (Carver, 2005, p. 241).

In sociology, trust is nestled in the interrelationships of love, commitment, trust, and communication (Braiker & Kelley, 1979, p. 166). Organizational dynamics are often studied by the commitment of employees tied to their level of trust in management and company goals (Rodger, 2010, p. 85).

In law, trusts and trustees are essential fiduciary responsibilities in estates, marriages, and business incorporation (Ponet, 2011, p. 1252).

Political science has looked at trust in people and political institutions. In a cross-sectional study of sixty-seven countries, only 28% of adults felt that "most people could be trusted." In general, the young and the poor were less trusting than those over age fifty and in upper-income groups. The Scandinavian countries were highest in trust of "most people" at 65%; the United States was slightly above average at 36%; and southern hemisphere countries were the lowest with Brazil, Uganda, Peru, and South Africa in the single digits (Inglehart, et. al, 2002, p. 165).

Gallup has been monitoring trust for many years. Trust in newspapers and television news is under 25%, having not been higher than 37% and 46% respectively in the 1990s (www.gallup.co). Trust in specific political offices is somewhat higher: 66% trust the judicial branch, 49% trust the executive branch, and 36% trust the legislative branch—levels that are dramatically lower than the 1980s when all three numbers were between 60% and 70% (Gallup, September 24, 2010).

Brand trust has been used most often in business in discussions about brand loyalty. Larry Light used the phrase "trust mark" in his 1990s writings on brand equity and brand loyalty. He wrote, "With the loyalty of its customers, a brand is more than a trademark, it is a trust mark" (Light, 1994, 63).

This is not to be confused with Trustmark Banking and Financial Solutions Company, a $9.6 billion in assets, diversified financial services company established in 1889. Trustmark Corp., ironically, was sued in a number of class action suits on its insurance and banking actions in the midnineties and settled them in November 1996 (www.allbusiness, 2011).

Trust has been shown to be an antecedent of behavior in personal selling (Doney & Cannon, 1997), brand sponsorship (Finch, et. al, 2009), and in relationship marketing (Morgan & Hunt, 1994). It has shown itself to be able to be measured with reliable and stable scales (Delgado-Ballester, et. al, 2003). Particularly interesting was the brand sponsorship study of two treatments of sponsorship in four different markets in Canada.

For a major mobile phone company, sponsoring an event was shown to increase levels of trust and intent to sign up with the same company again. However, in the markets in which the sponsorship occurred, this same effect could not be detected among those who consciously recalled the mobile phone company's sponsorship of the event versus those who could not. Thus, their measure of brand trust predicted subsequent levels of increased retention, even though levels of correct sponsorship identification could not predict the subsequent change in behavior (Finch, et. al, p. 69).

The Finch study showed four measures were related to trust: reputation and past experience, integrity (brand honesty and keeping promises), reliability, and shared values (Finch, et. al, p. 66). This corresponds to the two broad dimensions scaled by Delgado-Ballester: brand reliability (reliability and integrity) and brand intentions (reputation and shared values) (Delgado-Ballester, et. al, p. 37).

Advertising has been shown to be able to enhance a product's perceived trustworthiness both in the absence of past experience (new products) and with brands with previous usage (lapsed brands) (Li & Miniard, 2006, p. 103). When compared, brand experience has the greatest impact on future brand trust with, in this order, advertising, word of mouth, and brand awareness having the next effects (Xingyan, et. al, 2010).

Since reliable scales have been developed and changes in trust have been consistently found to precede changes in behavior, the number of articles on trust is growing as an important marketing and advertising subject.

References

Alhabeeb, M. J. 2007. "On Consumer Trust and Product Loyalty." *International Journal of Consumer Studies* 31, 609-612.

Braiker, H. B. and H. H. Kelley. 1979. "Conflict in the Development of Close Relationships." In *Social Exchange in Developing Relationships*, edited by R. Burgess and T. L. Huston. New York: Academic Press. 135-168.

Brudvig, Susan. 2006. "The Relationship between Trust and Commitment: A Meta-analysis," *Society for Marketing Advances Proceedings*. 31-35.

Carver, Charles S. and Michael F. Scheier. 2005. "Optimism." In *Handbook of Positive Psychology*, edited by C. R. Snyder and Shane J. Lopez. Oxford University Press.

Delgado-Ballester, Elena; José-Luis Munuera-Aleman, and María Jesús Yagüe Guillén. 2008. "Development and Validation of a Brand Trust Scale. *International Journal of Market Research* 45 (1): 35-53.

Doney, Patricia M. and Joseph P. Cannon. 1997. "An Examination of the Nature of Trust in Buyer-Seller Relationships." *Journal of Marketing* 61 (April 1997): 35-51.

Erikson, E. 1950. *Childhood and Society*. New York: Norton.

Finch, David, Norm O'Reilly, Paul Varella, and Diane Wolf. 2009. "Return on Trust: An Empirical Study of the Role of Sponsorship in Stimulating Consumer Trust and Loyalty." *Journal of Sponsorship* 3 (December 2009): 61-72.

Gallup Polls. 2011. http://www.gallup.com/poll/142133/confidence-newspapers-news-remains-rarity.aspx.

Garbarino, Ellen, and Mark S. Johnson. 1999. "The Different Roles of Satisfaction, Trust, and Commitment in Customer Relationships." *Journal of Marketing* 63 (2): 70-87.

Inglehart, Basanez, Halman, & Díez-Medrano. 2004. *Human Beliefs and Values: A Cross-Cultural Sources Book Based on the 1999-2002 Values Surveys*. Mexico City, Mexico: Siglo XXI Editores.

Laughton-Brown, Helena. 2010. "Trust in the Therapeutic Relationship: Psychodynamic Contributions to Counseling Psychology Practice." *Counseling Psychology Review* 25 (2): 6-15.

Li, Fuan, and Paul W. Miniard. 2006. "On the Potential for Advertising to Facilitate Trust in the Advertised Brand." *Journal of Advertising* 35 (Winter): 101-112.

Light, Larry. 1994. "Brand Loyalty Marketing: Today's Marketing Mandate." *Editor and Publisher 12/120/94* 127 (50).

Moorman, Christine, Rohit Deshpandé, and Gerald Zaltman. 1993. "Factors Affecting Trust in Market Research Relationships." *Journal of Marketing* 57 (January 1993): 81-101.

Rodgers, Waymond. 2010. "Three Primary Trust Pathways Underlying Ethical Considerations." *Journal of Business Ethics* 91 (January 2010): 83-93.

Ponet, David L. 2010. "Fiduciary Law's Lessons for Deliberative Democracy." *Boston University Law Review* 91 (May 2010): 1249-1261.

"Trustmark National Banks Makes Announcement. http://www.allbusiness.com/legal/legal-services-litigation/7290779-1.html. December 4, 2011.

Xingyan, Wang, Fuan Li, and Yu Wei. 2010. "How Do They Really Help? An Empirical Study of the Role of Different Information Sources in Building Brand Trust. *Journal of Global Marketing* 23. 243-252.

Chapter Two

Why Insights Have Built Trust Over Time

Thousands of Thoughtful Proofs That Advertising Works

Since 1980, the IPA (Institute of the Practitioners of Advertising) in the UK has published hundreds of case histories of advertising campaigns that worked. In each of the eighteen volumes, a jury of eminent business leaders judged case histories written by advertisers and their respective agencies. Half the points awarded were based on the excellence of the advertising and its impact, the other half on the sophistication of their ability to tease out the impact of advertising from the host of other effects that might explain the success of the brand. "The Effie Worldwide" made similar attempts to recognize advertising that works for North America, Europe, the Middle East, North Africa, and South America.

Advertising works because its cumulative impact interacts with product performance to create a relationship between a person and a brand that is enhanced by continuous communication. The reasons advertising works are certainly not based on naive trust; we expect advertising to be an advocate for the brand, telling only one side of the story. It is not even based on our ability to completely trust what an ad says. There are a host of words commonly used in advertising that are mere puffery. The law expects that when advertisers use these words (*best*, *most loved*, *ultimate*, *favorite*), people are not misled that the advertiser could prove these claims. In an extreme example, the FCC, in the name of protecting the freedom of political speech, explicitly exempts US political advertising campaigns from a need to prove, or even make provable, claims made against their political rivals.

Yet despite being a biased source of information, people seek out ads. We click on ads on the Internet, open direct mail that is clearly promoting a brand or cause, request catalogs, save and refer to the Yellow Pages, and call 1-800 numbers to request more information. We buy magazines that have more pages of advertising than articles and spend as much time with those ads as the articles. Year after year, polls reveal that advertisements run during the Super Bowl telecast were as well-watched and often valued as highly as the game itself.

The Relationship Model: Trust Enhances Willingness to Buy and Rewards by Being Trustworthy

Brand trust is always involved in purchase decisions. We can easily retrieve how we feel about a brand. These expectations have been influenced by all our experience with the brand—using it, seeing others use it, reading about it, seeing ads in a variety of media, online contacts, seeing it in the store, and the context of where it is available. As we are exposed to advertising, we are either involved enough to notice the ads or not, and the advertising's contents are perceived through the filter of our trust of the brand. Our level of trust in the brand is then either built upon or eroded. So the critical question is not how advertising influences purchasing but more precisely how advertising is incorporated into our relationship with that brand.

This model is a flow model: The model suggests that advertising is a dynamic part of the fluid relationship we have with a brand. To link a category to a need, it starts with a need that people feel, or could feel, is true. To link a brand to a particular benefit, it takes what we can see or feel about a brand in use and frames that for a brand. To introduce a new brand extension, advertising builds upon the strengths or image of the core brand. Importantly, advertising does this in a very visible way without coercion. The depth of trust potentially deepens with each contact; the trial experience is affirmed, and/or the reasons some prefer a brand are shared with others.

This model impacts how we should think about advertising insights. Does the insight that connects the viewer to the brand have the potential to deepen our trust for a brand? Since different people have different ingoing levels of brand trust, the reaction to the same insight offered will be very different across different people.

Advertising Is Shorthand for Brand Communication

In today's world of integrated media, the TV ad campaign does not automatically dominate brand communication. Social networking, online interaction, and in-store merchandising can have as large or larger impacts on the intangible aspects of brand communication.

The insights shared in this book are used across all forms of brand communication. However, I wanted the book to be interactive, to not just cite past or current campaigns that you may or may not be familiar with, but ones you could find and view on YouTube. I wanted to describe the insights that have built brand trust for so many great brands in the specific context of the advertising in which they were imbedded. Also, we can still find on YouTube the advertising that made critical mistakes and helped accelerated the demise of some formerly great brands like Schlitz and Oldsmobile. This choice lets you see the advertising as it ran recently or long ago, now with just a click. It is fascinating that all these examples are out there on the net via YouTube; it demonstrates that they were significant enough for individuals to find and post them.

Google and Facebook are changing the ad game by transferring billions of advertising dollars to something that cannot easily be captured in an after-the-fact example. When you are reading an e-mail from a friend or associate and the content of the e-mail suggests a product or service, Google, by simply clicking a link, will connect you to someone who has paid for that connection. When you view the content on a web page, Google will put on that page a display ad or a link that costs the brand only when you click it. When you actively read or click, showing you the ad that results does not capture the actual experience.

The new PR is to have brand content that a brand makes available, which is found through search-engine requests that each person makes. This requires the brand to develop useful, entertaining, and authoritative content that is worth viewing when found. They are rewarded if and only if they are actually actively read and used.

Facebook has created a model that invites brands to participate in peer-to-peer advocacy. The brand now has to earn the right to participate in private dialogue, which is forcing the brand to think more broadly about its ongoing relationship with its users and potential advocates.

Brand Advertising and Price Promotion: The Hydrogen and Oxygen of Advertising Effectiveness

Like two atoms of hydrogen and one of oxygen, brand advertising and brand price promotions fuse together into one substance. Many times they do so within the same stream of information; today, many car ads start with brand-building messages created by the brand's national agency and then cut to the local car dealer, which will most often carry a location and the current deal. National brands used to make "doughnuts," national ads with starts and finishes and in which a hole was left in the middle for the regional retailer's information. Most sponsored websites make it as easy as they can to get an offer and ordering page to you the moment you feel at all interested in finding out the potential cost of the brand.

The insight is that these two connected bits of information have quite different ways of working. Brand advertisements seek to influence perceptions, keep brand loyalists loyal, help interpret the usage experience, provide quality signals, build brand trust, and defend against rival brands. Price promotions from the same brand seek to induce trial, attract brand switchers, generate experience with the brand, provide price signals, harvest brand trust, and be an offense against rival brands. Like H_2O, each needs to be connected and in the right combination.

Shareholder Value of Brand Trust

When you buy a share of a company that advertises, you are buying the discounted future profits generated by the assets they possess and "goodwill." For branded companies, the brand trust results in goodwill and primarily resides in the relationships they have formed with their customers. In addition, the goodwill includes their sales partner relationships, the channels through which they sell, and even the added value people employed by the brand feel about their company. United Airlines' "Friendly Skies" was created in part to motivate their flight attendants to deliver a better level of service.

Some companies are valued for their collection of brands: GM, P&G, and Sara Lee are examples. The last is particularly interesting since Sara

Lee abandoned its collective name of Consolidated Foods Corporation for the better known but smaller brand they acquired—the Kitchens of Sara Lee. Sometimes the share price you pay for a company is almost a pure brand: Apple, IBM, Kellogg, Southwest Airlines, and Disney are examples of companies worth far more than their physical assets and discounted cash flow would justify. The multiple of sales that you pay for a branded company has traditionally been greater than for companies that produce products without brands.

In an extreme case, Coca-Cola's value to shareholders has accumulated over the years, building brand trust. In many places in the world, Coke is the safe liquid, far safer than the local tap water or even the local bottled water from an unknown source. This value has allowed the company to purchase the assets of many large bottling networks. The tangible assets come from their acquisitions, but they exist because of the goodwill produced by the brand, which built a level of trust with people who buy and use the brand. Quick responsiveness is required when you build trust. Coke can also make a mistake and recover (i.e., the well-intentioned but wrong-headed introduction of a reformulated New Coke). Coca-Cola was able to take it back, respond to customer ire, and revive. In 2011, Coke introduced a festive snow white "holiday" can, found it was confusing for customers, and withdrew it in early December. Responding to mistakes quickly, for brands like Coke, can actually enhance brand trust.

Many brands are inextricably linked to other brands. It may be Intel Inside, but it can only be bought working within another brand. Most software companies fit that description, with Apple the powerful exception. Automobile and beer brands often do not own their dealerships and distributorships, but their fate is dependent on those partnerships.

Advertising accelerates brand profits and thus increases the value of a brand. Specifically, advertising creates faster market penetration through speeding up brand trials, brand referrals from one friend to another, and faster adoption after trials into a repertoire of brands bought within the category. Brands often sustain higher average prices or permit the same or a lower cost to be charged because higher volumes allow lower per-unit pricing. Brands permit growth within the category through cost-efficient brand extensions and lower the cost of sales and service.

These effects of advertising accelerate and enhance the cash flows that the stockholder buys with their purchase of a stock; they reduce the volatility and thus the vulnerability of cash flows over time and enhance the residual value when that company is acquired by another.

Building Brand Trust Is about a Relationship with People, not Doing Things to Them

The most common mistake in thinking about advertising is to use language that explicitly states that advertising does something to people. Here are some common but ultimately wrong-headed statements used.

"Our advertising retains loyal customers." From a behavioral standpoint and from observing the sequence of products that are bought by a person across time, we know that no customers are loyal across all categories, and very few are totally loyal all the time. For categories that do not matter, I may buy the same brand out of habit, but if the pantry is bare and the store is out of stock, another brand goes into the basket. I may buy one brand loyally for months, but then my mother-in-law, whom I know likes another brand, stays at my house, and I purchase her favorite, thus interrupting the string of "loyal" purchases. A brand that I do not like as much is offered at half-price, and it is bought and used; my long-term trust of my "loyal" brand and the half-price brand does not change. In fact, the most loyal customers are those who buy less frequently because they stock up when the brand is on sale. For many nonloyal customers, they often pay higher prices than those who buy regularly (and know a good deal), are less likely to say in surveys that they are loyal (they really have no connection to the brand they infrequently use), and yet are 100 percent loyal within a given time span.

In all these "less than totally loyal" examples, advertising and brand communications participate with the people in a relationship, give them more information about the brand, inform them when it is on sale, entertain them, and reward them for their time spent interacting with the brand.

"We use promotions to gain new users." Advertising is consciously attended to by people who are and have used the brand dramatically more than by those who have not used the brand. For well-known brands, nonusers simply do not consciously process the ad as it washes over them. For relatively obscure brands, the benefits described and the involvement device within the ad are often assumed to be for the brand they use most often, not the one that sponsored the ad.

People who buy primarily for price are equally attracted by all price offers in the buying environment and, ironically, are greatly influenced by messages about the brand that let them choose which "cheaper deal" offers the better value.

"This advertising expenditure will be evaluated on its ability to gain share." Most people who say this are implicitly assuming that their current share is theirs and that advertising should be assessed only on its ability to have incremental effects. Ironically, most advertising and promotions are defensive by rebuilding the trust of somewhat regular customers to buy again in the face of rival messages, inviting an alternative purchase.

Often, even the concept of "share of the pie" is naive. It implies you are dividing a static pie and getting a bigger or smaller piece. However, most products today compete across category boundaries. The bottle of Clorox does not get purchased because Tide detergent offers a version that has a bleaching benefit. The compact disc loses out to an iTunes download. A smartphone app used in the car replaces the GPS stand alone. The PC you were planning to buy your student gets replaced with a tablet device from a brand you never would have otherwise considered. Calculating share in these cases is rarely as meaningful as it seems.

"We want people to become *aware* of our advertising, and then *interested*, and then come to *desire* our product and take the *action* we desire" (The famous AIDA model). Most first purchases of most products happen as conscious trials without desire, but with casual interest and experimentation or willingness to have a good-enough usage experience at a better price. Sometimes a piece of information that influences our buying connects with what we know about a brand, and we retain it, even though the ad that carried that message was never consciously attended and certainly not "retrievable" from our memory. Much of the power of advertising is in framing the experience of a product and purposefully transmitting information that happens after, not before, action.

McDonald's does not start advertising new products before they are already available and are being actively bought in their outlets. Over half of McDonald's buyers become aware of the new McDonald's product offering before it is advertised; over half of those who will ever buy it have already tried it before the ad runs. The advertising is trying to connect to both those who have already bought the brand and those on the fence who have considered it but not yet bought. The new product ad is trying to deepen that experience and invite another purchase to establish the product as another reason to visit McDonald's.

Product placements in movies are paid-for ads that are attempting to use celebrity power to form an association; most people do not even consider the brand at the time they are viewing the movie. Clark Gable, Joan Crawford, and John Wayne all appeared in moves after WWII in which the studio was paid for them to smoke Lucky Strike and Chesterfield. However, when the *American Idol* judges sip from their Coke glasses during the most-watched show of the season, everyone involved is aware of the ad nature of those cups.

Online advertising and social network interactions are the most fluid of all the media, adapting to each different person by the way they actively interact with the medium.

Online brand communication and overt advertising continues to constantly morph as billions of dollars of worth are created by each new exposure innovation, and more and more advertising dollars flow to where more and more people are spending more and more time purchasing more and more products.

Consider what happens when you click on a website. First, there may be a banner ad with buttons, which pops up and appears over the content when you stay on the page for a certain length of time; or perhaps a "daughter" window opens up. Second, the content itself might be syndicated, actually created not by the website but by the sponsor in the same "voice" as the site that was visited. Third, within the copy or visuals of the site, there may some integrated content from many different sponsors, which are shaped by the hidden cookies in the computer of the viewer, identifying their gender, past purchasing history, or even their willingness to purchase online. Fourth, the entire site may be sponsored by a brand that not only lets the site manage its own content but also hopes to get the favorable image of caring about the same issues as those who go to the site. And these are just the most visible forms of advertising.

Advertising on the web blends two different marketing concepts: advertising in traditional media and public relations efforts to influence the editorial content of media. It attempts to both intrigue and inform, to have style and substance, to prove and answer, to be persuasive and fact based, to both initiate and complete a sale. Like all advertising, most of it fails miserably. Less than 1 percent of people do a desired online activity wished for by the sponsor—click through a banner ad to learn more, "donate now," spend more than five seconds on a page, etc. Yet that tiny fraction has earned itself billions of dollars of ad revenue because the cost/benefit ratio is both sufficient, and the resulting actions have a tangible real aspect that traditional adverting in other media and traditional PR across media have never been able to isolate.

Google, Craigslist, and Groupon have changed the face and function of advertising. Facebook and Twitter are attempting to commercialize their millions of visits without sabotaging their reasons for being. Google's impact is constantly changing as users come to understand that those who will pay to appear first are influencing the searches received. Craigslist is being challenged by classified ads that can now be found in hundreds of places online, but the newspapers that were sustained by classified advertising as a highly subsidized media have had to shift to a user-subscription model online or wither in size and impact.

How Advertising Helps New Products Gain a Level of Trust Necessary for a First Purchase

In chapter 1, we saw that two of the five purposes of advertising are to enable the brand to extend its usefulness across a category with additional products (e.g., whiten teeth, diminish childhood cavities, freshen breath, remove tartar, guard against gum disease, and provide all-in-one protection) or across multiple categories (computer, telephone, television, and music storage).

Advertising reduced the risk perceived by customers of trying a new variant of a brand and, for the very same reason, increased the probability of gaining distribution in the places people buy the brand. We saw earlier that price buyers used advertising-influenced brand judgments to choose among several brands that were all featuring price reductions. Past advertising investments reduced the cost of introductory and follow-up marketing programs for the same brand. They also reduced the cost for packaging and labeling and modified existing package looks rather than invented from scratch.

The brand that successfully extends its brand horizon in this way is making an explicit guarantee to consumers by promising a certain experience and quality. People build a relationship with the brand based on this promise. Successful extensions make sense to consumers when they build from the core of what they know and do not neglect the base brand, even when that base brand is no longer a dominant part of the volume and profit of the total extended brand's volume and profit.

A brand can stretch within and across categories in several ways. The most common are to line extend in an existing category by adding new flavors, new packaging, and new sizes. A brand can extend its profitability with smaller sizes (travel and convenience sizes) and larger sizes (volume sales to giant "box" stores that are cheaper to provide to both the place of distribution and the customer). A brand can stretch vertically in an existing category, stretching up to compete with brands that are priced higher and stretching down to compete with brands that are priced lower.

Often, the most dangerous place to be in a market is around the average price. Hanes men's underwear faced this in the early eighties. In department stores, they were the averaged-priced brand competing with BVD, a higher-priced brand with higher perceived quality. In discount stores, they were the averaged-priced brand competing against

Fruit of the Loom with lower prices. The average price in a category is squeezed by volume brands at lower prices and high-margin brands positioned at higher prices. Effective brand stretching solves this problem. Ford, BMW, and Mercedes have stretched in this way, while Toyota and GM have used separate brands, depending on separate showrooms and separate advertising to do the same.

How Advertising Builds Trust in New Categories for the Brand

Brands can extend in a different category by opportunistic movement into categories that consumers see as a natural fit for the brand. United Airlines tried to extend their brand to hotels and other travel services without very much success, but Virgin Airlines has been more vigorous and, so far, successful. Also, a brand can partner with a dominant brand in another category by cobranding (M&M's in Pillsbury's cookie dough) or offer a joint product that makes two promises at once (PC brands with Intel Inside and Windows).

In all cases, the advertising insight that originally launched or sustained a brand must constantly be revisited and either modified, complemented, or connected. If care is not taken, the new brand can cannibalize the old franchise (Pillsbury Doughboy products), lower brand loyalty (does the mere existence of Lexus create an artificial boundary of prestige for Toyota?), weaken the logic of a line of products (Reebok offering NBA basketball shoes within a line of fitness running apparel), fragment the marketing effort (as advertising for the core brand disappears), or distract from new product development (limiting the company from launching truly "new to the world" products, for instance if Kraft stops launching new food brands as it adds brand variants to its existing brands: Oscar Mayer Lunchables, Oreo, and Triscuit).

A Friend Who Is a Brand Advocate Powerfully Builds Brand Trust

More powerful than the ad containing an insight is the advocate who internalizes that insight and then shares it with a friend or colleague. Advertising is noise that often gets filtered; we fast-forward the ad, a conversation in the room covers it up, our attention is distracted, we selectively read or hear only parts of it, or our own thoughts color it and we remember what we perceived, not what we saw. However, when shared by two friends or colleagues, a host of barriers to ads are overcome.

An insight shared bypasses the skeptical filter we use when we view advertising. Because each person has an idiosyncratic network of other contacts, the advertiser is no longer in control of context when a message is passed, and that's why the inherent truth of an insight is often more powerful than the way the ad is delivered. Three types of people are most likely to pass on information: experts, social leaders, and early adopters. Each have a different effect on the original insight.

Experts are listened to because they have proven that they have more knowledge about a particular brand or category. Your friends—the nurse, the mechanic, the frugal buyer, the "shop till you drop" buddy—all have source credibility. Social leaders are people who feel comfortable in their environment and see information sharing as a crucial part of their social capital, thus, the intensity in which they choose to deliver a message displays emotional intelligence that an ad created away from that "moment" could never have. Early adopters have the advantage of an actual product experience that carries with it credibility that the person who has not yet "opened a package" readily acknowledges they don't have.

Brand advocates tend to have more friends on Facebook, travel more often, have exposure to different often specialized media environments, are information hungry and seek out information about a category, and are simply more vocal about what they know.

Advocates are part of the stream. The role of advertising is not to create the stream but to acknowledge its presence, add to its content, provide channels for its flow, and monitor its path.

The Same Advertising Builds Trust in Different Ways with Different People

Filling up the deep pool. When people hold rich, deep trust for a brand, advertising works in three ways. First, it reinforces and reaffirms existing levels of brand trust. We try and defend the choices we make, and advertising for our brand often gives us the tools to do so. We saw that Rocky Mountain water and **kräusening** often served that purpose for Coors and Old Style beer. Second, it reassures us we are not alone. There is a sense that brands you see advertised are popular or prestigious, so advertising can provide a sense of camaraderie and shared trust with people you've never met. Third, it counteracts possible mistrust. The advertising gives us the tools to countermand the claims and users of other brands. If a competing brand proves it is less expensive, we can parrot our brand's claim of better value. If users of other brands say their brand is the best quality, then we can remember that our brand assures us none are better.

Giving us another reason to trust the brand. We notice the advertising of brands we have used much more than the advertising of brands we have not tried. Thus, after trying a product, the advertising can frame that experience, help us understand why we tried it, and perhaps deepen our feelings about why we liked the product. Some benefits are undetectable in use: Did the pain reliever really work faster? It did get rid of my headache. Did the shampoo revive my hair? It did seem to look nice.

Giving us the language to describe the reasons we trust a brand. As large brands expand into all facets of a category, there is the danger of distinctions between them fading. What is the difference between Crest and Colgate? As Apple is omnipresent in every category, what defines its soul? As the huge barns at Costco, Walmart, and Target expand, why did I really go there? Was it lowest price, or best value, or widest selection, or one-stop shopping, or for the brands I can only buy there? Advertising can help clarify why we trust brands, give new life to old slogans, and put a fresh face on a familiar experience.

Building Brand Trust Has Accelerated the Growth of Brands in Different Ways

Some brands have consistently had advertising that widened their appeal, either by running more often or being more salient. In a "share of mind" battle, Nike beats Reebok; Green Giant beats the bigger spender Birds Eye; Coke consistently beats Pepsi, not through more memorable individual ads, but more consistent contacts across all media; Levi's trumps Lee; and StarKist outperforms Chicken of the Sea.

Some brands have had strong likeability transferred from their advertising to the brand; we trust people we like more than those that we do not. Smucker's, Folgers, Heineken, IHOP, and Bubble Tape are all examples of brands that were outspent but dramatically better liked than many of their rivals.

Sometimes the advertising within a category leaves people feeling that one brand really is better than another. Hallmark achieves that over American Greeting Cards, Visa over MasterCard, Maytag over Whirlpool, and Toyota over Chevrolet. This is despite Consumer Reports ratings after Maytag started to be made by Whirlpool and during the times that Nova and Toyota shared the same assembly line in California.

Some brands achieve iconic status by a combination of consistent advertising, excellent product quality, and sensible pricing strategies. It is hard to parse what produces iconic brands like Disney World, Crayola, Gerber, Heinz Ketchup, or Jell-O, but when you look back at brands that were once icons and are no longer, it is clear that all these pieces have to continue to work together.

Different but similarly precious are niche brands viewed as almost indispensable by their users but still a minority interest to most. Starbucks, Tiffany, Kool-Aid, and Volkswagen Beetles are loved by their users and have advertising mightily appreciated by them but stumble when they try to appeal to everyone (like Starbucks as a breakfast destination, Tiffany counters in department stores, or the four-door Beetle Saloon).

The Theory and the Practice

Advertising works in many ways, but one of the most common and powerful is simple: advertising insights reinforce truths about the brand that deepen the trust between the consumer and the brand.

There are three main insight challenges for advertising professionals: looking for the insight that is best suited for the brand at this moment in time, identifying the advertising insight that resonates with potential users, and ensuring that the advertising is not only about the insight but also involving and personally relevant.

In the forthcoming chapters, we will look at advertising that succeeded and failed at building brand trust, and particularly at the insights that they sought to dramatize.

Preview of Chapters 3-15

Donald Gunn's
"Master Formats of Advertising"
Advertising Examples of Brands
into Trust Marks

Advertising Formats

When we go to a movie, our attitude toward that experience is vastly different when we are going to see a summer action flick, or an animated family movie, or a film with Oscar buzz, or when we go to be challenged by a documentary on a controversial subject. Our enjoyment of it is tied to our ingoing expectations and our judgment criteria of excellence differ. Advertising formats have that same effect. Unlike films, we probably lack labels for them, but since everyone is an expert of advertising (having been exposed to thousands of examples of each), we all know them when we see them.

When we watch a product demonstration, we focus on the visual and assure ourselves that we are watching reality, not a magician's trick. When we are engaged in a short-story vignette, we quickly decide whether we empathize with a situation like that or whether simply to vicariously observe a slice of someone's life. The brand's insight has to work within the format. When the insight is simply *said* in a demo but not shown, it doesn't work. When the story is not about the insight, it doesn't stick. When a celebrity presenter doesn't embody a facet of the insight, we end up taking away an experience not intended by the advertiser.

Donald Gunn's Typology

Donald Gunn has been an observer of the breadth of advertising creativity for thirty years. He worked as a creative in Paris, London, and Chicago. He put together a creative-resource advertising library, which classified most of the world's award-winning ads into categories so that creatives could request a short compilation of high-quality similar ads. He served as CEO of the Cannes Advertising Awards, the ultimate creative award event for advertising and the advertisers who enabled their work.

To help himself and other creatives, he observed that one way to break out of the straitjacket of me-too advertising was to first observe the format of advertising that dominated a category and then try to consciously adopt a different way to share the consumer insight. By having a short list of the different formats available, one can quickly categorize which of the twelve formats most ads in the category follow and then to try using other formats to add originality and depth.

All Ads Are Only the Picture of the Insight, not the Insight Itself

When we look at Donald Gunn's picture above, we are not confused that it is Donald himself. If we've had the pleasure of meeting this gentleman scholar, then we see in the picture the hints of a quick mind, the pleasure of someone who appreciates great creativity, and a gracious meeting host who delights in entertaining us as we are informed. For those who have not met him, they simply see a "caught in time" image.

The insight we expose to connect the consumer to the brand is exactly like this. In its richness, it is multidimensional and personal. It is nearly impossible to simply read a proverb like "Train a child in the way he should go, and when he is old, he will not turn from it." This proverb's wisdom has us reflect on the truths we personally carried into adulthood, or reflect on how we wish we had been clearer about this truth while raising our own children, or has us wondering about a child we know who seems to be going astray.

Great insights invoke many diverse personally relevant thoughts as they are viewed. These thoughts are influenced by the context of the entire ad and by the unique connections we make with those insights.

Great ads use the expectations of the format they've adopted to convey richer meaning. Because we have seen so many ads of each format, our frame of reference is not only the ad itself but also what we already expect the ad to be like based on similar ads we have seen, either from the advertiser or, more commonly, from all other advertisers that have used similar formats.

Understanding Advertising Insights in Context

Donald Gunn's typology lays out twelve different formats. Some ads are hybrids, uniquely blending two of the twelve formats in a creative way. Perhaps there are some ads that defy classification. But once you have thought about these formats, they will become a ready tool from which to view and appreciate both the style and purpose of the ad.

This book is about sharing how actual advertising makes the vital connection between the brand and the potential brand buyer. By looking at examples of ads within the context of the different advertising formats, I hope to unleash your ability to place different expectations on these insights, just as we all do when we watch different genres of film.

Chapter Three

Presenter, Testimonial, A Tells B
Directly Sharing the Insight

Present the Advertising Strategy

Perhaps the most common format for really bad advertising is the presenter, the trumped-up testimonial, or someone using marketing jargon to explain to their best friend over coffee the merits of a certain brand. There are lots of examples of how to do this successfully, which we will share in this chapter, but all too often these ads are painful to watch and a waste of a client's money.

You can understand how this happens. The client and the agency spend weeks poring through research, visiting the R&D labs, reviewing past work, and finally arriving at an advertising strategy. More often than not, the multipart strategy has everyone's pet idea retained. One person has a great thought about the target audience, another wants everyone to remember the brand's core essence, another person feels more comfortable with fresh language they are using that seems to capture a new insight, and another person on the team insists that the marketing objectives be clearly stated. The most recent copy slogan is added so the campaign will have continuity. They include all their thoughts, each makes sense and is well supported, so they approve the strategy.

The document the advertising team develops before the creative begins is called the creative brief. The first sign that the copywriter and art director are in for trouble is that most briefs are not brief. Many go on for several pages of single-spaced copy. Others insist on being on one page but have lots of different boxes, each of which have different thoughts. These boxes have various labels on them: background, objective/purpose, target audience/who are we talking to, mandatory elements, primary message, proof/support, brand personality, tone and manner, competition, intended media, key insight, and budget.

From inside the process, it was often worse than all these categories suggest. The author was able to find forty-two briefs for that many different advertising campaigns. They had an average of thirty-two sentences. They contained on average 240 words. Each sentence involved at least two to five conversations within the agency, with the client, and in agency-client meetings. Single words were discussed, edited, revised, and compromised. They were presented and presented again, until the agency and client team were convinced they had neared perfection.

But the advertising that is created from these briefs often disappoints the team. It misses many of the essential points in the strategy. It ignores some ideas altogether. It adds elements of execution intended to draw in the viewer, but those precious seconds require leaving out still more of the intended message.

This is when a frustrated creative team behind really bad advertising gives up and has a presenter read the strategy to the potential viewer. The briefing team feels like all their hard work has mattered. A skilled copywriter has polished the words of the strategy, and a trained actor reads them. All the ideas are retained—easy to approve, easy to review, and extremely unlikely to work.

Like a fine French sauce, advertising strategies must be a reduction of all you know. There are as many formats for advertising strategies as there are agencies and brand consultants. However, they all have one common problem: they contain far more ideas than one ad can communicate.

In the process we have described, sometimes the creative team is part of the long discussions. What happens is that they are usually terribly bored, they start doodling, and then—either late in the night or early the next morning—they have an idea. That idea is compelling. All the advertising begins to "write itself." In a burst of creative insight, they are able to see the idea work across different media. They talk with their creative partners, and good ideas spark more good ideas.

But they wait. They wait until the entire brief is agreed. Then they wait some more until they cannot be accused of shooting from the hip, or going off half-cocked, or rushing to judgment. They restate the brief in their upfront dialogue with the client, helping everyone know they have read it and internalized it. Then they show the idea to the client—relief! Everyone gets excited.

That's the magic of the advertising process, but it depends on what Leo Burnett described as "the lonely man," working late or early, doodling, letting his or her unconscious work, caring about each word and visual, being up against a deadline, working until that wee, small voice inside emerges.

The power of an advertising insight will be lost if the ad is not about just that insight. A powerful insight connects the brand to a potential brand buyer, understanding that an ad will only build brand trust if it works with the viewer, takes into account what they already know about the brand, about their needs, and about their history with the brand. If the now simple idea, that once stated is "blindingly obvious," is complicated by more words and more ideas to "fulfill the brief," then it probably will not work.

Building Brand Trust

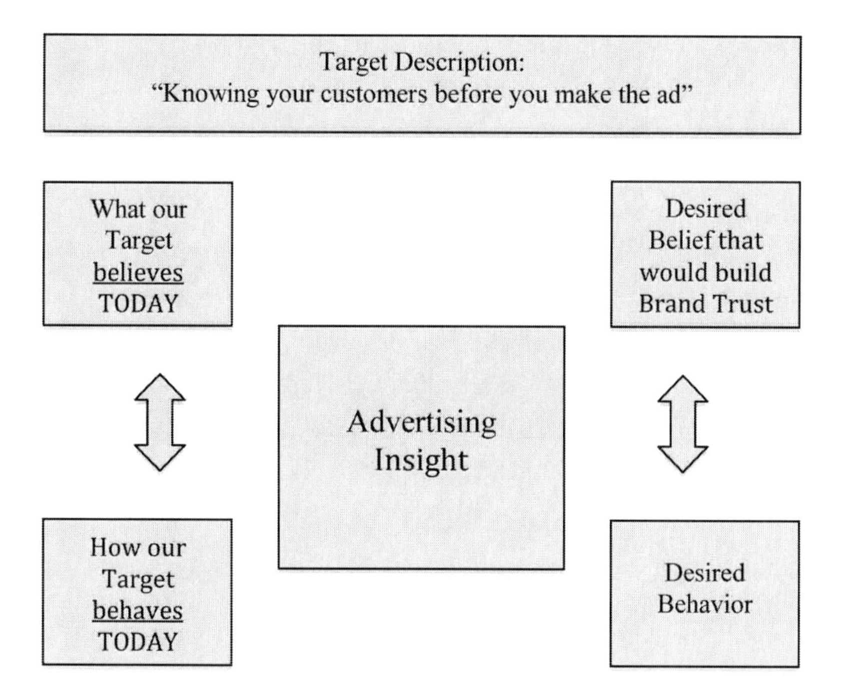

The goal of an advertising insight is to build brand trust. The person we want to impact holds a set of beliefs that interact with their current behavior. Some of those beliefs flow directly from, and were formed by, their behavior. Some beliefs preceded the behavior and were involved consciously or unconsciously in the decision to buy/use a brand. After being exposed to the advertising insight, both beliefs and behavior may change. If behavior changes, what are the beliefs we want to accompany that behavior? If beliefs change, what are the reasons that they may encourage different behavior?

Target Description: Knowing Your Customers Before You Make the Ad

One of the most common and misused concepts in advertising is the target. The phrase is inherently dehumanizing, militaristic, and misleading. It may imply that one can purchase media that efficiently or exclusively reaches the target. Highly targeted lists in direct mail get response rates of fewer than 2 percent. Behaviorally, targeted display ads get "clicked" in online advertising by less than 1 percent of those exposed. Other forms of media are probably even less efficient. Advertising works in many ways, but rarely exposes just the right people to just the right message.

The real reason to frame advertising insights in the context of a description and to share all the insights we have about those people is that we want to make the advertising more human and personal, not less. If we can create a private conversation between two people through the intimacy of understanding the person with whom we are communicating, then the advertising has a chance to have an impact.

For Horlicks (people drink a malted milk beverage in the evening to get a good night's sleep) the brand team knew a lot about the target. Those who suffered from poor sleep had bags under their eyes because they either tossed and turned finding sleep elusive, or they repeatedly woke up during the night. The brand team knew how the sleepless felt when their alarm sounded: frustrated, tired, slightly depressed, and resigned to rising before they had had sufficient sleep. The sleepless were more likely to be busy people who drank a lot of coffee or tea to get through the day. Their busyness also meant they were unable to take a nap during the afternoon. They could be almost any age, gender, or occupation. Half the brand team working on the advertising project not only knew someone like this, but they also saw their own grouchy, sleep-deprived face in the mirror each morning.

For Cadbury's Dairy Milk, the brand team also understood the target. Dairy Milk lovers were moms whose grocery budget did not allow for many extras. Buying an expensive, indulgent box of chocolates was certainly out of the question. These moms were buying selflessly and, for the most part, for the whole family. Dairy Milk, in the thick bar of chocolate with indentations to break off and share, was a nice family treat. We also knew that it probably would never make it to the family. Somewhere between the corner shop and a late TV treat, it would provide a satisfying reward of creamy taste and chocolate comfort.

While these are target insights, they do not define for the media person how to buy just the right media. However, if they are vivid enough, the media person can creatively design a media buy that more efficiently reaches them and, perhaps even more importantly, reaches them at the right moment so that the insight can be internalized by the target.

Current Beliefs in the Context of Current Behavior

There are literally hundreds of relevant beliefs people have that may or may not impact their behavior. They flow from who they are—their unique needs and individual personalities. What is essential to one person is often irrelevant to another.

We each have a bedrock of personal values that usually persist throughout our lives, and if they change, they change slowly. These values are tied to the relative importance we place on pleasing others or ourselves, seeking new experiences, or preferring the comfort of the familiar. These values put different importance on information, and what we retain in easily retrievable storehouses are those bits of knowledge that reinforce our core values. We hold attitudes about information, both good and bad. These attitudes color incoming information, making us try to avoid or counterargue those ideas that seem to conflict with our current attitudes—attitudes that are protecting our core values.

The resilience of this web of needs (personality, core values, knowledge, and current attitudes) limits the role of advertising. If these internal dynamic forces were few or weak, then advertising might truly be able to more powerfully persuade. But they are many, complex, and real. Therefore, advertising must find the unique combination of current beliefs and behavior that complement the desire to build more trust for the brand. Often, advertising works not by changing current beliefs but by powerfully reinforcing only a select few. Other times advertising can deliver a new thought, but only if it can be attached to other current beliefs that complement and reinforce the new thought.

Behavior

One would think that behavior is obvious, measurable, and easy to understand. You either buy the brand or you do not. You have either purchased the brand in the past or not. But it turns out that behavior is just as subtle and complex as the intangible set of beliefs.

People have repertoires of behavior. Over a relatively short span of time, they buy multiple brands at different prices. A few loyally buy only one brand, but often wait until they can stock up when it is on sale. A few buy the brand regularly as one of several brands and willingly buy it whether or not on sale. A few buy the brand regularly, but only when they can find it on sale. Many buy it occasionally, perhaps only once a year. A very few buy it once and then never buy it again. These patterns exist over longer time periods for products that are bought less regularly: cars, computers, mobile phones, and even homes.

In inspecting the same person's buying habits across many different categories across time, I found that someone who was a loyalist in one category would be a brand rotator in another category, a price shopper in a third category, and an occasional buyer in lots and lots of categories. Any one type of buyer was unlikely to be the most frequent in any category. Products that seem mundane and easily substitutable (toilet paper, kitchen cleaners, or brands of socks) had as many loyal buyers as did brands of perfume, expensive watches, or cars.

Desired Beliefs in the Context of Desired Behavior

For existing brands, the best place to find the connection between future beliefs and future behavior is in the current beliefs and behavior of the brand's core users. For almost all brands, 20% of a brand's users comprise anywhere between 50% and 80% of their volume and between 70% and 90% of their profitable volume. The problem with most research that is meant to find insights is that it reveals what most people who use the brand think, feel, and do. Unfortunately, the majority of users do not represent the core well. Relevant insights come easily when you talk to relevant users. The trick is simply to insist that whether you are talking to a few in focus groups or many in large-scale quantitative samples, you find those who are regularly buying high volumes of the brand willingly, not just because they find it on sale.

Insights that interest the existing, most valuable customers tend to work for three reasons. First, these insights help cement their reasons for buying and help retain the core volume and profitability of the brand. Second, they tend to resonate with the occasional brand users and thus support the group that is systematically associated with the growth of brands—additional volume from current users. Finally, they may connect with those who have not used the brand but share a similar set of wants and needs as the current users.

When you are introducing a new brand, the best group to seek insights from is among the frequent category buyers who currently rotate between brands in the category not for price but for the different features the different brands offer. These are people most attuned to the strengths and weaknesses of the current brands. They rotate for reasons: it may be that no one brand has the right combination of features for them, it may be that they see distinctions that loyalists of the other brands do not see between the different brands, it may be because they are continually searching for something that no brand currently offers. In all these cases, talking to them and listening to their perspectives is more valuable than talking to those who only buy one brand or who buy many brands based on price.

The Advertising Insight: Envisioning the Future

Which comes first, the chicken or the egg? Great insights lead to big ideas. Big ideas reveal compelling insights for why they could work.

When the advertising and brand teams, including the creative team, can settle on one advertising insight up front, there is added clarity for how to develop, judge, and produce the advertising.

The five-box strategy format is truly about imagining a new future in which the advertising insight has been communicated, internalized, and is now part of the mind-set of the people who will see the advertising. What is really different? What will really happen?

The insight becomes the idea that propels all the myriad details that make the whole believable. The ad has to pass the believability meter that is built into our collective unconscious, which rejects the whole because of minute pieces that are out of whack.

The big idea, poorly executed, fails just as fast as the poor idea brilliantly executed. When the advertising execution is approved by the brand team, the clarity of the insight must then propel hundreds of decisions about casting, lighting, choice of media, flow, editing, music, and if on the web, sequence of click pages.

Clean, simple, intuitive design became the compelling insight that propelled Apple across many different product platforms. It was Steve Jobs's ability to envision the new world that his products could help create, if they integrated with simplicity and ease. He raised the bar so high that few other companies could emulate his standards and no others could anticipate them.

Nike desired to inspire activity, activity that they could enable with shoes designed for custom activities.

Allstate Insurance focused on inspiring trust, protecting their customer with "good hands."

Cheer connected with people wanting to wash all types of clothes in all temperatures of water, not just getting their dirty whites bright, but keep their wash-and-wear safe and colorful and their ground-in-dirt jeans clean.

Pert Shampoo showed the convenience and end results of combining a shampoo and conditioner into one shampoo.

Walt Disney World convincingly showed that a magic trip to Orlando should be on your agenda this year, at this life stage, and that each type of age and activity focus could be wonderfully served.

Corn Flakes simply reminded people that the unadorned great taste of their cereal was worth tasting again, as if for the very first time.

All these simple insights transformed beliefs, reinforced trust in the brand, and grew sales.

Trusting Nike

Like Apple, Nike has a transparent strategy of helping people envision a more active future in which Nike's sports gear is an integral part.

Their insight as foresight sets their advertising apart from the "how we make the shoe" or even the "how it helps you perform" of their rivals.

This ad for Nike women's athletic gear does not even show Nike's sports gear. Their goal is to focus on category motivation, linking Nike to the very reasons why people participate.

It is a brilliant use of onscreen presenters as young women directly tell you the benefits they will experience as adults because of their sports participation. It disarms the parents' apathy and low expectations about their daughters' sports activities and positions Nike as the brand leader.

Nike: Women's Athletic Gear

http:/ / www.youtube.com/ watch?v=AQ_XSHpIbZE

"If you let me play ..."

"If you let me play sports,"

"I will like myself more."

"I will have more self-confidence. I will suffer less depression."

"If you let me play sports,"

"I will be 50% less likely to get breast cancer."

"I will be more likely to leave a man who beats me."

"I will be less likely to get pregnant before I want to."

"I will learn what it feels like to be strong."
Nike
Just do it.

Retrieved from rossknights, Mar 5, 2007, "Nike ad: If You Let Me Play (1995)"

Presenters Do Not Have to Be Dull

The following ad wants people to feel the shiver of cold that comes from having freezing conditions outside and windows that do a poor job of keeping the heat inside.

They opt for the straightest line between two points and simply tell potential customers just the facts. Safestyle window protection, like Gecko car insurance in the United States, has created an interesting spokes-avatar for their commercials to tell the otherwise straightforward message.

The challenge for both brands is to make sure that the balance between the extra involvements created by use of the avatar does not subtract from the net takeaway of the brand story.

Safestyle's

http://www.youtube.com/watch?v=TGZVgoFpGcw

Safestyle
window protection

"Oh no. Here comes trouble."

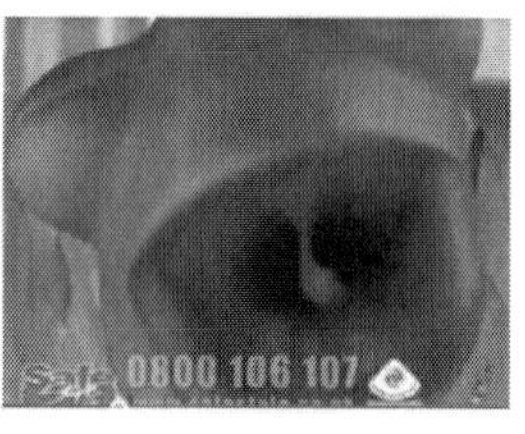

"They're freezing my fins off."

Time to call, "Safestyle"

With Safestyle.co.uk energy efficient doors and windows

you now get their award-winning installation, for Free!

Energy saving glass to keep your house warm. For FREE.

Safestyle will come now, give you a free quote, and you can pay later.

So get your free quote today. At www.Safestyle.Co.UK. Or dial 0800 106 107 now.

Retrieved from safestylewindows, Dec 14, 2010, Safestyle's "fishy Presenter" TV ad

Trustworthy Spokesperson

Some actors become as famous for their advertising roles as their acting career. Many people may have seen Dennis Haysbert, the Allstate spokesperson, as President David Palmer in his four-year run on *24*; or in the TV series he led, *The Unit*; or in his guest-starring roles on a variety of TV series. However, he has had the most exposure for his nine-year stint as spokesperson for Allstate.

His signature deep voice, commanding presence, and trustworthy persona is ideal for telling the serious stories of potential loss and good value that Allstate wanted to communicate.

The advertising insight is that using a talent like Dennis is a strong, implicit statement about a brand that you buy on trust, pay for in advance, and hope to never use.

Allstate

http:/ / www.youtube.com/ watch?v=TscHTLOL9bY

"In the last year, we've learned a lot. We've learned that meatloaf and Jenga

can be more fun than reservations and box seats.

And who's around your TV is more important than how big it is.

That cars aren't for showing how far we've come,

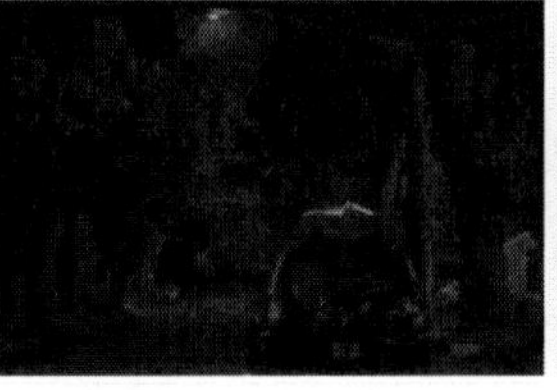

but for taking us where we want to go.

We've learned that the best things in life don't cost much.

And at Allstate, they don't cost much to protect.

So protect them.

Put them in good hands."

Retrieved from libtechsk8er, August 1, 2011, "Allstate Commercial – Best Things in Life"

Sharing Your Brand's Values in Slice-of-Life Advertising

Some slice-of-life commercials are really about the story of the brand, or portraying a problem that the brand can better solve, or depicting the brand's benefit coming to the fore.

A variant is when one of the actors takes on the straight role of the product pitchman. The on-camera dialogue stops trying to be "overheard real life" and becomes exactly what an off-camera announcer would say.

The brand is solving a common need, and the brand presents itself as uniquely able to solve that need for all different types of clothes in all the different water temperatures.

In the Cheer ad following, our familiarity with hundreds of commercials we have seen before makes this believable, not because of her authentic role as mom, but because we assess whether we believe the product does what it says it does and whether that would be of benefit to us.

All-Temperature Cheer

http://www.youtube.com/watch?v=yNep-l_iWUsc

"All right. Pro got nothing on this arm, baby."

"A pro wouldn't want what's on that arm. Off. Off.

"I'll have these clean in no time."

"In the same temperature?"

"It's the same mud."

"Not on the same clothes." "So?" "This sweater goes in cold. These go in warm,

and your socks go in hot."

"Three temperatures?"
"Three types of clothes."
"Three detergents?"

One detergent
All-Temperature-Cheer

"Hey, the mud came out. Everything is clean!"
"Hey this is the pros, kid."

Retrieved from eithecat, July 31, 2011, "Cheer All Temperature Detergent commercial"

When in Doubt, Sing It

Like country music with its well-worn earthy stories, jingle commercials rely on the melodic quality of the music and the hook of the lyrics to quickly communicate the brand's premise to the potential customer. It is not a coincidence that many of the songwriters in Nashville make a substantial part of their living writing jingles and music tracks for TV advertising.

The strategic insight of Pert Plus, a shampoo and conditioner in one, was that men were the number one users of these combination products. While women accepted that a laundry detergent could have multiple formulations inside one product, they found it less believable that the same product that removes dirt can add oil to their hair at the same time.

Men, on the other hand, were not replacing two products but surmised that any conditioning benefit would be a plus, especially if it is simple.

Pert Plus

http://www.youtube.com/watch?v=nsaONhqKaBU

Music up

"You give your all to all you do.

Don't settle for less from your shampoo.

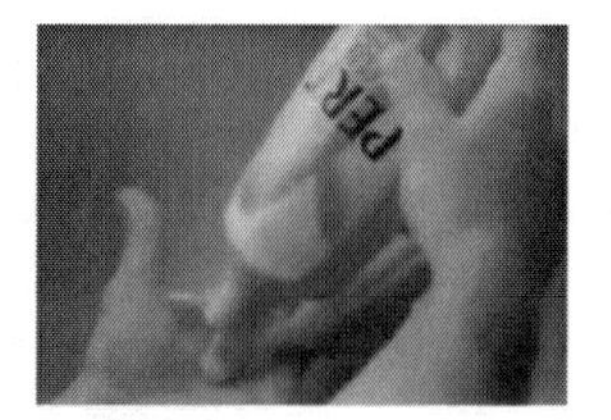

Wash 'n Go Pert Plus

"You don't need separate shampoos and conditioners, get it together.

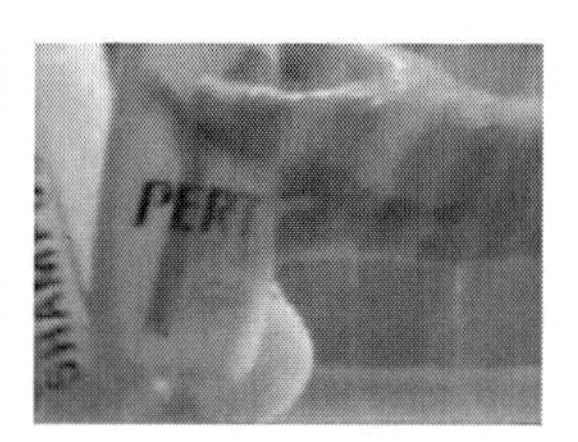

One step gets your hair more clean, more manageable.

With control you can't get from shampoos.

Wash n' Go

Shampoo and conditioner in one--
Pert Plus

Retrieved from 80sCommercialVault, July 31, 2011, 80s Commercials Vol. 5

Problem Detection

In many ways, finding out the barriers to buying more of a brand is more difficult than finding out how to positively encourage people to repeatedly buy. The behavior we can observe and ask directly about is the positive choice of a brand. While there may be many unconscious reasons we use brands that are based on previous experiences and expectations, we are more consciously aware of our recent past behavior and, therefore, can describe only the surface reasons why we made the decision to use the brand or service.

The reasons why we avoid a brand are much harder. Just like the ads we see but do not seem to notice, our unconscious is very good at steering us into habitual choices that make life easier.

After we learn to drive a car, our unconscious takes over most of our mundane driving decisions, so much so that we can drive for miles and have very little memory of the signs we saw, the traffic we passed, the familiar turns we made, the reasons for lane changes, and the speed we were going. Trying to ask someone why they did not drive in the same lane or why they did not speed up to the speed limit when other cars started to pass forces them to guess. They will give an answer, but it may not be accurate. The real reason was tied to their ability to do many things without consciously thinking about them.

Sometimes the most valuable insight that we can have for a brand is why people are not using them more often, or why former users have stopped using them, or why people are reluctant to try and find out more about them. Why don't the 45 percent of women who don't color their hair choose not to do so? Why do people shopping at a supermarket avoid the meat counter and go to the local butcher instead? Why do people who enjoy the taste of beef more than chicken and who do not have health concerns about beef still eat more chicken than beef? Why was the US Army the last choice among the branches of the service for most eighteen—to twenty-four-year-olds? Why were American cars with high consumer reports ratings not on the list of "cars I would consider" in California but were on the list in Oregon?

As individuals, detecting the problems we have with a brand turns out to be difficult. The real problem may be masked. We feel uncomfortable buying the cheapest brand, but it is easier to see that it does not have all the features we might want. The problem may be a number of small pesky irritants, not one major issue, and we have a hard time integrating all these to form an answer.

A store may be inconvenient because all the parking spots nearest the entrance fill up quickly; each store in the chain has a different layout, and you feel lost when searching for a product; the system for adding checkout lanes is haphazard and you get stuck in a slow line; and prices are marked differently from one department to another, making it hard to find the price. All these add up to the major problem of inconvenience, yet none pop to mind when you are asked why.

Because it is hard to articulate the reason, we guess. We guess that whatever we liked about the brand we did buy and the place we did shop in must be absent in the brand we did not buy or the place we did not shop in. So when people in focus groups are asked about problems, someone guesses, and the other people in the group, uncomfortable with their inability to articulate the problem, jump in and agree.

However, the group moderator or the people viewing the group know that factually, that is not a problem or that the brand in question actually outperforms the brands they are currently using on that characteristic. If confronted with the disparity, the person being interviewed "shuts down" and stops offering their opinion. If not confronted, that nonproblem keeps people from searching their own feelings more firmly.

While we cannot often recall why we did not buy a particular brand, we can recognize the reasons offered. We can tell which problems with a brand are common and which are not. We can tell which are important to us and which are not. And we can tell which problems we have actually experienced with that brand.

Trust and Distrust Are Highly Emotional Concepts

We use our emotional "good/bad" sense to sum up our feelings about problems with brands, but when asked, we are more likely to generate rational reasons. Rational reasons are rarely retrieved in the process of evaluating a brand; instead, we rely on emotional reactions that are the instantly retrievable. These are feelings of trust or mistrust that we have formed about brands. If asked whether we feel good or bad about brands, we can go through lists of dozens of brands in only a couple of minutes. If asked whether these brands are good or bad value, high or low quality, or more or less expensive than other brands, it takes over six times as long to answer about those brands. Emotional reactions are faster, and we rely on them.

When asked whether we are confident about our answers to whether that brand is trustworthy, we tend to answer that we are very confident—even about brands we have yet to buy, even about brands we say we have never heard of, and even about new brands that have yet to be seen on the shelves. When asked whether we are confident about our answers to more rational evaluations of brands (quality, price, or value), we tend to be less confident and admit to being not confident at all about brands we have never heard about or new brands that we have not seen before. So emotional reactions are more trusted.

In an actual store visit where we are buying dozens of brands, we are making hundreds of decisions not to consider or not to buy other brands. Even for considered choices like cars, we tend to have a shopping list of only three or four cars, despite an average of twelve different models that all meet the same set of eight to ten rational criteria for what we want in our next car. So our short list of products we might buy is more likely defined by our instantaneous emotional reactions than by our rationalizations of the problems we might have with those we did not short-list.

Emotional words have three characteristics: valence (good or bad), intensity (how good or bad), and referential direction (internal or external source of emotion). The best way to understand the source of a brand's problem is to help someone articulate how they *specifically* feel about the brand. They will not be able to recall the exact word, but they can recognize it. Once they recognize how they feel, that word will help the brand team know whether there is a potential problem (negative valence), how serious it may be (intensity), and whether it is caused by past personal experience or social norms (referential direction).

Walt Disney World's Challenges Were the Barriers to Returning, Not the Desire to Return

For those who have gone, Walt Disney World has the highest level of satisfaction and desire to return of any vacation destination we have been able to offer. For those who have not gone, it is usually on the short list of places "I someday want to visit." Getting long lists of the positive motivations to visit did not separate those who went more often and those who had only gone once. The challenge was to detect the problems that those who love Disney had about going "this year."

In the late eighties, Walt Disney World was running two types of commercials. The first was aimed at their most frequent visitors: families visiting for the first time. It was under the "when in doubt sing it" version of simply singing "Come be together at Disney."

It was visually full of the theme park on a nonbusy day, with the family taking full advantage of all the different facets of the park. It captured why people who go, or might go once, would go.

Disney World: 1988

http://www.youtube.com/watch?v=dkTX2tmIJUE

Song: "Come be together at Disney.

These are times you'll always treasure.

Now your dreams come true.

Golden days that last forever,

shining just for you.

Feel the joy that's all around you, share the drear come true."

"It's Mickey."

Together,

together at Disney.

Retrieved DisneyVideoMagic2, Nov 26, 2010, "Walt Disney World Commercial"

The second type of ad running during this period could be described as "something new" ads. Disney was investing in spectacular new rides at Magic Kingdom and Epcot Center. Each new adventure was usually celebrated with a commercial in the hopes it would spur return visits or be the final straw in getting someone to stop putting off the trip to Disney World.

In 1989, Disney World had even bigger news to share. They opened a new adventure area within Walt Disney World in Orlando, Disney-MGM Studios.

The strategy was simple: announce the new park, show its fun, and wait for visitors to arrive. Although this created a short-term increase in visitors, the longer-term trend was discouraging. Park attendance at Magic Kingdom and Epcot Center both decreased from 1990 through 1994, with their losses more than offsetting the new visit to Disney's Hollywood Studios.

Disney MGM Theme Park: 1989

http://www.youtube.com/watch?v=r4UJ67YnGFE

Anncr: "First came the Magic Kingdom.

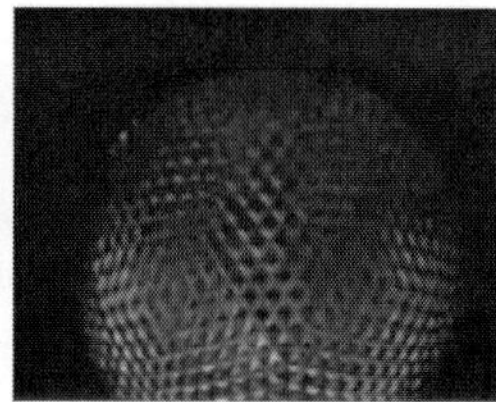

then the incredible Epcot Center,

Now comes the new Disney MGM Studios

theme park.

Music, action sounds.

Music, action sounds. Scenes of Indiana Jones Attraction.

Scenes of various avenues, including main street.

Scene of animation studio, with cartoon jumping to life.

Anncr: The Disney MGM Studios Theme Park at Walt Disney World in Orlando.

Retrieved xxGalacticGeminixx, Jun 19, 2009, "Disney MGM Studios-1989 Ad"

In Order to Build Trust, Make Sure You Keep Doing What Built the Trust

The folks who managed Disney did not make the same mistakes as the folks who managed Oldsmobile and Schlitz. In the attempt to seek new opportunities, they did not abandon their brand essence and the first-time visitors who had made them more successful.

The ad opposite is very much like the ads they ran before rethinking their business model and very much like the one we saw earlier.

A pleasant song sings the strategy, the visuals are all the exciting scenes of their park, and the emotional moment is around the heartfelt thrill of seeing their favorite Disney character come to life.

Disney World: 1994

http://www.youtube.com/watch?v=brvybZkFn-E

Song: "Be our guest, be our guest, put our magic to the test.

Bring a heart that's full of wonder and let Disney do the rest."

Music continues

"Come to our world and be

part of our family.

Come be our guest."

"Good night, Mickey."

Walt Disney World in Florida.

Call 407-W-Disney.

Retrieved from mikerichardson, August 1, 2011, "Walt Disney World Commercial"

These core commercials improved and sharpened over time as they focused more on the child's wonder of being at Disney World.

It was clear from a parent's emotional response to planning a first trip to Disney World that it was the anticipation of how much their young children would enjoy the visit that encouraged them.

It was also clear from those who had just been there that those expectations were not only met but also exceeded. The longer people stayed at Disney World, the more money they spent to be in a hotel inside the resort and the more satisfied they were. So getting the child experience right would encourage both first visits and minimize any "buyer regret" that often comes with major expenditures for high-ticket products.

Walt Disney World: USA 1995

http://www.youtube.com/watch?v=I6Ftsx1vzrU&NR=1

"Hello."

"It's time to get up."

"It's Goofy."

Kid laughter

"Hi!

I saw your movie 3 times.

Well, I guess you've seen just about everybody.

I've been waiting my whole life to meet you."

Call 1 – 407-W-Disney
And make the dream come true.

Retrieved from MegaRock64, August 1, 2011, "Walt Disney World (Wake Up Call)"

Picking the Right Moment to Go Back to Disney World

Every family probably has an optimal time when they think it would be *perfect* for their child to go to Disney World. For some it might be age five, for others seven, for others ten. The problem is that Disney World is a family vacation, and if one child by definition is the optimal age, another child in the family *feels* too old or too young.

This next commercial takes on this barrier by having a wonderful conversation between two children, one who has been to Disney World and one who has not yet had that chance. As in many families, the older child becomes the mentor, playacting the role of the parent, becoming the "onscreen" presenter within a delightful slice-of-life story.

Walt Disney World

http://www.youtube.com/watch?v=4x3poLxJjzw

"Larry, this is like no place you've ever been in your whole life.

First thing you've got to remember about Disney World is to pace yourself.

This is a mistake that a lot of first timers make. They've got all these rides and

cool things to do, and if you try to do them all, you'll be sleeping like a baby.

Number two, don't eat just before you go on Mr. Toad's Wild Ride.

Number three, Goofy is hug I know he's only this big on TV, but in real life

Goofy could beat up Dad. Well, I guess that's all the important stuff. You're going to love this place, Larry.

It really brings out the kid in you."
ANNCR: "There's never been a better time to make the dream come true."

"We'll be leaving in about three weeks."

Retrieved from MotherAtHeart, Jun 23, 2010, "Disney World Commercial - 1994"

Reaching Others Beyond the Young Family

The breakthrough insight for Disney World was that every age group had slight barriers to coming this year that were overwhelming their interest in returning to Disney World. Some of these were economic; taking the whole family to Disney World is a major expense for most families and not one that some can afford to do every year.

However, the emotion-based reasons were more important. Parents worried that their teens might not want to go or might not enjoy themselves once there. Childless couples wondered if, as a couple, they could have the fun they had as a child. Older couples wondered if they should wait for that elusive grandchild to be born and be old enough to go, or if they could possibly have fun on their own.

Disney World developed marketing material for each of these groups: commercials, planning videos, and websites.

This commercial reached out to pre-child couples.

Disney World: USA 1995

http://www.youtube.com/watch?v=7xqiD6tEZTo

"So Hal, I heard you took Sally up to the lodge in the woods."

"Well, sort of."

"She didn't mind roughing it,"

even with all those wild animals?

Yea. I bet the fish were biting.

Man, that's the life.
A little boating. A little swimming.

Just you and Sally alone in no where. Where is it?"
"Disney World!"

Laughing and saying "Unbelievably." "Yea."
Disney World

Call 1 407-W-Disney and make the world come true.

Retrieved from mycommercials, August 1, 2011, "Wal Disney World Commercial (1995)"

Expanding the Magic to Other Joint Products

The success of the new efforts reversed the decline, and for the next few years, the total numbers attending Walt Disney World increased annually. There was also the addition of a fourth attraction: Disney's Animal Kingdom. The fun rides, safari and river excursions, parades, and resorts gave even a wider range of appeal to different age groups.

The increased interest of all ages opened up other opportunities. One of the most successful has been the combination of a visit to Disney World tied to going on a Disney cruise ship in the Caribbean. The following commercial announced this joint experience for what has turned out to be a success for the Walt Disney Company.

Disney Cruise Line: USA 1998

http://www.youtube.com/watch?v=jpqHvMn7_M8

Music: Saharazad

Music continues

Music continues

It's a first

from the dream makers of Disney.

Introducing Disney Cruise Line.

Imagine combining a visit to Walt Disney World

With our own private island in the Bahamas.

Call and discover uncharted magic.

Retrieved from DisneyParkVideos, August 1, 2011, "Disney Cruise Line – Commercial #1"

Renewing Interest for an Older Brand

If Kellogg's Corn Flakes had a *tiger* for a presenter, then he would probably say that they taste "Grrrrreat." The problem for the brand was that other smaller brands spent more advertising money and were aimed exclusively at young families or teens. Thus, the brand, which is truly liked and eaten by the whole family when purchased, had a nostalgic image of being "for old folks."

Rather than bring back Cornelius Rooster, their old mascot, Kellogg's Corn Flakes let a "typical potential eater" become their presenter. The dialogue between the off-screen announcer and the actor tells the insight that this cereal really does taste surprisingly good—good and simple. The brand responded with a record sales increase.

Kellogg's Corn Flakes

http://www.youtube.com/watch?v=RYv2sPqnTZI

Open on screen saying, "Introducing a cereal from Kellogg's."

Man, "I've just got two things to say about this cereal. Boring. Too simple.

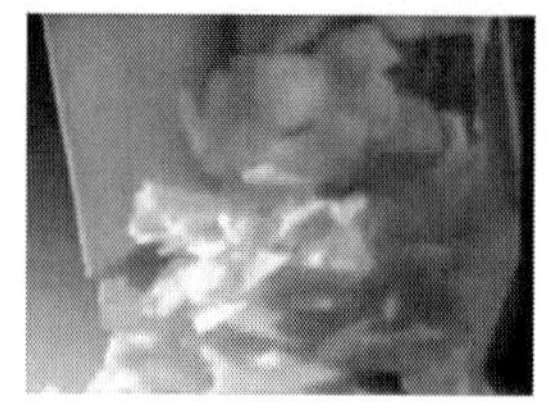

These days you have to have oats or straw or hay or something. This is nothing

but flakes. But the taste, the taste is good.

Kind of shocked that something this simple tastes this good.

I think that this simplicity angle might just work. This cereal might make it."

Anncr: "Kellogg's Corn Flakes."

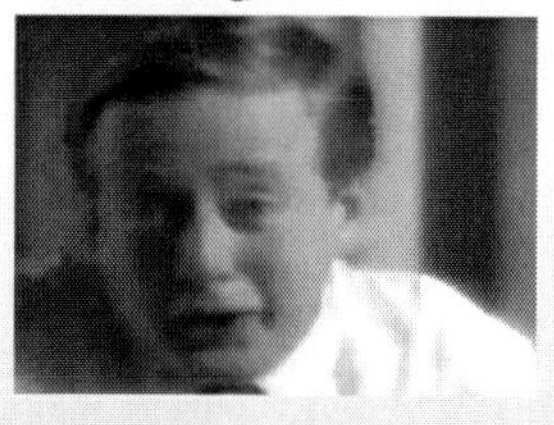

"Hey, can I pick a winner Or what!"

Kellogg's Corn Flakes. Taste them again for the first time.

Retrieved from GloopTrekker, July 26, 2011, "Kellogg's Corn Flakes "Taste Them Again"

Presenters Keep It Simple

Throughout the year, Grace Bros. Department Store in New South Wales, Australia, talks about the fashion, fun, and flair of being a non-price-focused department store. They focus on their range, the importing of fashionable brands from around the world, and their intense desire to showcase local high-quality Australian clothes, appliances, and products for the home.

Twice a year they have storewide sales, much in the manner of Harrods in London. The price reductions are incredible, and some customers hold off purchasing products that they have seen and liked, just waiting for these sales.

The use of a serious store personality created for the commercial is a powerful way to use a presenter and to give a sense of newsworthiness to a promotional event.

Grace Brothers Department Store.

http://www.youtube.com/watch?v=ynYoHuPHYIM

At Grace Bros. we only have two sales a year, so they've got to be good.

The Winter Sale will be one you can't afford to miss.

Store-wide, the best brands, the greatest ranges,

and most importantly, true sale prices.

Up to 50% off in women's Fashions.

Up to 50% off in mensware.

And up to 50% off in Homemakers.

Huge Savings. Don't miss the winter sale at Grace Bros.

I certainly won't."

Retrieved from GrubcoTV3, July 26, 2011, "Grace Bros commercial [1984]"

Trusting an Animal Presenter

Dozens of commercials are made every year that feature a winsome animal as the presenter. Sometimes they become a spokesperson, like Morris the Finicky Cat, Charlie the Tuna, or the Geico Gecko, but often they are one-time presenters simply delivering the strategy onscreen.

Diet Pepsi has used a chimp; Philips vacuum cleaner has used a talking mouse; Jeep a singing squirrel, pigeon, and coyote inside the new Jeep Liberty; Budweiser's Clydesdales got disturbed by a streaking freshly shorn lamb; and EDS (a consultancy) shared the challenges of cowboys herding cats.

Of course, many of these are borrowed interest only. Cadbury, on the other hand, followed in this tradition with an onscreen presenter, a rabbit announcing that the short season for buying Cadbury Crème Eggs was here, but only through Easter.

Cadbury’s Crème Egg

http:/ / www.youtube.com/ watch?v=Q596AhiyU7Q

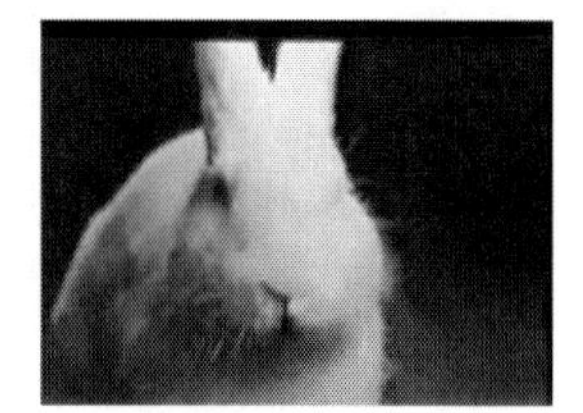

Shot of rabbit clucking like a hen.

“You’re looking at a very unusual type of egg from Cadbury.

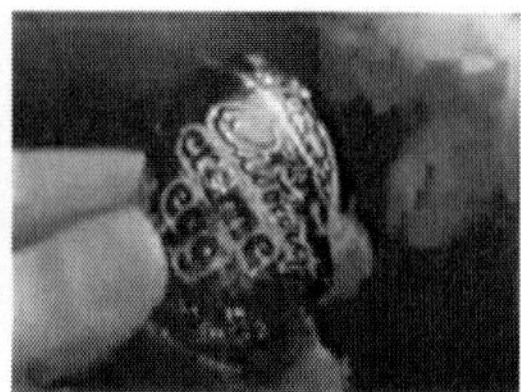

That will only be around until Easter.

It’s shell is pure rich Cadbury’s chocolate.

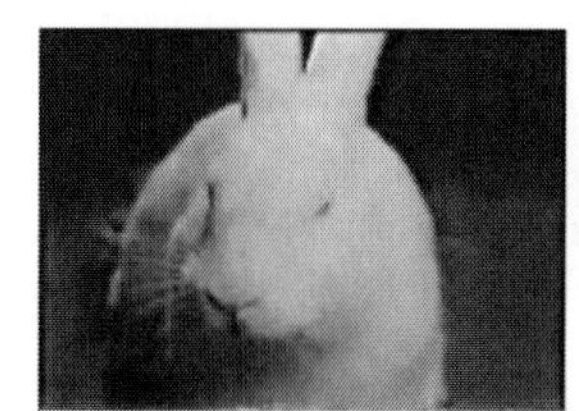

But look.

Inside sits a sweet creamy yolk surrounded by delicious white filling.

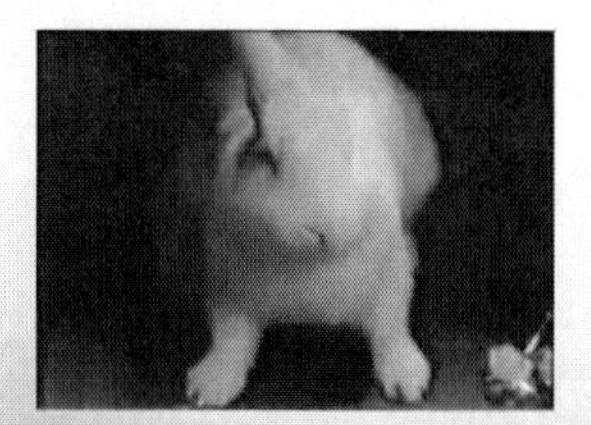

Crème Eggs from Cadbury.

“Why they are the best thing to come along since the Easter bunny.

And when he’s gone, they’re gone.”

Retrieved from michend2003, July 26, 2011, “80s Cadbury Eggs Commercial”

Who Is More Trustworthy than Hawaiians Inviting You to Visit Hawaii?

The final example is that of an off-screen presenter who lets native Hawaiians tell the reasons why it's worth flying to Hawaii and, of course, doing so on United Airlines. This commercial is based on the insight that the exotic yet American nature of the island is extraordinarily appealing to all Americans in the many mainland cities that United Airlines serves.

Presenter ads can effortlessly transition from face to feature when the dialogue runs continuously throughout the commercial. That's an insight that every documentary maker has learned and used in their films and which commercials like this creatively leverage.

UAL to Hawaii

http://www.youtube.com/watch?v=t5qgS0gpBh8

Hawaii has many faces,
all calling you.

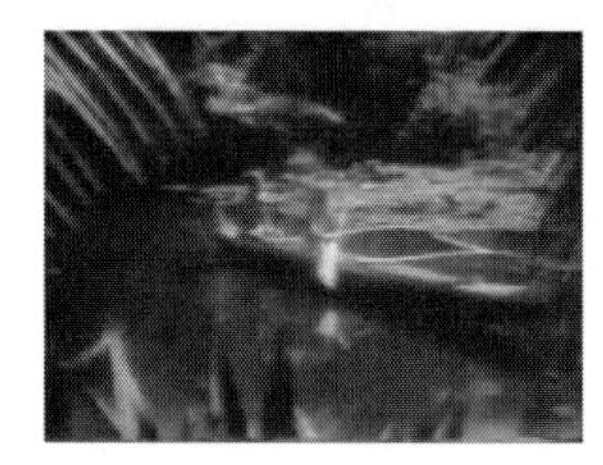

Come.
paddle my quiet lagoons.

Discover my miles of
endless beach.

Come walk across the
face of my volcanoes.

Explore my mysterious
caverns.

Come play in my
tropical wonderland.

Come fly my airline to
Hawaii. United.

We built the largest airline
in the free world.

Song, "Fly the friendly
Skies of United."

Retrieved from MrClassicAds1970s, July 26, 2011, "United Airlines Hawaii commercial 1979"

Chapter Four

Unique Personality Properties "Embody" the Insight, Building Brand Trust over Time

Creating a Branded Celebrity

Over time, some companies have built trust in their brand via their own celebrity personality properties. Unlike the celebrity, they take time to develop. However, with consistent use, they create an instant sense of familiarity and involvement in the ad. Their image in the store or on a web page calls out and reminds the potential buyer of the brand's name and also the associated imagery of the brand.

Sometimes the personality property flows from the brand name: the silver Jaguar, the black-and-white Panda brand on Asian specialty products, the softly descending gold Dove at the end of soap commercials, the puffy Fruit of the Loom characters, the big-nosed controversial Camel cigarette figure, and the Green Giant are examples. The Green Giant character was actually created to protect the brand name that came from importing, growing, and marketing the larger English pea (i.e., Green Giant). By associating the name, which was at first only a hard-to-protect descriptive name, with the iconic figure of the mythic giant, the Minnesota Valley Canning Company in 1928 was able to trademark and protect Green Giant.

Sometimes the property flows from associated products. Perhaps the most famous is the Mickey Mouse black-and-white visual for Disney, or the image of Tinker Bell magically opening the doors to Walt Disney's Wonderful World of Color. The silver-haired KFC colonel came from its founder, Harland "Colonel" Sanders. Hugh Hefner's Playboy Bunny logo, with its distinctive tux tie, was used in advertising for twenty years. The red-and-green Kellogg's Corn Flakes rooster went from the package to the advertising and back again several different times.

Some of the most well-known personality properties were created out of whole cloth for the specific purpose of a broad campaign to sell their brand. The Clydesdales, Kool-Aid Pitcher, Planters' Peanut, Mr. Clean, Michelin Tire Man, Trix Rabbit, Speedy the Alka-Seltzer conductor, and the Geico Gecko are great examples.

Creating and Evolving the Property

The personality property may have started as a logo image of the brand, a once-off promotion, or a single ad that seemed to have instant appeal. However, nurturing and evolving the image over time and across international boundaries has been the crucial differentiator between those images that have endured and those that have come and gone.

The boundaries of what constitutes a property are not well defined for they are constantly expanding. Apple started out in the cheeky mold of the Beatles "Revolution." Its iconic "Bite out of the apple" logo ties firmly to the Adam and Eve danger-of-knowledge motif. It launched the Mac computer with the once-shown 1984 image of the hammer breaking through the gray world of big business me-too IBM clones. The Apple image has constantly evolved into connoting clean and simple design and user-first cloud-based life enhancement.

Heinz used the cool buzz of the "Fonzie-like" cheekiness to relaunch its ketchup from side-by-side product comparisons to contemporary music and innovative packaging. The KFC Colonel has transformed Christmas in Japan to the time when bringing home a barrel of chicken defines the holiday. Geico has made its Cockney-accented gecko move from a spokesperson to the inspiration of better service and better prices.

On the other hand, the Playboy Bunny image seems dated, revived only by nostalgic TV series like *Mad Men* and *Pan Am*. Mr. Clean never evolved. The image of a genie-like character helping a woman whose fondest desire is a really clean kitchen seems as dated as the "Man from Glad" attempting the same task; it's lost in a different era and different set of values. These characters simply stopped evolving and investing in keeping a brand relevant.

Find the Best Way to Tell the Brand's Story

In the sixties and seventies, ads for Niblets Corn, Green Beans, and Peas were set in the valley of the Jolly Green Giant, a huge, shadowy figure that appeared on the packaging and opened and closed each ad with a deep baritone "Ho ho ho."

The announcer described the reasons to believe that Green Giant vegetables would taste crisper and fresher than other brands. The lower volume of water in flash-frozen Green Giant, the diagonal cut of the green beans, and the "just-picked freshness" of the larger peas all complemented the cute valley farmers who cared about quality and freshness.

The insight of creating a cast of characters who can be the pitchmen instead of the iconic Green Giant has worked brilliantly for over fifty years.

Green Giant 1965

http:/ / www.youtube.com/ watch?v=Q8ilBsr9n3o

In the Valley of the Jolly
"Ho Ho Ho"
Green Giant.

Every year at the valley fair
they judge Green Giant's
Niblets Corn against all comers

and Niblets Corn always
wins ...

"The Green Ribbon"

The judge explains, an
ordinary can of corn has
lots of water

to keep his corn crisper
the Giant's corn has almo
no water."

Niblet's brand corn is the
Giant's own special kind
grown to be sweeter.

For the crispest, freshest
tasting corn, try Green
Giant's Niblets Corn

Good things from the
garden. Garden in the
Valley, "Ho Ho Ho"
Green Giant.

Retrieved from communicatrix, Dec 22, 2008, "1960s Green Giant TV commercial"

In the late seventies, improved animation made the stories more visually interesting. The Giant evolved visually, but for two decades the same format was used.

The advertising insight that helps the personality property work harder for the brand was the creation of the Giant's helper, Sprout. Suddenly the main character could be the spokesperson. The Giant stopped being a visual logo and, in the persona of Sprout, could tell far more involving stories with humor and charm.

One of the key insights about effective advertising is that when you have to tell about the product to tell the story, then the intended information is more memorably communicated. As the ad opposite shows, Sprout is discovering that "just-picked vacuum packing" is the everyday reason that Green Giant Niblets Corn tastes crisp and fresh.

The Giant's "Ho ho ho" still opened and closed the commercials, but it is his little helper Sprout who evolves and improves the effectiveness of the story.

Green Giant 1989

http:/ / www.youtube.com/ watch?v=zCCrjjqWrQ8

Up in the Valley of the Jolly Green Giant

"Hi Sprout.

Lovely day isn't it. "

Not for packing corn I'm afraid.

"Don't worry Sprout. The Giant vacuum packs his special Niblets Corn

with very little water

That's why his sweet Niblet's Corn always tastes crisp and fresh.

Another perfect day for corn, Mrs. Duck.

"Ho Ho Ho" Green Giant.

Retrieved from Crommy5, Nov 15, 2010, "Green Giant Niblets Commercial 1989"

Pillsbury Dough Quality Cues in the Commercial

Like the Green Giant, the Pillsbury Doughboy was chiefly used as an opening and closing brand visual. The body looked like a chub of fresh dough, the baker's hat communicated the "home baker" image, and the lovable "He-he" giggle created a sound cue as distinctive as the Giant's "Ho ho ho."

The stories were set in real households, with cutaways to the product rising in an oven, being buttered or iced, and pulled apart with steam wafting in the air for a visual just-baked goodness.

The advertising insight was how to integrate the opening and the middle. The device that was used for more than a decade was "Mmmm, ahhh, ohhh . . . Poppin' fresh dough." The appreciative appetite sounds were appropriately placed and then reprised just as the finger tickled the nonexistent belly button of the Doughboy, eliciting the famous giggle.

Pillsbury Cinnamon Rolls

http://www.youtube.com/watch?v=4TeuDUAjSts&feature=related

There□s nothing like waking up to my fresh-baked Cinnamon rolls.

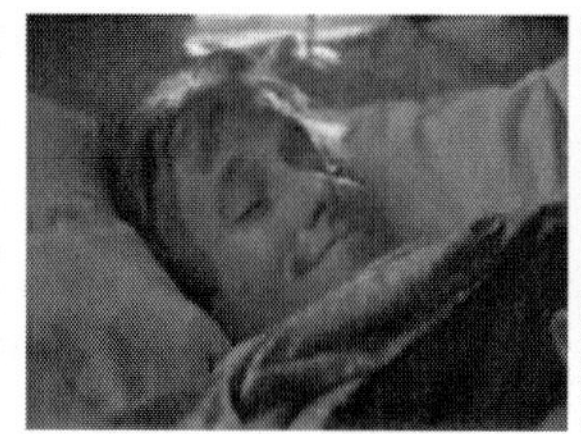

Mmmm,

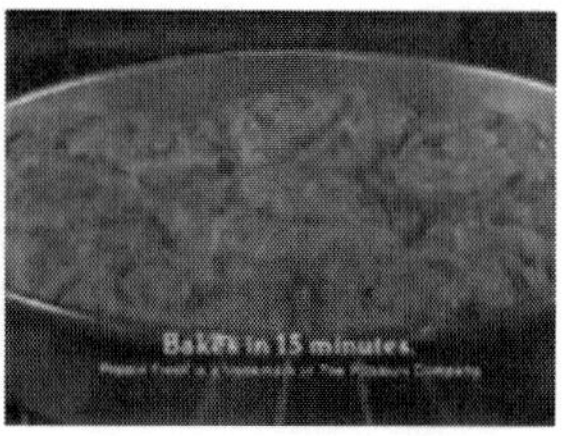

that poppin□fresh dough.

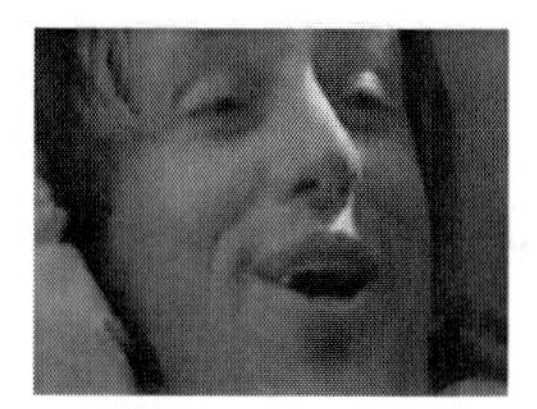

"Hot cinnamon rolls."

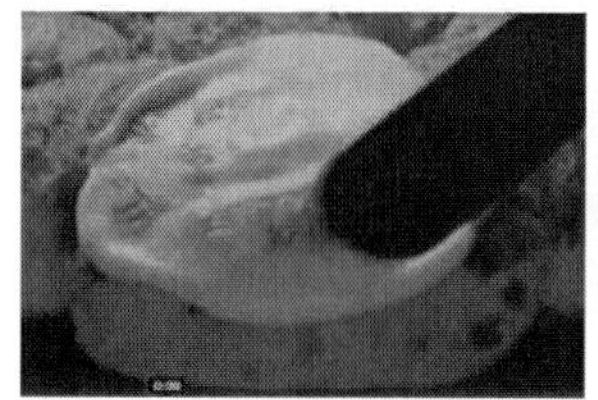

Ahhhh!

"I can see them rising in the oven. All that cinnamon."

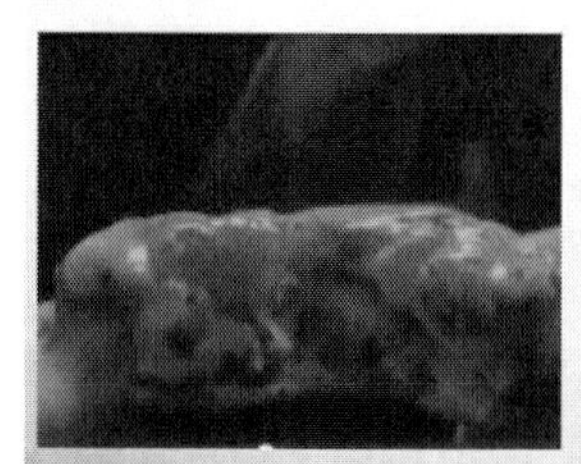

Ohhhh. That poppin□ fresh dough.

Mmmm, Ahhhh, Ohhhh. "Cinnamon fresh dough."

"He He!" giggle.

Retrieved from TheVideorougue, April 14, 2011, "1983 Pillsbury Cinnamon Rolls"

Personality Properties as Part of a Broader Campaign: The Clydesdales

The Clydesdales have been part of the promotional face of the Anheuser-Busch brewing family from the time August Busch Jr. presented them to his father to celebrate the repeal of prohibition. They were used to deliver two cases to Al Smith, the governor of New York, who was instrumental in the repeal.

They have been used alongside many different eras of Budweiser beer advertising. Their physical presence in parades across the country and their use in Super Bowl ads, like the one following, have given a distinctive, proud, authentic, heartland image to the beer, consistent with Budweiser's brewing imagery.

One of the most memorable iconic images appeared on air only once, when the two lead horses of the hitch knelt down before the post-9/11 Manhattan skyline.

Budweiser

http:/ / www.youtube.com/ watch?v=_NXIv28HYOA

The final horse for this year's Hitch Team is Thunder.

Maybe next year Hank.

Woof. Woof.

Theme music from the movie "Rocky"

Welcome aboard, Hank.

Retrieved from BudBowlLLII, Feb1, 2008, "budweiser Clydesdale Team commercial"

Creating a Cast of Characters

Another insightful way to avoid a superficial image from a personality property is to create a cast of characters that can represent different aspects of the brand, create more interactive stories, and represent different products under a brand umbrella. The Keebler Elves are a classic example.

In the UK, McEwan's extended their traditional beer into the growing can lager segment by creating the Grousebeaters and telling strong Scottish stories that revolved around their endless appetite for the beer.

In a category where young men and women were swilling beer, flirty and full of fun, this campaign stood out and allowed a new entry into a crowded category to thrive.

McEwan's Lager

http:/ / www.youtube.com/ watch?v=7NbqXOTKWjU&feature=related

"Here we are at the start of The Grand Nationals and

here's the latest favorites by Wee Little.

They're off.
He's refused.

But what's he doing?"
He's over--and look at him go.

He's over the last obstacle.
And it's Grousebeaters taking the flag."

"Well done, General."
"How about me, Tush?"

"Ah, John. You really used your head, for once."

(Aside) "Daft boy."

Anncr. "Only McEwan's Lager satisfies the Grousebeaters."

Retrieved from neilnblack, July 26, 2011, "Inverbraw Grouse Beaters 4"

Distinct Visual Properties

Many ads create properties not through the use of characters but in the distinctive visual style of their advertising. Louis Vuitton uses black-and-white silhouette figures. iPod uses black-and-white dancing figures on bright green, yellow, and orange backgrounds, which match their outer covers. Dewar's Scotch uses close-ups of famous people with their Dewar's profile alongside.

In the UK, Cadbury's Flake developed an incredibly sensuous style of ads of women in beautiful settings, enjoying the crumbliest, flakiest chocolate.

Cadbury's Flake

http:/ / www.youtube.com/ watch?v=JrKUwUGwQfs

Only the crumbliest,

flakiest chocolate

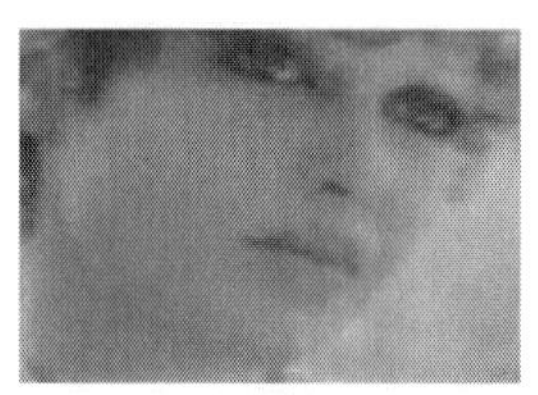

tastes like chocolate never tasted before.

Only the crumbliest

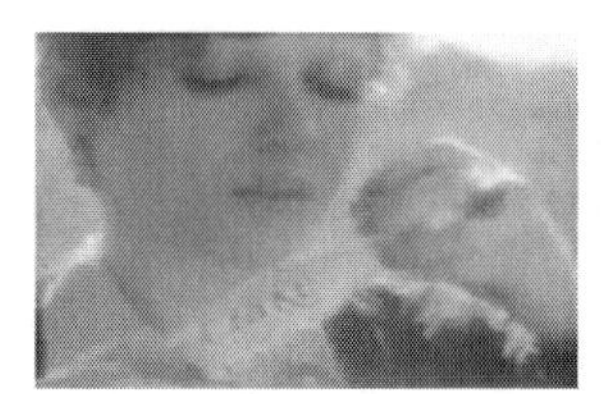

flakiest chocolate

tastes like

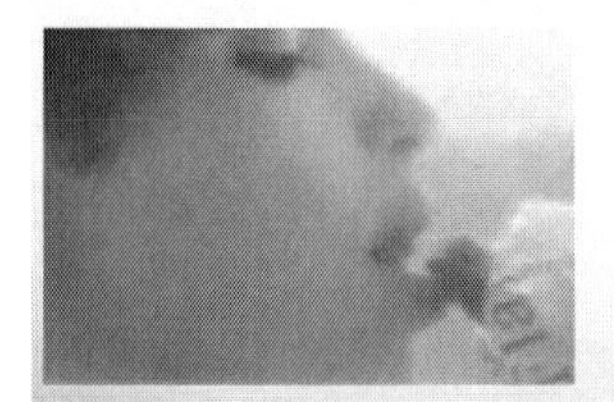

chocolate never tasted before.

Tastes like chocolate

never tasted before.

Retrieved from glunglun, July 26, 2011, "Cadbury's Flake Advert"

Chapter Five

The Demo: Visual Proof of the Insight

Tangible Reasons to Trust a Brand

We've all walked away from an in-store demonstration owning the showcased product. A great salesman makes the product seem so inviting, easy to use, helpful, and answers the questions we had and the new questions that came to light during the product's use. A great product demonstration ad captures the tangible believability of that experience.

"Seeing is believing" is an idiom testifying that physical, concrete proof is a powerful form of persuasion. Interestingly, people find product demonstrations in advertising mesmerizing, even for products that they do not use. These two facts combine to produce a format of advertising that is often used and, when done well, is incredibly effective.

There are two clear parts to brand trust: the tangible facets of the brand that you can see and the reputational ones that you believe. Demonstrations can move some of the reputational elements into the tangible column. Shampoo has been called hope in a bottle, but the visual transformation of hair from before to after is what makes that hope a reality. You might think about beef as a good-tasting source of protein, but beef producers would rather you think about it as "sizzling good" in interesting easy recipes, not as a thick bloody-red blob staring back at you from behind supermarket cellophane. Similarly, Pillsbury would like your mind's eye to visualize hot popping-fresh buns, not a chub of gooey dough languishing in the refrigerator case.

A clever demonstration can take something you cannot see—the incredibly light touch required by power steering, the ability of a pan to withstand burner temperatures your stove can't create, or how a conditioner actually makes your hair feel silken—and make them visible and memorable.

A demonstration is trying to answer questions you have in your head that might be keeping you from buying a brand. Is it real cheese? What would basic training be like? Would that new product actually look good in my home? Will I feel comfortable on an Asian airline?

Overcoming Skepticism Based on Life Experience

When new technology or product features transform the usage experience from what has been reassuringly familiar, it is hard to make it believable. No one expects to go to the Department of Motor Vehicles, be summoned for jury duty, or return a purchase without a receipt and say they had a pleasant time. Similarly, *new and improved*, two of the most overused words in advertising, have come to mean "more expensive, more complicated, and not meaningfully better" to many people.

Understanding the real challenge of healthy skepticism demands an advertising insight. Look at how BMW 321i introduced "incredibly responsive power steering."

BMW 321i "Mouse"

http://www.youtube.com/watch?v=Qf0jvHfTODw

Classic music intro

Classic music intro

Classic music intro

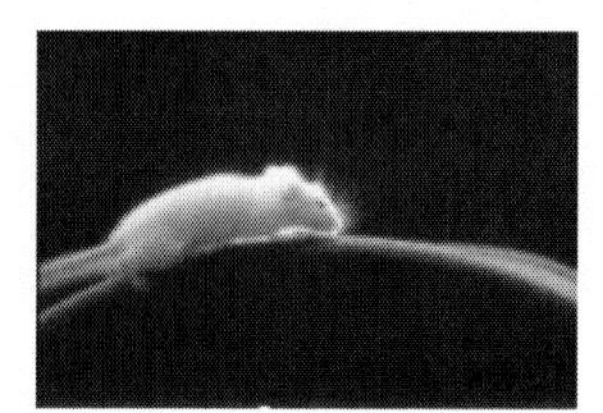

Blue Danube orchestration, mouse runs around wheel, wheel easily turns.

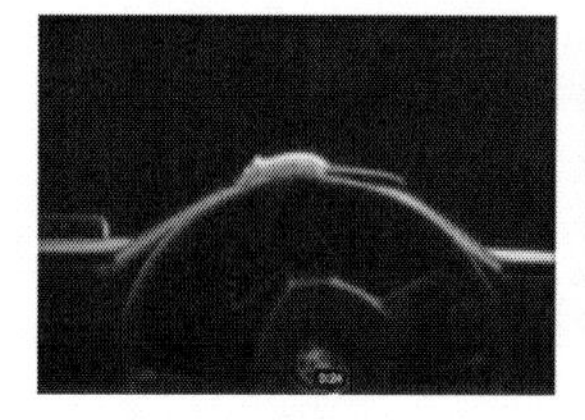

Blue Danube orchestration

Blue Danube orchestration, mouse turns, runs other way, wheel turns other way.

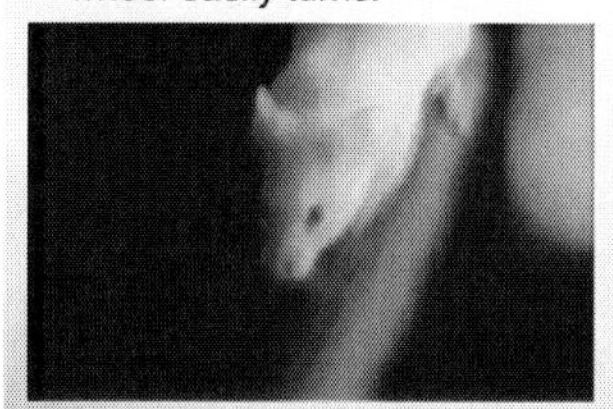

Blue Danube orchestration

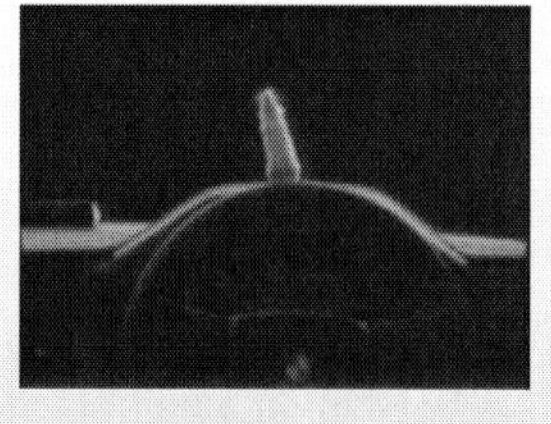

The BMW 321i

Now with power steering.

Applause

Retrieved from ConvergingArrors, October 6, 2006, "BMW Mouse Ad"

Torture Tests

We've seen monkeys throwing Samsonite luggage, wristwatches in extreme peril so Timex can claim "Takes a lickin' and keeps on tickin'," and a Vision Saucepan subjected to 850-degree heat that melts the aluminum pan it is holding. These are all other versions of the demonstration—the torture test. The ad implicitly asks you to say, "It would never break or fail with me. I would never subject it to that much abuse!"

Again, these ads are in search of an insight that will permit them to bypass the skeptical test. "In my experience, baggage handlers ruined my suitcase"; "I bought a cheap watch, and it just didn't last"; and "Could a clear saucepan really be safe?"

Vision Saucepan

http://www.youtube.com/watch?v=f1HXqh8YadA&NR=1

A new Vision saucepan has many advantages

over an ordinary saucepan.

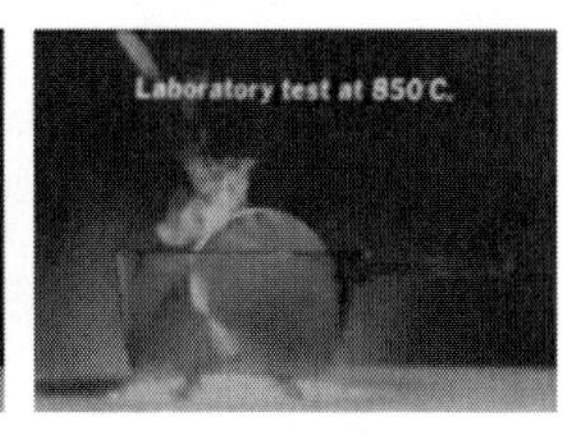

It will never stain, and it's easy to clean.

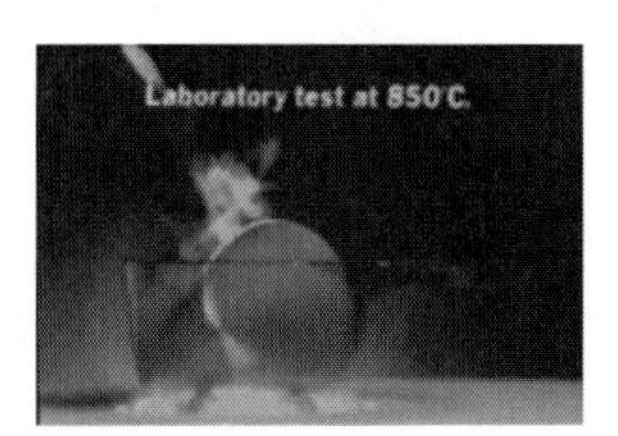

It's handle can't work loose.

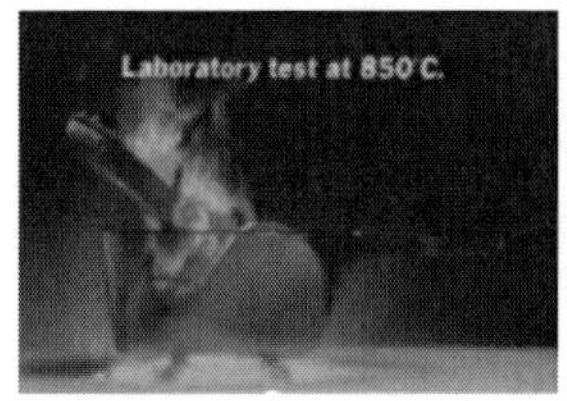

And, as you can see, it's not a bit perturbed by a heat that can turn an ordinary

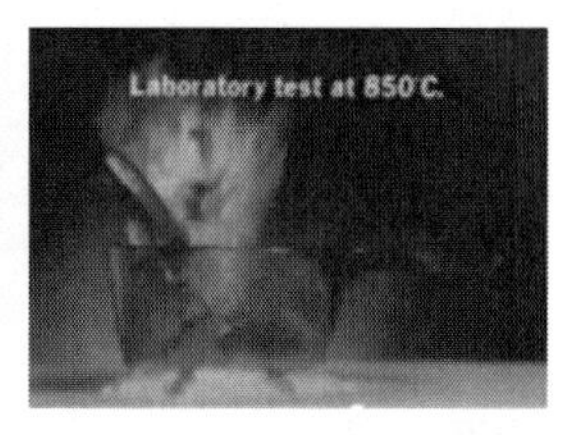

saucepan into a sauce.

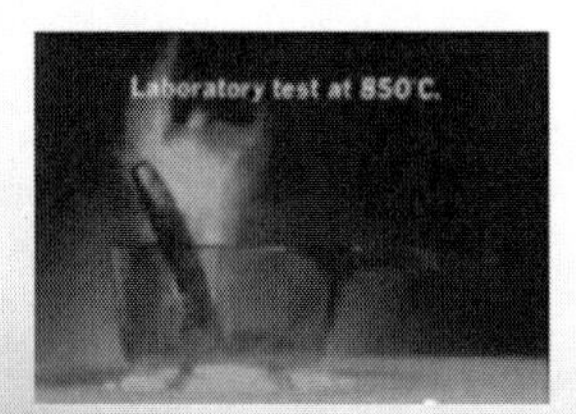

Vision. Designed in France with an remarkable new material called Xeleon,

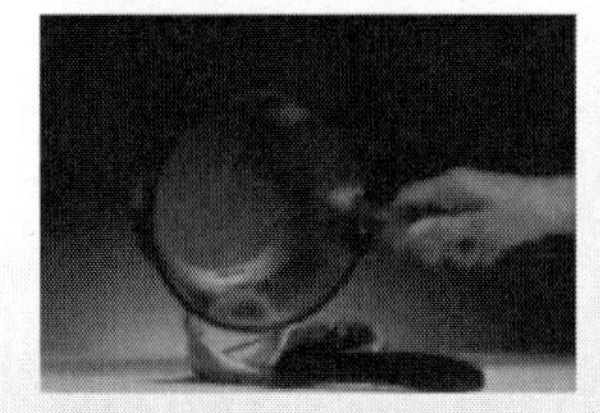

with a 10-year warranty from Dow-Corning.

The future in saucepans is absolutely clear.

Retrieved from donkeyshines, Nov 3, 2008, "Vision Cookwear"

Real-Life Torture Tests

While many ads devise truly imaginative torture tests, equally effective are the torture tests that brands often experience in real households. DieHard batteries preventing waking up to a dead car that had its lights left on overnight in winter, Apple's online ad showing the new iPhone surviving a fall from a shirt pocket onto a tile floor, and Sealy presenting their mattress as an indoor substitute to a child's trampoline.

These have the advantage of being both real and extreme and yet believable through the flash of recognition.

Sealy Posturepedic

http://www.youtube.com/watch?v=kw9U3bIBX6E&feature=related

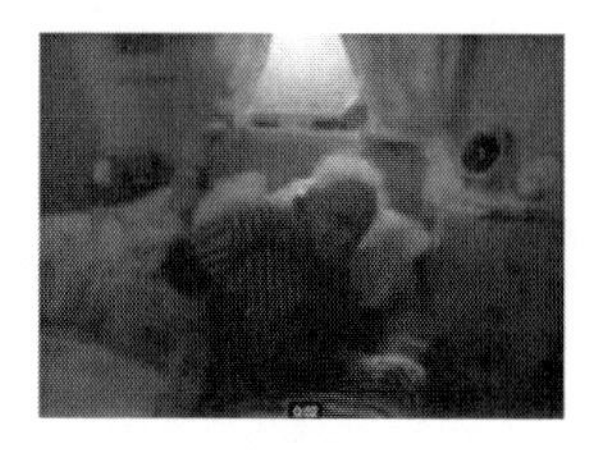

Some beds do this.
(man struggles to get out)

Some beds do that.
(couple literally fall out of bed)

Some beds bounce, but they don't bounce back.

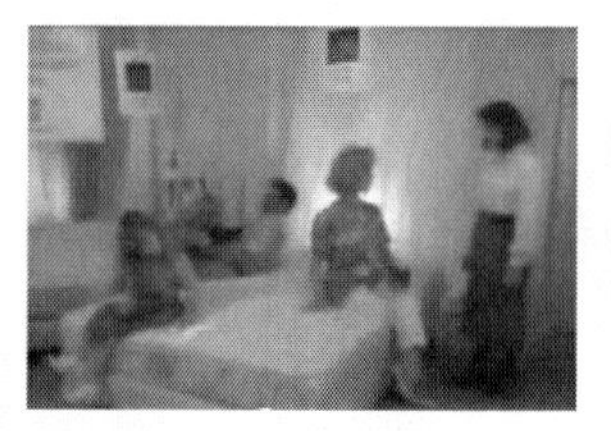

But of all the beds that you might try,

there's only one bed you should buy.

Wake up with that
Sealy Posturepedic feeling.

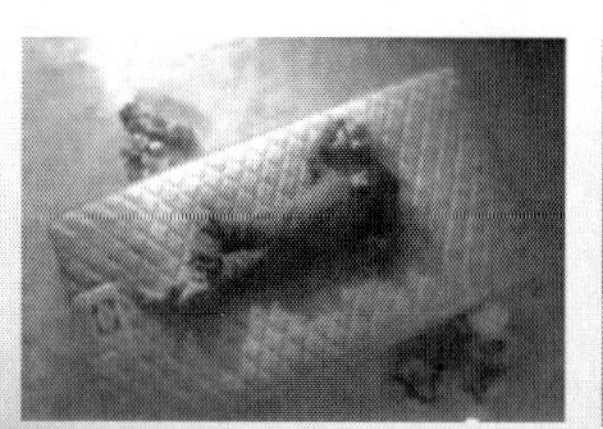

We're years ahead.

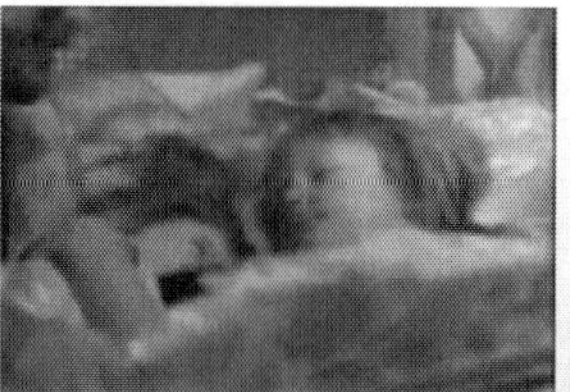

Wake up with that
Sealy Posturepedic feeling.

The world's best bed.

Retrieved from tramman82mk2, Nov 25, 2010, "Sealy Posturepedic 1989"

Before and After

This classic Agree shampoo ad rolls out the full demonstration in an upbeat style that matches the casual nature of "hope in a bottle."

Rather than dramatize the "before" of its sister "Help stop the greasies" ad, this one focuses on the insight that hair's dramatic transformation is all the proof young women need.

This commercial's song, "I Do, I Do, I Do," was bright, and the hair stylist's tone was sexy as well as authoritative, helping move Agree to the number 1 position in Australia.

Agree Shampoo

http://www.youtube.com/watch?v=mwqc1m7mCJc

Do you know the shampoo that helps stop the Greasies?

Song, "I do, do, do ...

...I don't, don't, don't"

Agree shampoo works two ways to help stop the Greasies between shampoos.

First, it cleans your hair.

Then it cleans your scalp so your hair stays cleaner between shampoos.

No matter whether your hair is oily, normal, or dry, you can still get the Greasies.

Song, "Don't you think it's time you Agree?

I do. I do. I do.

Retrieved from AustralianAds, July 26, 2011, "Agree Australian ad, 1981"

Demonstration Insert

The most common use of a demonstration is as a short insert in a thirty-second ad.

The “seeing is believing” nature of a demo lends itself to the quick visual that illustrates how a product actually works, particularly if you could not physically see how it works while in use.

Hundreds of pain relievers, aids to indigestion, stomach remedies, and other “internal” products use the demonstration insert.

Here Silkience uses the way its formula coats drier areas of the hair more than naturally oil-coated areas to show how it “goes only where it is needed.”

Silvikrin Silkience Conditioner

http://www.youtube.com/watch?v=0J5YMTupjVA

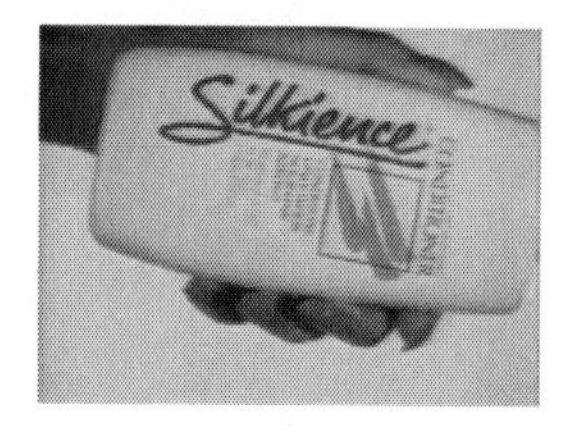

Song (lyrically version of Tommy Song) See me

Song: Touch me

Anncr: Science brings you Silkience,

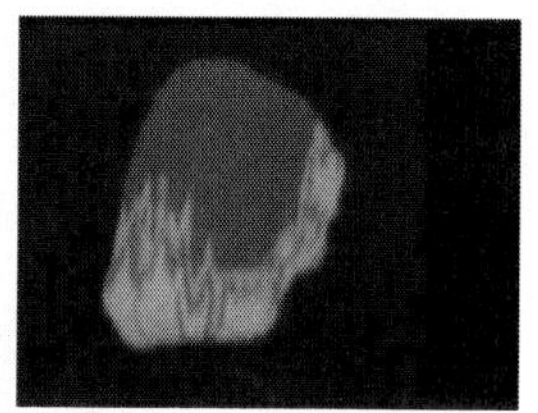

a conditioner that goes only where it is needed,

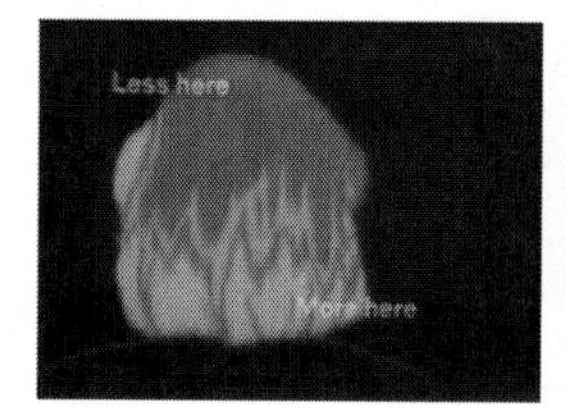

like this,

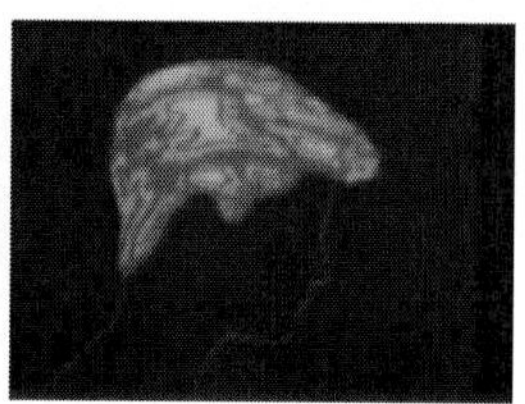

or all over like this.

What you don't need goes clean away.

Feel me.

For beautiful conditioned hair, give it the Silkience touch.

Retrieved from NinaOPerez, July 26, 2011, "Silvikrin- See Me, Touch Me, UK Advert"

Demonstration's Ability to Combine Benefits

The focus of most advertising is the benefit thought to be most important—this is what is fully dramatized.

Kleenex Boutique Tissues had two potentially quite different benefits: the generic use of taking off makeup and the Kleenex-specific new designer boxes. Since facial tissue is left out in the open, its packaging is somewhat important to most buyers.

Here Kleenex shows both at the same time: fashionable women demonstrating use and also imbuing the packaging with a sense of attractiveness.

Kleenex: USA 1978

http://www.youtube.com/watch?v=0ClOXz_Mld0

Song: Do do do do do

Song: Get away

Do do do do do

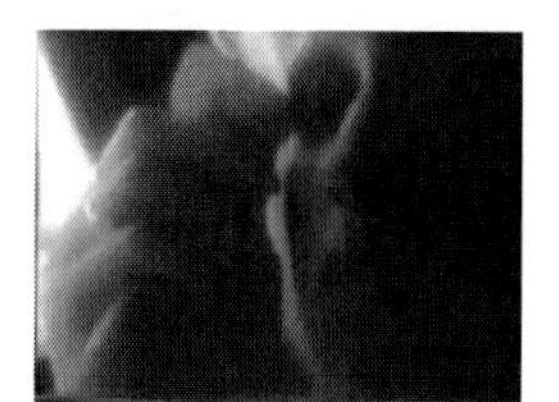

Get away

Do do do do

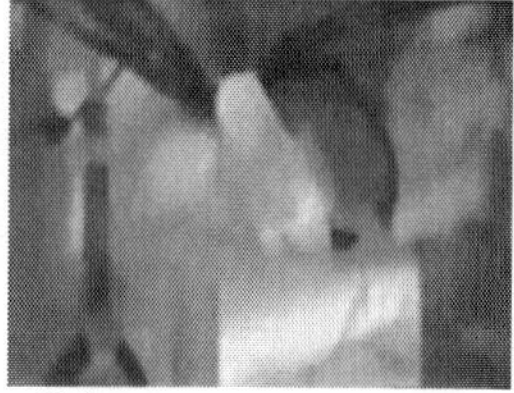

Get away

Do do do do do

Kleenex Boutique
10 blending colors

In beautiful new boxes.
Song: Do do do do do

Retrieved from haribokey, July 26, 2011, "1978 Kleenex Boutique Tissues"

Creating Trust for a Career Choice: The US Army

When a young man or woman decides to enlist in the army, understanding the context of the life choice they are making is central to finding the right insight to advertise. There are two quite different contexts to consider: choosing the army instead of civilian life and choosing the army instead of one of the other armed forces.

The army as the backbone of the military, with the proverbial "boots on the ground," faces some of the toughest recruiting issues. The ability of recruitment to attract sufficient numbers to meet the needs of what is a high-turnover career for the vast majority of recruits is a critical mission in an all-volunteer military.

The insight that attracts someone to apply has to do several things at once. It must turn interest into belief and take the person either down to the local recruiting office or have them begin the application process online. Since a small minority of young people will both qualify and be interested, the insight has to be relevant to the mind-set of very specific small subgroups. Most important, it has to feel authentic and dramatize a specific benefit unique to the army.

The Air Force has the top-gun advantage of cutting-edge technology and has the reputation of being best at preparing its people to obtain high-paying civilian jobs after service. The navy promises travel, adventure, port cities, and the perception of being both intellectually challenging and safer. The marines have the reality of a much smaller recruiting goal, offering the elite feel of the Air Force and the physically challenging job of the army.

In a competitive context, it is not surprising that the army has always lagged behind the other forces in its ability to meet its higher manpower goals.

This issue came to a head in the nineties when the baby bust of the seventies produced far fewer potential young people than either the eighties or the coming wave of age-appropriate young people "in the pipeline" for 2005-2015. The economy was robust, unemployment was low, and the life choices outside of serving in the armed forces were high. Coming at a time when joining the army meant shipping out to dangerous Middle East duty, the challenge to advertise the army was high.

Young people recognized the practical benefits that the army could offer; enlistment meant training now and dollars for college when they graduated. But financial incentives had two drawbacks: they had not generated sufficient recruitments before when they became the featured reason to join, and they might attract only the recruits with the lowest job potential—not ideal for any branch of the military that requires using technologically advanced aids and needs to integrate real-time field information with the other services.

The army delivers three emotional benefits: self-direction, personal challenge, and honor. It enables the recruit to gain experience that would help them later in life—build new skills and self-confidence. For many, the army would help the young person demonstrate their personal courage to themselves, develop the strength and stamina to meet a physical challenge, and garner respect for becoming mature and responsible. Additionally, service in the army allows the young man or woman the opportunity to be part of something they, their family, and the country recognizes as making a significant sacrifice, giving what few can give.

One of the strengths of the army is its history of formidable leaders. Our most memorable leaders have come from the army: George S. Patton, Dwight D. Eisenhower, Colin Powell, Douglas MacArthur, Norman Schwarzkopf, Stanley A. McChrystal, and David Petraeus.

Their common ethos: tough, straightforward, mentally strong, willing to step in harm's way, and able to make intelligent decisions in the heat of conflict.

Thus, leadership opportunity for everyone—not just for officers—was the advertising insight that potential recruits could trust. First came "Be all that you can be." This sweepingly powerful message in the early nineties was at first very successful. Key was the demonstration of what that line meant. Advertising for the army has very negative movie imagery to overcome: recruits being bullied in boot camp, waves of soldiers becoming cannon fodder and dying, dysfunctional Vietnam-era draftees fearing the front lines. The power of demonstrating army life becomes vital.

Army: USA 1994

http://www.youtube.com/watch?v=DDbNtFL2TUI

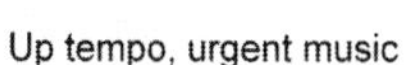

Up tempo, urgent music

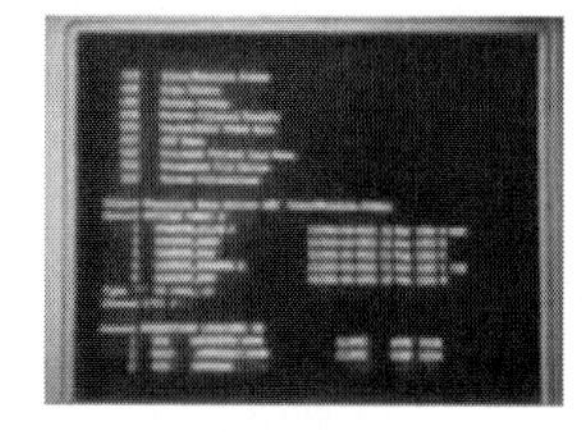

Up tempo, urgent music

Up tempo, urgent music

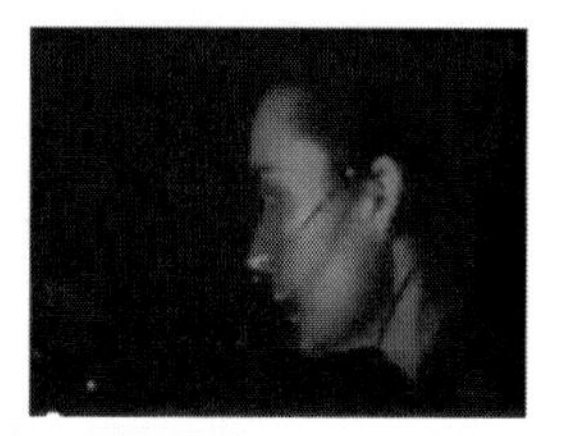

Up tempo, urgent music

Up tempo, urgent music

Up tempo, urgent music

So what's on your resume?

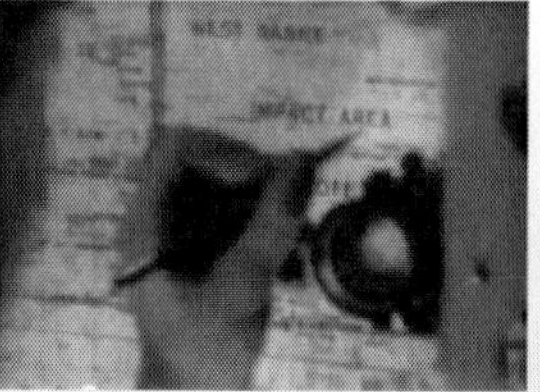

The Army develops qualities that 9 out of 10 employers look for.

Be all that you can be.

Retrieved from commercial2000, July 31, 2011, "Army be all you can be (1994)"

Recruitment started to drop just before 9/11. "An army of one" reversed that situation. The advertising insight was sharper, recognizing that this generation needed even more assurance that their service would be reinforced.

The power of the campaign came from its full use of media. The TV campaign encouraged the potential recruit to go online. There the demonstration insight was heightened. The online effort allowed a young person to examine all aspects of boot camp, to see what it would really be like to serve in the Middle East, and to see the mix of actual recruits. One effort followed real recruits in real time going through their initial training. Undergirding all this was the ultimate emotional benefit: the promise of courage, determination, and spirit being delivered to every enlisted soldier.

Army: USA 2001

http://www.youtube.com/watch?v=aqcDfE6ePLg&NR=1

What we do are the same things American soldiers have been doing for generations.

Soldiers now and soldiers then.

Same courage, determination,

willingness to serve.

What changes are equipment, technology,

but the spirit of a solider, that has never changed.

And that's what made the difference.

Make history.
Become a soldier.
GoArmy.com

An Army of One.

Retrieved from DigitalCyclone, July 31, 2011, "Army of One – Cut from the Same Cloth"

Overcoming Distrust

Cathay Pacific flies mostly Commonwealth citizens to mostly Asian destinations. The competitors are the flag carrier airlines of their country of origin: British Airways, Air New Zealand, and Qantas.

The advertising insight came from realizing that the real issue was the distrust of the unknown. Cathay's better arrival times and room in business and first class were offset by superior features from the Asian airlines: Singapore Airlines, Japan Airlines, Emirates, and Qatar Airways.

Cathay demonstrated their claim of "arriving in better shape" by showing their unique advantage: incredible service from their Asian staff and safety of the British crews.

Cathay Pacific: Australia 1985

http://www.youtube.com/watch?v=QsNZwOtK-_U

Cathay Pacific will make you feel at home,

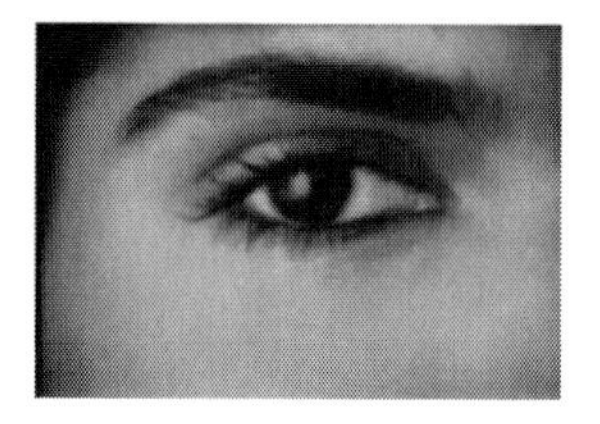

anywhere in the Eastern World.

In Japan

or Thailand

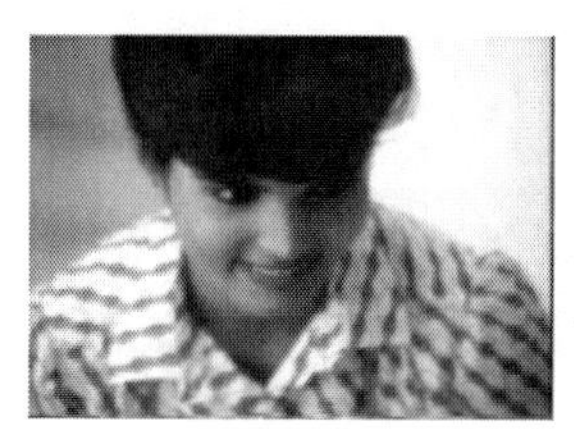

The Philippines

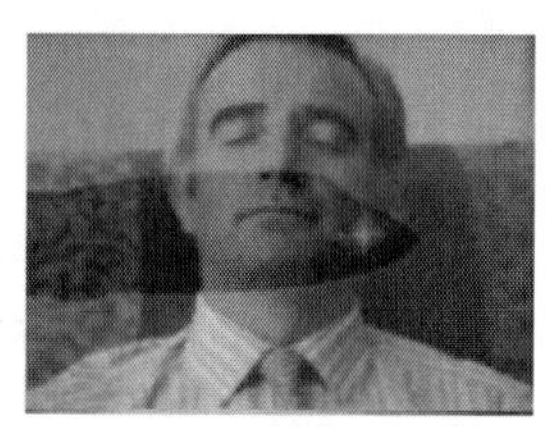

Singapore

and Hong Kong.

Or, for that matter, in good old East Sussex.

Cathay Pacific,
Arrive in better shape.

Retrieved from CheshirecatTV, July 26, 2011, "Cathay Pacific Advert 1985"

Making the Expected Interesting

One of the most common features of advertising promotions is the package deal, adding more and more elements to a low price to add increasing value, both real and perceived.

More for less is a proven formula. The potential challenge is how to make that offering interesting enough to attend to all of value. We've heard "Wait, there's more!" perhaps a hundred times too many.

This Austin Metro ad demonstrates the usual package deal of buying a new car in a fascinating way: by simply visualizing the package and the size it would have to be to have all these features.

Metro: UK 1980

http:/ / www.youtube.com/ watch?v=qldn4mAIC8k

Anncr: We're giving motoring a new dimension for the budget conscious driver.

You can now get the Metro in a unique package

that includes delivery and number plates,

12 months Road Tax,

a full maintenance plan covering labour and parts,

including batteries, tires, and exhaust.

And full AA membership with a full range of Services.

A small deposit, payments starting at around 27 pounds a week can give you two years of carefree motoring.

Then you can return it with no more to pay, or keep it with one final payment.

Retrieved from haribokey July 26, 2011, "Austin Morris Allegro"

Demonstrating Appetite Appeal

The Beef Council was faced with rapidly declining per capita beef consumption, dropping by over one-third in the period from 1975 to 1995. The assumption was that the main problem was health issues since chicken consumption had grown while the total consumption of protein had been level.

However, the advertising insight was that the consumer faced a confusing array of beef cuts in the supermarket. Beef had the image of taking too much time to prepare. Many younger women felt ill equipped to cook the different cuts of meat correctly. They no longer trusted beef as the core meat for their family.

This series of ads demonstrating fast, mouth-watering beef recipes help stopped the decline of beef consumption in the United States.

Beef Council

http:/ / www.youtube.com/ watch?v=tviyAIS9c_U

Music: Copland's Rodeo,

Music continues

Music continues

Music continues

Music continues

Music continues

You can have a great beef dinner in no time at all.

Well, almost no time at all.

Beef. It's what's for dinner.

Retrieved from espionageenterprises, July 26, 2011, "Beef It's What for Dinner – Circa 1993"

Food ads across the spectrum require finding the perfect demonstration of why we like to eat a particular food. Since taste happens out of sight in the mouth, the job of creative is to visualize the product in a way that captures both appetite appeal and mouth feel.

All the different ways food feels in the mouth turn out to be as important in deciding what to eat as good taste since most foods we eat for enjoyment do taste good.

Crunch, sticky sweetness, melts in the mouth, and the velvety feel of liquid chocolate when demonstrated by the advertising tend to help you anticipate the experience.

Pillsbury is a master of visualizing the anticipation of great taste and mouth feel.

Pillsbury Soft Breadsticks

http://www.youtube.com/watch?v=fc0iHhElbDM

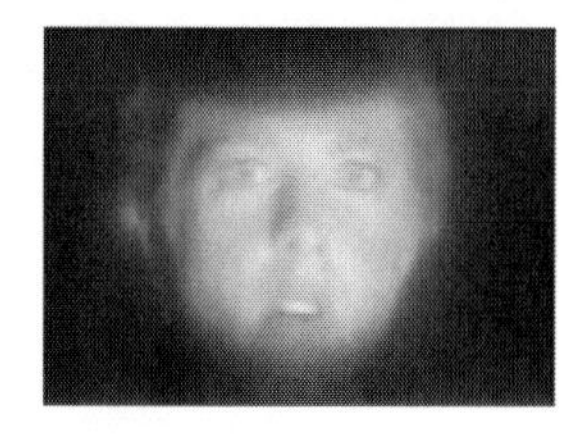

Music: Slow rising cresendo.

"Mmmm"

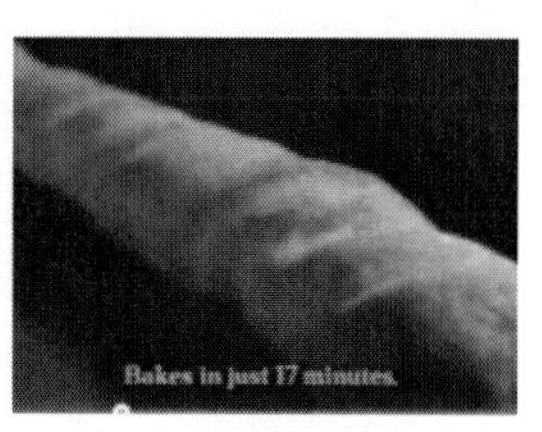

Music continues

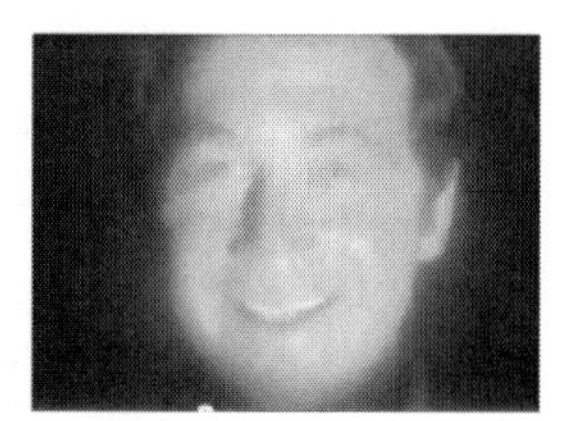

"Ahhhhh"

"Ohhhhh"

Pillsbury introduces soft breadsticks.

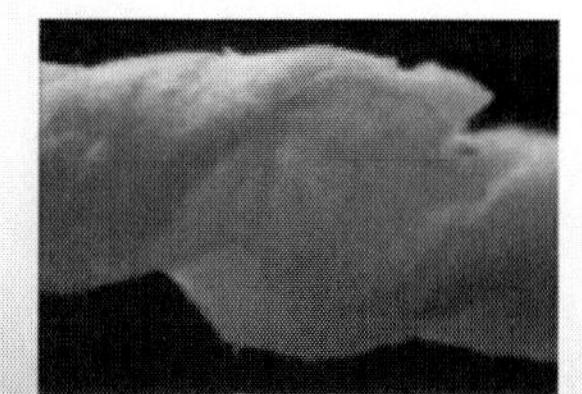

So crisp outside, yet so soft inside.

The most incredible breadstick you'll ever eat.

Mmmm, Ahhh, Ohhhh, Poppin' Fresh dough

Retrieved from Burninschit, July 26, 2011, "Pillsbury Soft Breadsticks 1984 Commercial"

Overcoming Fears, Appetite Appeal, Demonstrating the Benefit . . . All at Once

Velveeta is "ooey, gooey, yellow magic." Millions have loved its lower melting temperature, its ability to pour and to potentially coat the undesirable (soggy potatoes and mother's favored broccoli), not to mention its "eternal" shelf life.

However, the fear is that high-sodium processed cheese is not "real cheese."

In this lively ad campaign, which reinvigorated the brand, the advertising takes on the task of demonstrating both the positive benefits and overcoming potential negative worries, all in one smooth-flowing ad.

Velveeta Cheese Spread

http:/ / www.youtube.com/ watch?v=ecoBoeyjoL4

There's no single cheese like Velveeta

because Velveeta is more than one kind of cheese

Colby, Swiss, and Cheddar

blended all together

for a creamy taste that melts with ease.

Velveeta Processed Cheese Spread tastes so fine.

Lots of natural cheeses do it.

Velveeta really knows how to please.
You know it's great when they clean their plate.

There's no single cheese like Velveeta.
Original or Mexican.

Retrieved from WRFB79, Jan 17, 2011 "Velveeta Cheese Spread"

Chapter Six

Dramatize the Need

Linking the Brand to the Central Category Need

Apple has been spectacularly successful in helping create the need envisioned by Steve Jobs for a cloud-based set of devices that interact with our lives. From music to computer functionality to video entertainment, the devices and software they sell help facilitate making Apple's vision part of our lives.

We trusted Apple that the 99¢ we paid for each song that were merely digits in a computer would be more useful and entertaining than the solid disc we perused at the record store, just as we had trusted that compact disc would be better than the round of vinyl we bought twenty years ago.

Insights that Connect Our Core Needs to Categories and a Particular Brand

So many products in our lives that we now take for granted are relatively new. Insurance for our retirement and life were absent not so long ago. Similarly, we took our environment for granted and regarded seat belts as an invasion in privacy. On a more trivial level, we did not use plastic bags to collect our garbage, disposable diapers for our children, or change our hair color to enhance our self-image.

Someone had to "invent" the product's features, but then it took advertising insights to help connect those new brands to our lives and thus accelerate the development of mass markets, which in turn could sustain the new industry. Along the way, millions of us have had to develop trust not only for the brands that embody these new concepts but also for companies within whole industries, which started as only ideas and which introduced products that rapidly looked dated and often failed as better-resourced and fine-tuned brands that replaced the early entries. DEC and Atari computers came and went. Set-top boxes on TVs came, were played, and disappeared as computer-based gaming transformed the world. Our parents may live in nursing homes with long-term health insurance that no longer makes financial sense for the companies that developed them. American Express developed premium health care insurance, sold it, found it to be a bad idea, exited the market (although making good on the policies they sold), and we had to shift our brand trust from one brand to another.

Advertisers in this sea of turbulent innovation have to link these new products to something with a deep foundation. It cannot be product features because, up to this time, we have not known anything about them; and besides, these features may be irrelevant in five years or less. Think of the features offered by the first "brick" mobile phone that practically required a briefcase to haul it around.

It cannot be to established brand names when more nimble new brands can move faster, offer better value, create new channels of distribution (since they do not have to protect the old channels for their old products), and source more funding money to expand quickly since they can offer spectacular returns to first-mover investors.

Trusting Brands That Satisfy Our Core Needs

The foundation for the new rests with an understanding of our unchanging core needs. If a new brand speaks to a core need we have had, have now, and anticipate that we will always have, each person can test whether he or she can trust this new product to a better job of helping satisfy those needs. We can try the brand if it is affordable. We can talk to someone who has tried the product and have them relate it, not to the features of the brand, but to how it is making their life better or more satisfying or more fun or less expensive.

There are four different sets of core needs that we all have. They rest in a dynamic relationship with each other because to satisfy one set of needs, we are putting the other at risk.

We Need and Want to Grow; We Need and Want to Have Some Stability

We love being creative, to have our freedom, to think new thoughts, to have variety in our lives, to learn, to be rewarded for taking new risks, and to play a game where the outcome is not yet known. We love the familiar, order, the return to that which always gives us delight, to rest upon a foundation that feels stable, and to know the rules of the game will not change midstream.

We trust Apple, Ping, Econscious, Crayola, Sharp, Samsung, L'Oreal, Google, Song, Costco, and Starbucks to offer us a stream of new, fun, cutting-edge products. We watch programs that feature innovations, buy magazines to peruse the pages and pages of new fashions, troll the Internet looking for new ideas, and go window-shopping when we have a few minutes to spare.

We trust Kellogg's, Tide, Levi's, Kraft, Timex, IBM, Chevrolet, Nike, Walmart, Schwinn, Allstate, and Brooks Brothers to offer us a stream of traditional, safe, well-thought-out brands, new and old. They line the aisles of the familiar stores we frequent, making our shopping faster and more efficient, assuring us of quality as they have met the test of time.

We Need Autonomy to Show Our Individuality; We Need Connectedness to Enjoy Our Friends and Family

We want to be independent and self-reliant, express our individuality, and have our liberty. We celebrate the geniuses and the artists whose lives are symbols of breaking conventions. We like to indulge and reward ourselves; we feel strongly that we must find personal fulfillment before we can be stable enough to give love to others.

Harley-Davidson, body art, Brooklyn Jeans, Godiva Chocolates, Ben & Jerry's Ice Cream, Smartphone apps, iTunes playlists, craft beers, local wines, and spa treatments all allow us to express ourselves.

We enjoy social support and a sense of belonging. We love being loved. We think about our school, our family, our friends, our job, and our networked lives.

Facebook, Twitter, and YouTube are built on the network sharing of our lives. Coca-Cola and Budweiser celebrate their wide appeal. Volkswagen and Toyota celebrate their products for the masses. McDonald's and Walgreens thrive because they appeal to the whole family.

The Practice: Examples of Brands Connecting to the Category Need

Insurance

Around the world, insurance providers are constantly trying to connect with people who do not feel the need to purchase insurance. In a world of uncertainty and risk, they seek to provide assurance. They need you to consistently buy something you hope you never will use.

Large shares of their intended audience are people who are just entering the life stage that needs insurance. For life insurance, it is when the family would be devastated by the removal of a prime wage earner from the life plan of the family. A medical emergency or the death of a family member instantly changes the expected course of a life. Insurance is the way most societies have enabled the catastrophic financial events that happen to a few to be financed by the thousands who may or may not ever experience the loss or emergency that necessitates them.

Advertising is there to remind us that these events do happen.

This first example from the UK is for those people who privately fund their supplementary pensions through insurance. Most people set up their scheme, pay the monthly charges year after year, and then use the benefits many years later. However, life has a way of interrupting prudent planning: babies arrive after a gap of several years, some of our children are born with greater needs than others, we get divorced and remarry. These events should cause us to rethink our insurance and savings plans. The companies that service these needs have to find ways to memorably remind us without appearing too self-serving.

The Allied Dunbar Pensions ad is definitely worth linking to YouTube to hear the wit and charm of the situation of a middle-aged couple finding out their family is expanding in unexpected ways.

So human, so believable is the bellwether of superior advertising. Slice-of-life advertising succeeds when it weaves a wonderful story around the advertising insight. It can either lead inexorably to the insight, or it becomes impossible to share the story without sharing the insight. The key for this format is that the brand, Allied Dunbar, is linked to the establishment of the category need—not whether it is less expensive or better valued or more easily obtained or has helpful agents.

Allied Dunbar Pensions

http:/ / www.youtube.com/ watch?v=IOhtIdu5c8I

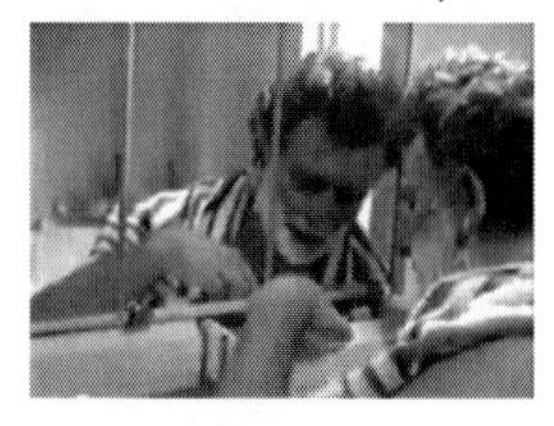

"Have you seen my razor?"
"It's on the cabinet."

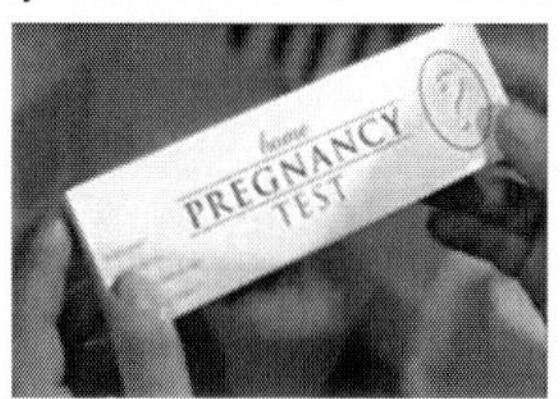

"Whose is that?"

"Nothing to do with me!"
"Don't look at me!"

"I thought we told you to be careful."

"John … I think we're the ones that should have been careful."

Man singing Nat King Cole standard, "There may be trouble ahead,

but while there's moonlight, and music, and love, and romance, let's face the music and dance."

Anncr: If your family suddenly grows, so too will your responsibilities. That's why Allied Dunbar's plans adapt.

Let's face the music and dance.

Retrieved from NinaOPerez, Dec 30, 2007, "Allied Dunbar: Trouble Ahead"

Centraal Beheer Insurance

The basic category need of accident insurance is protection when life doesn't go as planned.

This Dutch insurance company has won many international awards and has become synonymous with this concept with advertising solely focused on dramatizing those unexpected moments of life.

Centraal Beheer Insurance

http://www.youtube.com/watch?v=Pcj8uOVDub0

Mix of Iron Band and Calypso music

Tra la la

Bitty da de, tra la la

Brakes screeching,

gear roars, and tires screech.

Music re-starts

Bitty da dee, tra la la

Expect the unexpected.
Just call us.

Centraal Beheer Insurance.
055 579 8000

Retrieved from oonai5000, Sep 20, 2008, "Centraal Beheer commercial (Hedgehog)"

Seat Belts: Lifesaving Category

In 1984, only 14% of people used seat belts. Today 84% do, saving twelve thousand lives a year.

The critical insight was that seat belts were primarily associated with horrible deaths by fast-moving cars on highways and therefore were easy to ignore on quick trips to the store, picking up the kids from school, and running errands (local trips that actually accounted for over half of fatalities).

The game changer was to switch from the image of death (which we all try to deny) to personal stupidity (which we all grudgingly admit) through the use of Vince and Larry, seat belt test dummies.

The first ad creatively helps us understand the risk of not using seat belts.

National Safety Board: 1985

http://www.youtube.com/watch?v=UFlsJcZjwzc&feature=related

Somber, eerie, music

Sound of crash, tree shakes

Somber, eerie, music

Somber, eerie, music

Gregorian chant music

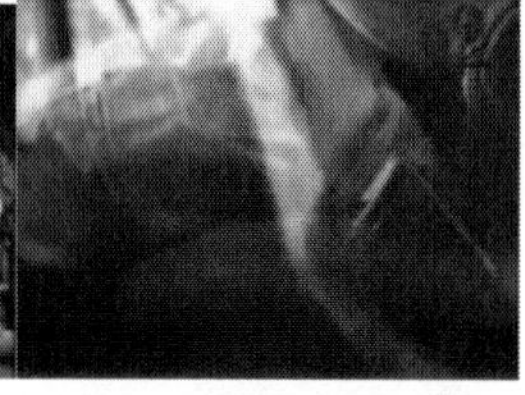

Gregorian chant music

Gregorian chant music

Gregorian chant music

Heaven Can Wait

Retrieved from luisbriseno, August 1, 2011, "This is why you should use safety belt"

The Crash Dummies ad goes beyond the risk and connects us to the easy yet wrong decision to not take the moment to buckle up.

A second insight is that people need to be involved in the ad if the relevant message is going to be imparted. Vince and Larry took a taboo subject, death and dismemberment, and kept you engaged.

These campaigns focused on the personal benefit to the seat belt user. The next two campaigns resonated with our interest in being connected to our friends and our community: littering and drunk-driving prevention.

Crash Dummies PSA

http://www.youtube.com/watch?v=e5IWaNLyc0M&feature=autoplay&list=PL018E23CE794C98E9&index=3&playnext=3

"Now thanks to these airbags this job is now a piece of Cake."

"But Vince ..."

"I'm telling you partner, I might just stick around a few more years."

"But Vince ..."

orr Vince under glass."

"But Vince, look out!"

"No more dashboard du jour

"Even with airbags, you still have to remember to buckle your safety belt."

"Now you tell me."

You could learn a lot
From a dummy.
Buckle your safety belt.

Retrieved from Videotimemachine, August 1, 2011, "Crash Dummies PSA"

Drunk-Driving Prevention

The critical insight of this campaign was that people who become too impaired to drive safely are the least likely to put their keys in their pocket and either take a cab home or bum a ride from a friend. Instead, this campaign focused on getting people to make the effort to save the lives of their friends.

Two different campaigns were run: "Drinking and Driving Can Kill a Friendship" and "Friends Don't Let Friends Drive Drunk."

According to the Ad Council, more than 68% of all adults exposed to this advertising have tried, in the past six months, to prevent an inebriated friend from driving.

Drunk Driving Prevention: Crashing Glasses

http://www.youtube.com/watch?v=-jFAvIuAev0

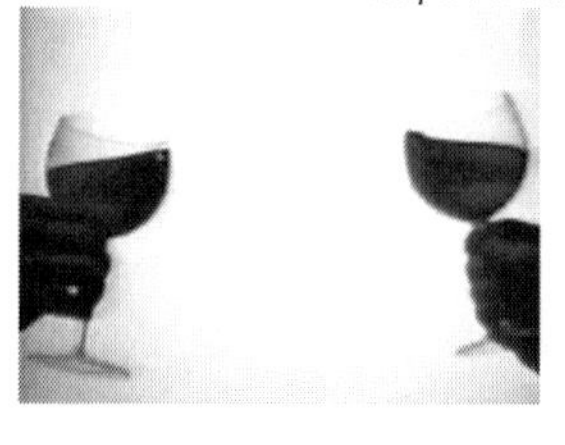

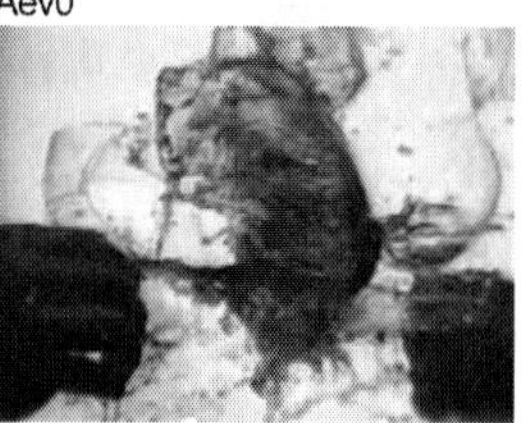

"When friends don't stop friends from drinking and driving.

(Sounds of screeching brakes, and horrible auto crash)

Friends die."

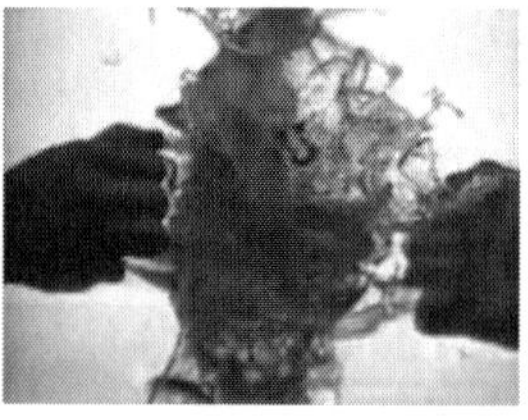

"from drinking and driving.

(Sounds of screeching brakes, and horrible auto crash)

Friends die"

"from drinking and ...

(Screeching brakes ... but no crash)"

Drinking and Driving Can Kill a Friendship

Retrieved from adcouncil, August 6, 2007, "Drunk Driving Prevention"

Pollution: Keep America Beautiful

One episode of *Mad Men* set in the sixties evoked the spirit of the country before this famous campaign. The Draper family is seen leaving a park after a picnic. They toss their paper plates and cups to the ground as they fold up their blanket and pick up their picnic hamper.

Across the country during this era, thoughtless litter routinely trashed campgrounds and roadsides.

The "Crying Indian" campaign is credited with changing that notion as it became one of the most memorable images in advertising history: the crying Native American, saddened by the waste, with the memorable tagline "People start pollution. People can stop it."

Anti-Litter Campaign: Keep America Beautiful

http://www.youtube.com/watch?v=_R-FZsysQNw

Music swells

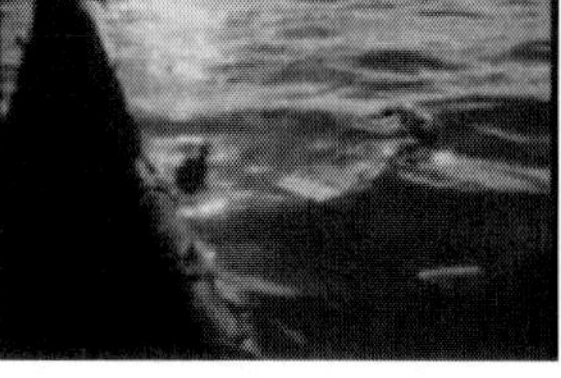

Music continues

Music swells

Music slows down, ebbs.

Some people have a deep abiding respect

for the beauty that was once this country,

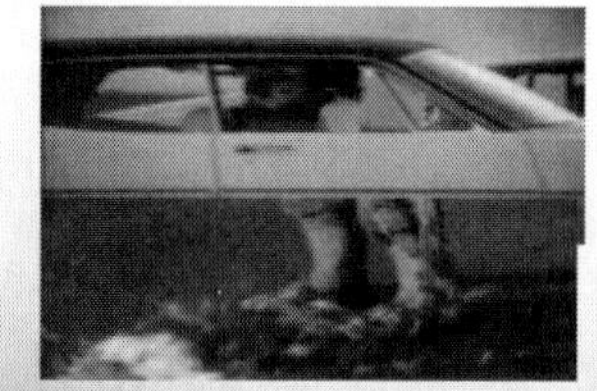

and some people don't.

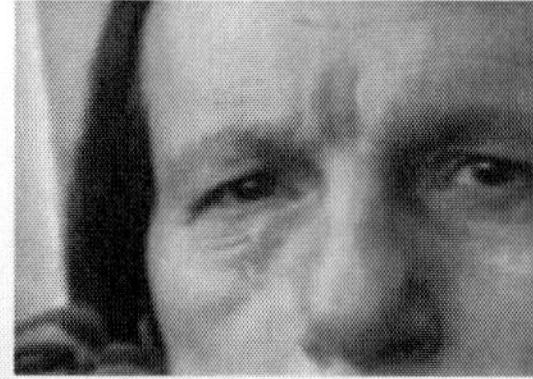

People start pollution.
People can stop it.

Music stops

Retrieved from michend2003, Dec 16, 2008, "70's PSA Keep America Beautiful"

Establishing Category Need: Glad Disposal Bags

There are two images that do not go together: clean, safe, shining kitchen floors and germy, unsafe, slopping garbage.

Glad's job was to *disconnect* these two, but more importantly to associate their premium two-ply plastic bags as the saving grace that prevents this minor disaster.

This spot in the campaign pulls out all the emotional triggers: the soothing voice of Tom Bosley (from the *Happy Days* sitcom), an innocent helpful young child, plus a nasty staining mess and the simple question: "Why take chances? Get Glad."

Glad Disposal Bags

http://www.youtube.com/watch?v=4lde9dgoZkk&NR=1

Why take chances with weak bottom bargain bags?

"Oh, Joanie"

"I'm helping!"

Glad Kitchen Bags have three plys

to resist the tears and punctures that cause leaks in other bags.

Thank you Joanie.

Why take chances?

Get Glad.

Kitchen Disposal Bags.

Retrieved from mycommercials, Aug 13, 2006, "Glad Garbage Bags Ad"

Gender-Specific Diapers: Luvs Deluxe

For a short time, Luvs succeeded in establishing a new disposal diaper need: pairing the right diaper to the right gender. It made sense that the need for absorbency would be different for boys and girls.

When Luvs introduced boy and girl diapers, they were a huge success. So much so that Pampers (also made by P&G) and Huggies (made by Kimberly-Clark) quickly introduced their boy/girl versions as well.

However, stores could not accommodate double the number of boxes, and all three brands were forced to go back to the one version that fits both genders.

Luvs Deluxe Diapers

http://www.youtube.com/watch?v=Fi_T2R2010A

In the beginning, there was man and there was woman.

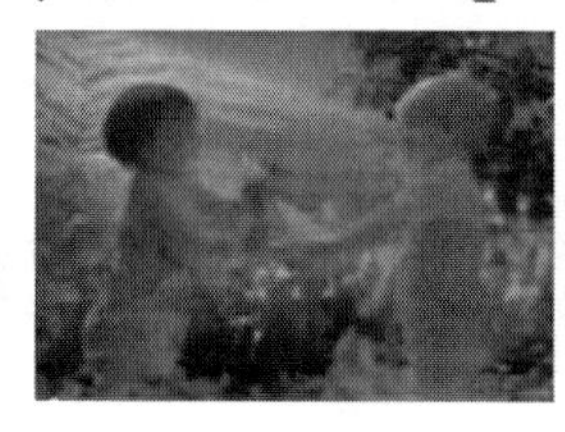

"Want some apple juice?" Equal in all ways, but one.

Boys get wet up front. Girls get wet in the middle.

Two different problems, yet all diapers were created alike. Till now.

Introducing Luvs Deluxe for Girls and Luvs Deluxe for Boys.

Both with the exclusive leak-guard system that can absorb wetness again and again.

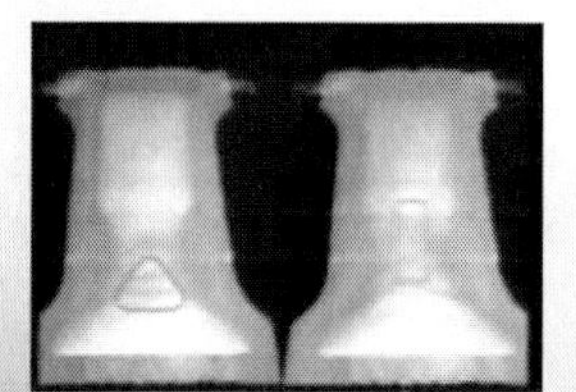

Now placed where baby wets most. Up front for Boys, in the middle for Girls.

Made like no other diaper before to help stop leaking.

Luv Deluxe for Girls. Luv Deluxe for Boys. We know they won't change, so we did.

Retrieved from zyber9, Jan 13, 2010, August 11, 2011, "Luvs Deluxe Adam & Eve (1988)"

Motivational Cues About the Category: Herbal Essence Hair Color

Seventy-five percent of women color their hair. They want reliable color that gives consistent and foolproof results. Since most women color their hair themselves, they want the product to be easy to use and long lasting, with a simple way to select the right color and shade. The shade itself is very individualistic. Twenty years ago it was most likely to be a shade of blond; today, some hint of red is most frequently bought.

Brand trust is required to believe that a brand can provide a consistent, individualistic color. The major brands have held similar shares for many years. Clairol had seen its share slowly slip as its franchise got older and older. Its quest was to develop a brand that would help its total franchise get younger.

There are two times when women who have not been coloring their hair begin to do so. The most obvious is when the first strands of gray appear. However, for many it is when the oils of youth decline and their hair no longer looks as shiny and luxurious as it did in their late teens and early twenties.

More common for those under forty is when they decide to make a distinct fashion statement. Becoming a brand, which younger users try and like, would be a powerful way to start out because these women have the opportunity to stick with the brand they first chose for a much longer time.

The five golden needs of hair coloring are great hair, quick and easy application, beautiful color, durability, and color with depth and highlights. Three of these are judged solely by the person coloring their hair: the great hair results of healthy, lustrous, and revitalized; the clear/quick/easy application process; and the durability of color ensuring that it lasts as long as it promises without fading or washing out. Two of five often require external approval: the shimmering color and color that has the highlighting and shadings that attracts the gaze of others.

Most advertising in the category fell into two distinct types. Some brands seemed to focus on the "external" nod of interest, either by men or other women. Nice 'n Easy focused on "You, only better" and mentioned how "your guy will notice." For Brunettes Only relied on subtly different shades, but all with a male appreciation shot after each different hue was shown.

Other brands relied on celebrities to rub off their glamour onto the brand. L'Oreal hired Diane Keaton to sell their "gray to beautiful" promise and Gwen Stefani to guarantee "luminous color." Sarah Jessica Parker sold Garnier customers on its "incredible softness." Revlon showcased Sheryl Crow as a working woman on tour with six weeks of newly radiant hair. Over time, Revlon has highlighted Halle Berry, Susan Sarandon, Kate Bosworth, and Eva Mendes.

Herbal Essence was the brand that Clairol wanted to use to attract a younger segment, which was focused on making a fashion statement by changing their look and feel. While the name and reputation (*Herbal*) promised "gentle," that part of their brand image would not offer the boldness that a fashion statement demanded. The crucial advertising insight was to link the brand to what would create category growth: younger women wanting to reawaken their sense of style and sexy self-confidence by starting to use a hair color as a fashion statement. In the early 2000s, that meant changing from blond or brunette to some shade of red.

The commercial opposite uses classic foils: the tone-deaf husband and the hot pool guy. However, the story is about the need that the category can deliver: a sense of renewal, excitement, and personal satisfaction in making a change—a change that will draw favorable attention, but most importantly will renew self-confidence. Of course, the advertising draws on the branded "permission to believe," the "sniff" shot of Herbal Essence's distinctive, fresh smell. But the payoff is the category promise of more intense, vibrant color that makes a visible difference to the woman in the mirror, restoring her inner feelings of sexy confidence as well as the outer reward of having a great new look.

Herbal Essence Hair Color

http://www.youtube.com/watch?v=Qxub4mtRtRI&playnext=1&list=PL2D43EE35F692EFAA

I think our relationship needs a little more intensity, more color.

You want intense?
You want color?

Herbal Essence has that exhilirating fragrance with herbal extract

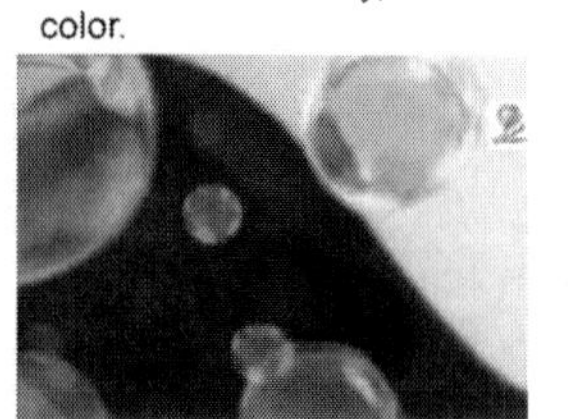

for color more intense,

more vibrant than it has ever been.

Wow! Great color!

You did all this for me!

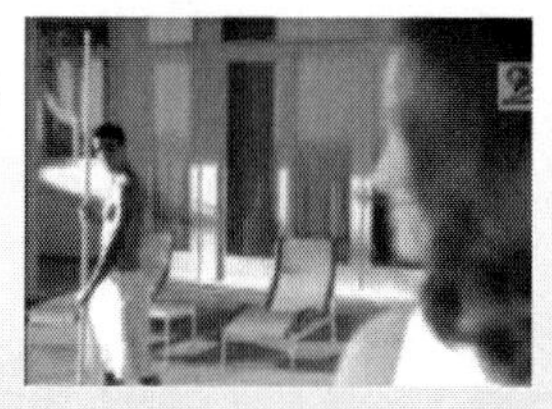

No. I did it for me. And maybe a little for him.

Herbal Essences. A totally organic experience in color.

Retrieved from clou9r2, July 9, 2007, "Herbal Essences Hair Color Ad"

Establishing the Need and Trusting a Promise

Horlicks Malted Milk solves two of three sleep problems.

Some people have a hard time getting to sleep; the warm milk supplies the tryptophan required to make them drowsy.

Some people fail to get to deep sleep; their insulin levels fluctuate, and they are never allowed to reach the deep sleep they need. The carbohydrates in malt are released steadily for a number of hours, helping reduce insulin bumps that wake them up.

Some people need less sleep and wake up early, unable to get back to sleep. The only cure for them is to get up, sleep less, and enjoy the genetic gift of more healthy hours of wakefulness.

This ad tells and shows the way Horlicks addresses one poor sleeper's needs.

Horlicks: Australia 1984

http://www.youtube.com/watch?v=BCQXsbUrnzo

Getting to sleep is difficult for many people

and other's find it hard to stay asleep, through the night.

When sleep doesn't come easily,

Horlicks can help.

Medical research has proven that Horlicks' unique blend

of ingredients in warm milk can help you sleep

the whole night through.

Wife opens shade, "Good morning." Husband, "All ready? Ah, what a sleep."

Horlicks. The natural way for a good night's sleep.

Retrieved from panalouis, July 26, 2011, "Ad for Horlicks"

Remind People of the Cold in the Summer

For Australian Gas Light, the problem is always one of establishing the need for the category since they are the monopoly supplier of natural gas heating.

A key problem for AGL is that Sydney winters really are not that cold; many houses seem to do just fine with only sporadically space heating the brick homes, which tend to hold heat in the mild winters.

A second problem for the company is that the only time to efficiently install gas heating is during summer, when the last thing that seems relevant is a cool Sydney winter.

This ad for AGL did the trick by cleverly exaggerating the need and offering AGL's solution.

Australian Gas & Light: 1983

http://www.youtube.com/watch?v=enAORdrAlmc

Is the pattern of the world's weather changing?

Could Sydney be next?

Man, "It's cold."
Friend, "Nice weather for Eskimoes."

Whatever happens, there is something that we can all take comfort in

Natural Gas.
Natural Gas gives you natural heat

that will see you through the most trying cold snaps.

Cozy heat that gets into every corner of your room.

And when your bill comes, and no matter how the weather turns, your Natural Gas supply is reliable.

So don't get left out in the cold. Get in touch with your Gas Center now.

Retrieved from GrubcoTV3, July 26, 2011, "Natural Gas (AGL) commercial"

Going Back to Basics: The Need for Frequent Flights to Popular Destinations

In the middle of fare wars and frequent-mileage-club offers, United Airlines rolled out the lush music of Gershwin's "Rhapsody in Blue" and reconnected to frequent fliers' desire to fly out and return in the same business day.

This insight is that sometimes the best way to combat an aggressive category competitor (in this case American Airlines in Chicago) is to link the brand to the essence of the category: on-time departures to and from cities like New York.

This ad's use of a professional mom elegantly linked the brand to the category need.

United Airlines

http:/ / www.youtube.com/ watch?v=CjbEpxtdUcl

Gershwin music intro

Gershwin music intro

Gershwin music intro

Gershwin music intro

Gershwin music intro
goes under

For a half century and more,

business travelers have depended on United to get them to their most important meetings.

United.
Re-dedicated to getting the service you deserve.

Come fly the friendly skies.

Retrieved from wildav713, July 26, 2011, "80's United Airlines TV Commercial"

Chapter Seven

Symbol, Analogy, or Exaggerated Graphic for the Need/Problem

Big Enduring Idea

Leo Burnett's very Midwestern motto was "When you reach for the stars, you may not quite get one, but you won't come up with a handful of mud either." Often that meant trying to find a campaign idea that would last past the execution being presented for approval. It required an advertising insight that was truly about the nature of people and the nature of the brand, not a clever execution device that would quickly wear out.

Many of the greatest were built by big enduring ideas. The Kodak Moment. "Kellogg's: The Best to You Each Morning." The Green Giant Company. The Michelin Man.

But there are many equally successful niche brands that have leveraged big enduring ideas. The blue Tiffany box. The stylized Celtic knot of Chrome Hearts Eyewear. The exaggerated flow of a Porsche. The compact usefulness of Swiss Army Knives. The pronged crown of Rolex.

Our brains are better at recognition than recall and better at retaining details of stories or myths than long lists. Many of the ideas that endure are encoded in powerful symbols connected to familiar analogies; they remind of us stories and myths or are wrapped in exaggerated graphics like the "idea bulb" visual above.

In this chapter, we will look at a powerful way to use these visual devices. We will look at symbols that connect the need for the category (or the problem the category solves) with a brand we trust.

Stuff of Our Dreams

One of the most bizarre campaigns of all time was for Dunlop Tires. It ran around the world and garnered many creative and effectiveness awards. A stream of demonic figures, as if from our dreams, tested the driver of a black car that drove through bizarre landscapes, depending on Dunlop Tires.

If "seeing is believing," then this commercial works by having you suspend your filters for advertising and get caught up in the sheer audacity and excellence of production values.

Dunlop Tires "Tested for the Unexpected"

http://www.youtube.com/watch?v=NLWWtgqDG2M

Bizarre music collection of African and Indian instruments

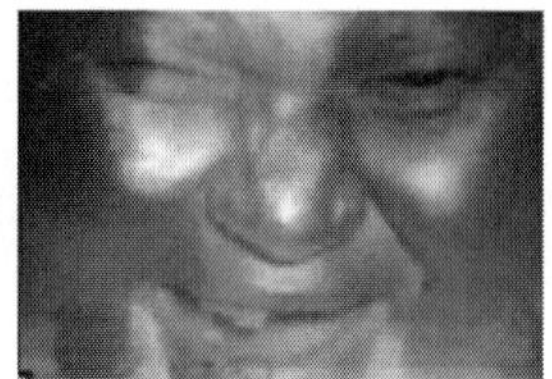

Scenes of car "attacked" by demons
Soundtrack, "Venus in Furs, Velvet Underground

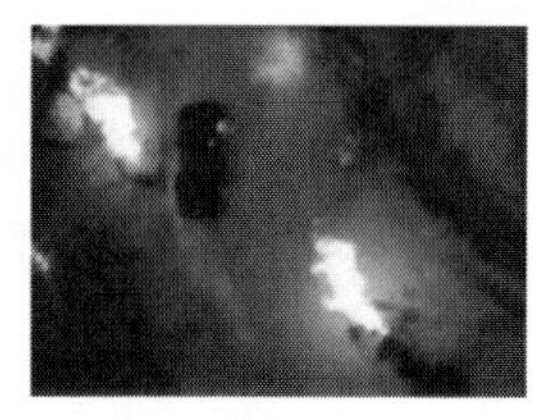

Shiny, shiny boots of leathers, whiplash girl child in the dark,

Downy sins of streetlight fancies, ermine furs

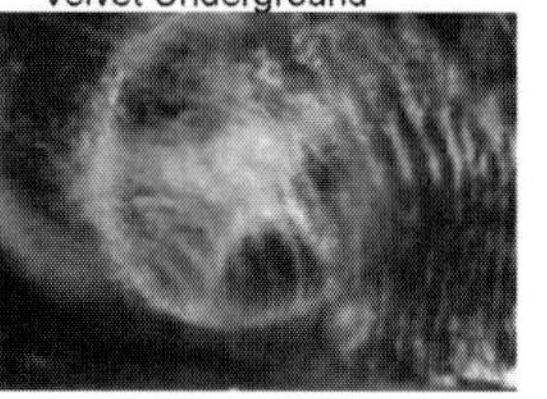

Adorn the imperious, Serene awaits you there

I am tired,
I am weary

I could sleep for a thousand years

Tongue of thorns, the belt does await you, strike dear mistress, and cure his heart

Car avoids demons and traps on
"Dunlop Tires, Tested for the Unexpected"

Retrieved from Leodegan, Oct 8, 2007, "Dunlop – Tested for the Unexpected"

Impaired Vision

In the last chapter, we looked at anti-drunk-driving that worked through getting friends to stop friends.

The ad following speaks to the drinkers themselves with the visual device of the empty glass. Glass after glass adds to the blur, resulting in slower reaction times until finally, after the fourth glass, the inevitable sound of brakes and a crash drives home the danger of drinking and driving.

Since ultimately, the decision not to drive must rest with the potential driver, constant repetition of the real risks they are taking by driving drunk must be regularly refreshed.

Anti-Drunk Driving "Glasses"

http:/ / www.youtube.com/ watch?v=MrhV3QTkNyw

Clink, one glass appears in front of point-of-view speeding

car in city lights

Clink another glass is added in front of the driver's point-of-vew

Clink, a third glass is added in front of the driver's point-of-view

Clink, a fourth glass is added and sounds of brakes and crash

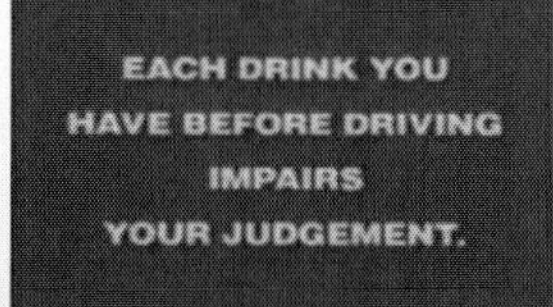

Screen, "Each drink you have before driving impairs your judgment."

Support Safe, Sober Driving. MADD (Mothers Against Drunk Driving) 1 800-665-MADD

Retrieved from fmaddcanada, Nov 20, 2007, "Glasses – Public Television Campaign"

Drugs Altering Your Brain Chemistry

Public service ads invariably try to tie the recognition of human needs and problems to the actions that you can take to improve your life or community.

This public service ad example is one of the most famous; the very compelling analogy that taking drugs is literally frying your brain, changing its chemistry forever.

The power of the visual analogy is that it leaps past counterargument and postrationalization, which are the strong defenses of those who have come to use drugs as part of their lifestyle.

Drug-Free America "Fried Egg"

http://www.youtube.com/watchv=nI5gBJGnaXs&feature=autoplay&list=PL9BCAA2CC2ECB86B8&index=7&playnext=4

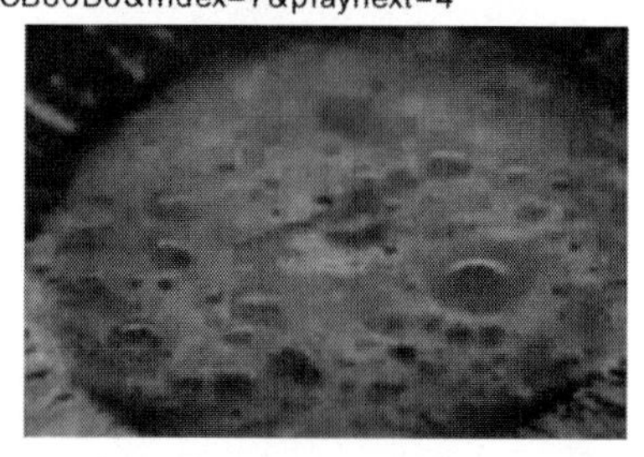

This is drugs.

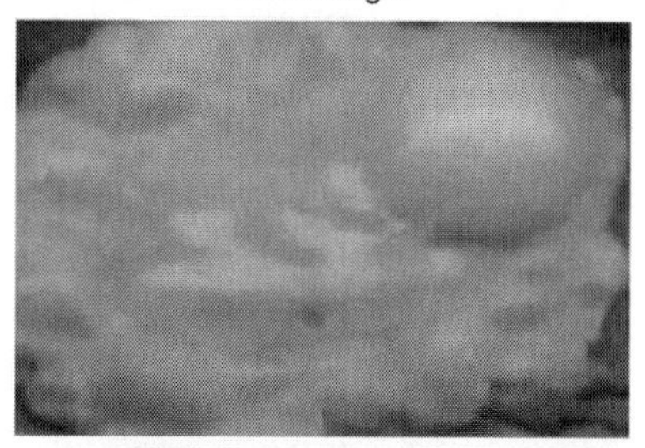

This is your brain on drugs.

Any questions?

Retrieved from pushthefire, Nov 9, 2006, "Brain on Drugs"

Maytag—Trust Dependability

For several decades, Maytag used the lonely repairman as its visual symbol of a need/problem.

The problem for high-quality washing machine makers is that most washing machines look exactly alike. It is the quality of the individual parts, the precision of the production line, and the investment in research and development to improve the washing and drying process that can make a brand like Maytag stand out from the others—but only over time as they service thousands of loads of wash over many years. The problem for the buyer occurs after several years when the repair bills start and potentially add up. Of course, when they do break down, time becomes important. Trips to the coin-operated Laundromat are frustrating and costly, not to mention the expense of replacing a washer or dryer.

Most people setting up their first house choose an average—or below-average-priced washing machine. A high-quality Maytag could never compete for that first purchase. However, the second purchase is usually when the first one breaks, is determined to be too small, or does not have features now deemed important. Enter the lonely repairman.

The brilliance of this advertising campaign is that it visualized what cannot be seen—the absence of a problem. All brands eventually fail, so Maytag could not claim perfection. But rather than get into a cost/benefit numbers game, they visualized and verbalized what the potential buyer wanted: dependability.

Like most categories, there is no single attribute that can "win the battle." Laundry machines compete on six main characteristics: quality, functionality, convenience, innovation, impression, and uniqueness. For many years the last two were related to innovation:

changes that made the machine quieter, the ability to use cold water to truly clean and thereby safely handle a broader range of clothes, more sensitive internal sensors to gauge the state of the clothes being dried, and precise timing mechanisms for separately delivering detergents and fabric softeners.

Functionality, convenience, and quality are interrelated and tied to price. Since most machines come in standard sizes, the dimension of the interior space is tied to how strong the materials are that hold the core rotating drum. Stronger materials permit larger more convenient and more dependable operation. More sophisticated electronics permit a range of features that give the owner more control and more precision with different types of loads.

Different owners valued these six characteristics differently. First-time buyers found the various features confusing. A good salesman could sell the first-time buyer a machine—on which they made more profit—that was not the most expensive brand on the floor. GE dominated this market for two reasons: they were made by a company people had learned to trust for other products, and they offered salesmen good profit margins on average-priced machines. Because GE offered a wide range of different price points across a number of different appliances found in the home, they could work effectively with home construction companies to put the right-priced machine into a new home.

Kenmore was a company that sold exclusively through Sears, the dominant retailer during most of this period. Without the additional markup of a wholesaler and sales force, they could compete effectively with GE at each quality level at a lower price. Maytag's reputation for dependability (upon which it delivered) and innovation (they consistently had unique features based on their commitment to constantly improving their products) won them an enviable position that attracted fanatical belief and rewarded the buyer with years of trouble-free use.

Visual symbols like Mr. Lonely uniquely brand the commercial, quickly present the core problem (other machines break), and when crafted carefully, can endure across many years.

Eventually, Maytag hit the ceiling of their growth after they owned the high-quality higher-priced position. Internal efforts at cutting costs backfired, quality sank, and its reputation got zinged when Maytag's top-of-the-line Neptune series had to be recalled for defects. In 2006, Maytag was acquired by Whirlpool; suddenly, a Maytag was simply a Whirlpool with a Maytag label.

Maytag "Old Lonely"

http:/ / www.youtube.com/ watch?v=aXFkREnrWUY

We do less each day than most people do before sunrise.

No this job isn't for everyone.

But if you've got what it takes you can be one of us.

The few.
The patient.

"The lonely."

MAYTAG.
The dependability people.

Retrieved from TownsendServer536, Dec 30, 2008, "Maytag (1995)"

Visualizing an Otherwise Invisible Problem: Kellogg's Bran Flakes

Many people use cereals for the roughage it provides to help them achieve regularity. Of course, talking forthrightly about the problem being solved doesn't make for appetizing commercials.

The advertising insight was to use a visual analogy. Regularity is very much like exercise; do the right thing consistently, and you get great results.

This commercial tries to speak to two different sets of ingoing judgments. For the older audience, which has more problems of this nature, while they might not vigorously exercise, they could at least eat right—Kellogg's Bran Flakes.

For the younger audience, which does take the time to exercise and realize those benefits, the discipline of eating Bran Flakes might also make sense.

Kellogg's Bran Flakes

http://www.youtube.com/watch?v=r5aiO3t2Gyc

Staying fit takes two kinds of exercise.

Exercise for your outside,

and exercise for your insides with Kellogg's Bran Flakes.

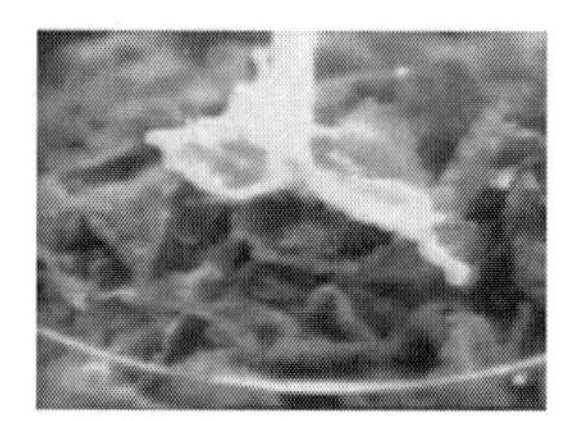

Kellogg's Bran Flakes are loaded with fiber

to exercise your insides as only fiber can.

Plus, Kellogg's is the only Bran Flakes to give you a full day supply of iron

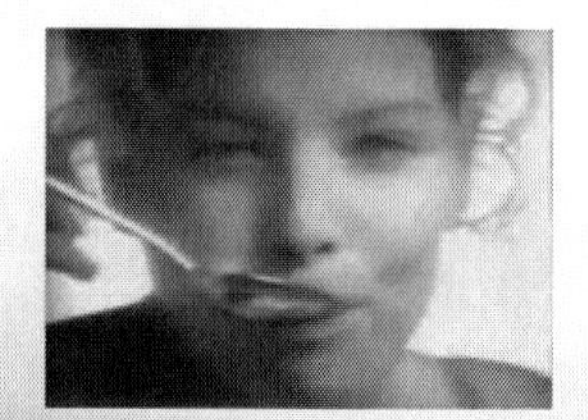

in each delicious bowl.

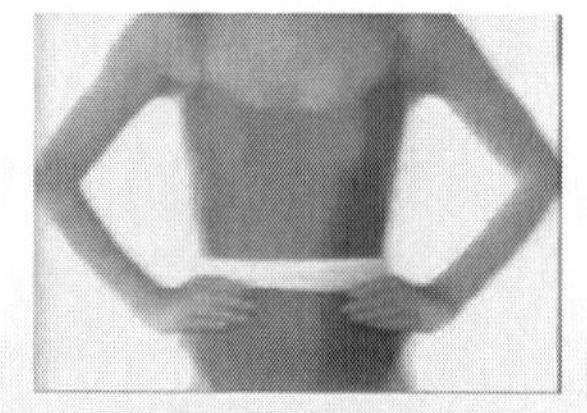

So, if you plan to stay fit, don't just go half way.

Get Kellogg's Bran Flakes, they help you keep fit on the inside.

Retrieved from Genius7277, July 26, 2011, "Commercials: Kellogg's Bran Flakes"

Cats Need Variety

Cats are not dogs. Most medium to large dogs will chow down the same food, meal after meal, year after year. Cats will not.

Lions, tigers, and other wild cats roam wide territories and eat a varied diet to survive. House cats crave change and will suddenly ignore the food that their owners provide, unless they regularly change the varieties they serve.

Morris, the finicky cat, has visualized this core cat need/problem for owners since 1968. The original cat was rescued from an animal shelter in Chicago. There have been only three Morris the Cat, and all have been rescued from shelters before coming to live the luxurious, pampered lives of advertising superstars.

9-Lives Cat Food

http:/ / www.youtube.com/ watch?v=uCja1WGZx-E

9-Lives presents
Morris.

Your castle almost finished
Your Highness." Morris, "Good,
reserve the dungeon
for yourself."

"Here's your enchanted
castle."

Morris, "This is her second
childhood today."

"Hungry?" Morris,
"Lower the drawbridge,
I'm leaving."

Don't be finicky, here's 9-Lives.
"Hark, the sea wind brings a
message."

"9-Lives Savory Stew ...
Mmmm"

9-Lives. Nutritious foods
cats really like.

Even Morris.
Morris, "Only fit for a king,
9-Lives."

Retrieved from Genius7277, July 30, 2011, "1978 9 Lives Morris the Catch Commercial"

Chapter Eight

Direct Comparison: Framing the Competitive Advantage

Rivalry between Established Competitors: Which Brand Is More Trustworthy?

Professor Michael Porter powerfully outlined the five basic forces that determine the state of competition in any one industry; one of them was the rivalry between established competitors. Coke versus Pepsi, GM versus Ford, and Kellogg versus General Mills—the list is long. It also morphs across time: Microsoft the Monopolist, Microsoft versus Apple, Apple versus Google, Google versus Facebook.

Often missed in the one-on-one battle is the collateral damage to multibrand competition when these rivalries get fierce. When the cola wars broke out, there were a number of soft drink brands that were viable before but extremely weak afterward: 7UP, A&W Root Beer, Dad's Root Beer, RC Cola, Dr. Pepper, and Orange Crush. Both Coke and Pepsi grew volume and share as the war continued, with sometimes Coke and sometimes Pepsi having slightly larger shares between them.

Certainly these rivalries do not have to be transferred to the advertising, but they tend to be like a red flag to a bull: once a competitor names a brand in an ad, the named rival feels driven to address their concerns in the same medium, and an advertising battle breaks out. But unlike an election, the buyers in a category have lots of choices. They can choose between the two, rotate between them enjoying the price discounts that usually accompany the advertising, decide to buy the other brand, or even opt out of buying completely.

United and American Airlines saw each other as their main competitor and engaged in "mileage reward" program wars. Meanwhile, Southwest Airlines delivered more efficient local service at a lower price and thrived. GM and Chrysler raced to Washington for help during the financial meltdown, while Ford toughed it out and is prospering.

Borders and Barnes & Noble were rivals and fought for locations, services, and prices. Thousand of specialty bookstores across the country failed, but when the battle shifted, only Barnes & Noble saw that Amazon.com was the long-term competitor and tried to adapt. Borders expanded, discounted, added services, and went bankrupt.

Framing Effects

Pointing out the polar bear (did you see the seal first?) makes it harder to see the seal. Pointing out that the Escher cube could not really exist forces you to look closer and see the visual anomaly. This is the huge impact that framing has and one of the chief reasons that comparative ads work. The advertising insight required is "What, when pointed out, gives our brand a more sustainable basis for trust?"

7UP tried "The difference is clear." Coors talked about Rocky Mountain water. Which is more important: lower fares or more flights daily? Is it how many tons you can haul in your pickup, or how many can ride in it? Is it better gas mileage, or a comfortable ride? Each side has one brand with a competitive advantage trying to change the evaluative structure used by potential buyers.

Better Is Better Than Best

Whenever an advertiser says "Best to you each morning," "The finest fried chicken in the world," "The world's best aspirin," "The most advanced home gaming system in the universe," or "Lose weight fast," they are making claims that are not capable of measurement and, therefore, viewed as unlikely to deceive consumers.

However, when a competitor says their drink "tastes better," "is lower in sodium," or "has a better on-time record," they have to prove that to the FCC. If the competitor named or implied protests, they may have to take their ad off the air, run corrective advertising, or cease and desist and pay a large fine. Thus, comparative advertising has not only creative challenges but legal risks as well.

Brand Positioning

Sometimes the advertising for a brand is about helping potential customers understand the brand's relationship relative to other competitors. The extremes are easy but usually filled with small-volume stores, luxury boutique stores that carry the highest-quality and highest-priced goods, and dollar-type stores, which carry the lowest-quality and lowest-price goods. However, the volume is in the middle. By comparing yourself to competitors, you may be helping customers locate you in the muddled middle.

The Cola Wars

From 1975 onward, Coke and Pepsi have often called each other out in many of their ads. Pepsi started the war with the "Pepsi Challenge," national blind taste tests in which Pepsi won.

Coke responded with comparative advertising and marketing. The pressure may have forced their hand in launching New Coke, which was a disaster forcing a retreat to Coke Classic.

The advertising insight featured next was an attempt to "lower the temperature" of the war by having fun during a temporary truce with two truck drivers sharing a moment that included a taste of each other's cola.

Since Pepsi is the sponsor of the ad, it is no surprise when the Coke driver won't return the can of Pepsi but finishes the can with dire consequences.

Classic Coke vs. Pepsi

http:/ / www.youtube.com/ watch?v=qy4_XKYo0rQ

Pepsi Driver:
"It's cold. Whew."
"What can I get you?"
"Blueberry pie and Pepsi."

Song, "C'mon everybody, come together."
Pepsi Driver: "Good Song"

Coke driver, "Great song."

Pepsi Driver "Working late on the Holidays?"
Coke Driver: "Yep."

Coke: "It's hard on the kids."
Pepsi: "Yeah."

Coke Driver slides his Coke over to Pepsi Driver.

Pepsi Driver does the same, Coke driver won't return can of Pepsi.

Sound of breaking glass as something breaks through the window of the diner.

Retrieved from Hitman 799, July 21, 2010, "The Classic Coke Vs. Pepsi Commercial 1995"

Visualizing the Difference from Competitors

Dove soap chooses to take on the whole world of soaps in this visually simple yet striking demonstration format ad.

While Dove does not visually say they are comparing themselves to Irish Spring (the deodorant family soap) or Ivory (the baby soap), these two brands are so distinctive that their users would recognize them instantly.

Dove uses the framing technique that the comparative ad permits. Soap works in part because of its alkalinity, so to imply that alkalinity is bad because it can dry your skin is to shift the very way they work into a potential disadvantage—beautiful, simple, and a clever advertising insight.

Dove Soap "Bar None"

http://www.youtube.com/watch?v=Zr9bNOHjstM

This paper measures alkalinity: the darker, the more alkaline.

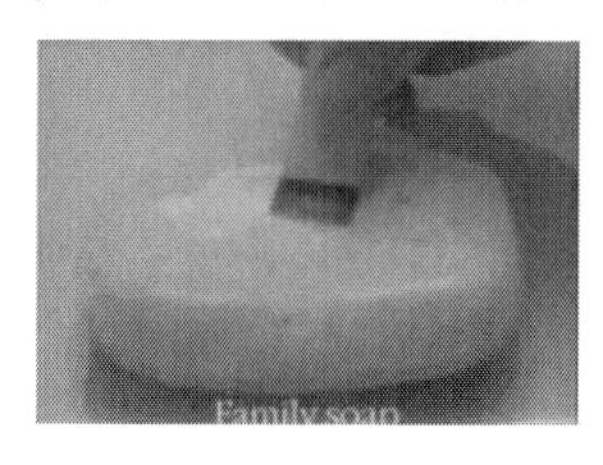

Family soap

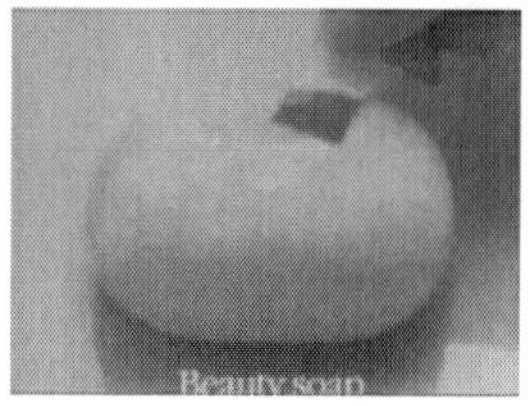

Beauty soap

Baby Soap

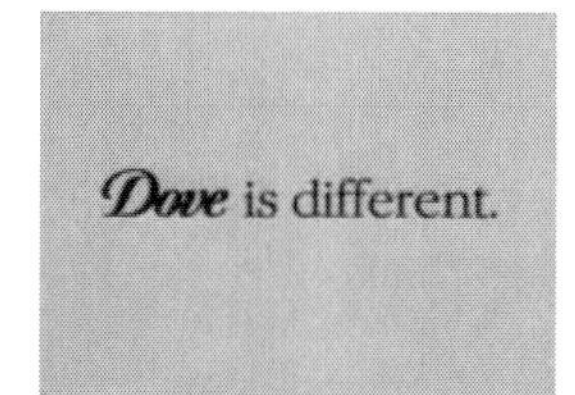

Dove is different

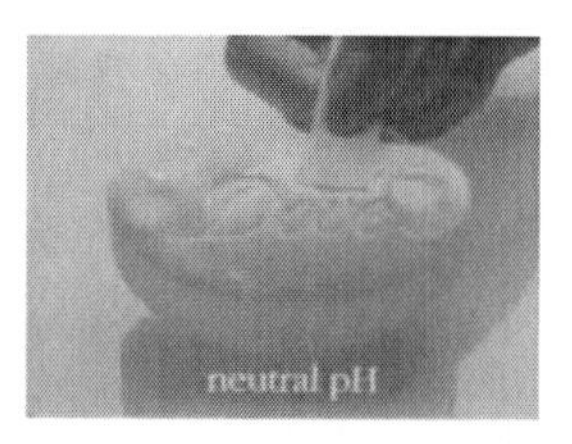

Neutral pH

Dial contains neutral cleaning agents and ¼ Moisturising Cream

Dove

Won't dry your skin like soap can

Retrieved from Thesurus05, "Thesurus05's Advert Collection #6"

Apple Takes on Microsoft

This comparative ad campaign works at so many levels.

Apple is known for being hip; its spokesperson in this ad is just that.

Apple's product advantage is a simple, well-designed, integrated interface and applications—these ads follow that pattern by being visually clean and arresting.

The war between Apple and Microsoft has often been bitter.

Apple was winning the editorial battle in PC magazines (where Microsoft was so often the monopolistic bad guy) until Microsoft offered several PC editors really high salaries to come work at Microsoft after their time as editors. A trick they might have learned from Washington DC lobbyists.

Apple and Microsoft are often in court battling over patents. But in this campaign, Apple is lighthearted, using humor to deflect the very serious intent to take on Microsoft and Windows PCs directly.

Macintosh Computers: Apple vs. PC

http://www.youtube.com/watch?v=2W8d7EyFSrs&feature=autoplay&list=PLA01C423891ABCBCF&index=3&

Hello. I'm a Mac

And I'm a PC

Hey Mac. Did you hear the good news? Windows 7 is here and it won't have the problems of last operating system.

Trust me!

It seems I've heard this before, PC.

Windows Vista is here and it's not going to have any of the problems Windows XP

It's not going to have any of the problems Windows ME had.

Not going to have any of the problems Windows 98 had.

Not going to have any of the problems Windows 95 had.

Not going to have any of the problems Windows 2 had.

This time it's going to be different. Trust me.

Retrieved from MSBusted,Oct 22, 2009, "Apple welcomes Windows 7"

Hypercompetitive Food Advertising

Competition, thy name is brand choice in the supermarket.

Huge megabrands dominate the retail space: Kraft, Campbell's, Stouffer's, Pillsbury, Sara Lee, Heinz, and Kellogg. They compete on the big four areas of food: convenience, taste, nutrition, and indulgence . . . And no one brand can promise all four in one offering.

Heinz Ketchup is an interesting brand; its thickness makes it less convenient. Compared to its rivals, it is equal in nutrition and indulgence.

That leaves taste, and better taste is usually idiosyncratic.

If you eat at a diner, you probably prefer to have a squat Heinz bottle at your elbow. But if you buy from Burger King, Del Monte is what you squirt on your burger.

So Heinz takes its thick formula and challenges its competition in this famous strainer test.

Heinz Ketchup

http://www.youtube.com/watch?v=TRpdmXIM3U8

"If I take some Heinz Ketchup,

and put it in a kitchen strainer,

and do the same with the other national brands,

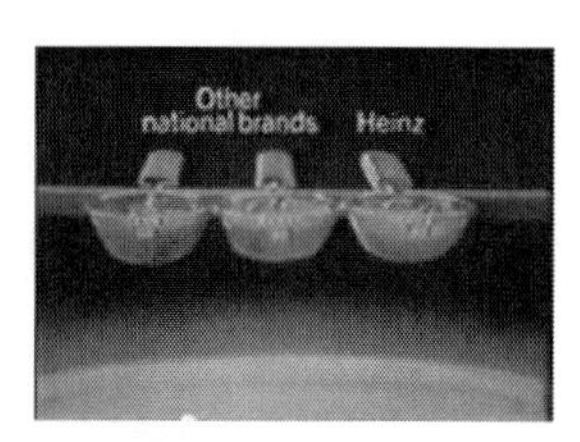

something amazing happens.

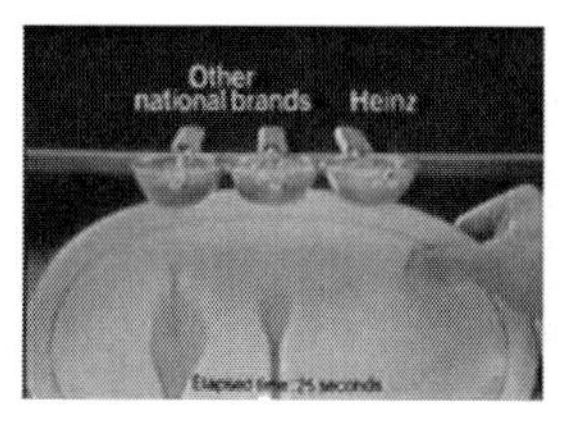

See the difference? How about this.

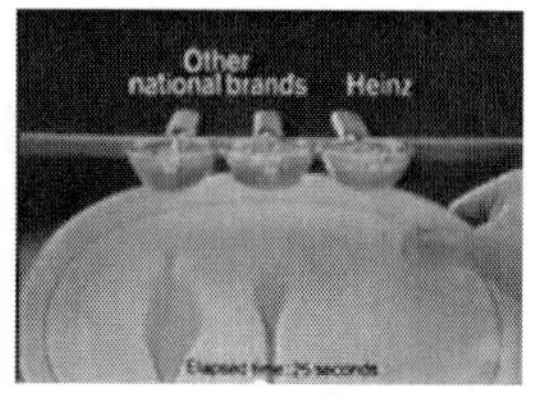

Yep. We challenged the competition and they ran.

Heinz Ketchup is thicker and really pours on the flavor.

Now which one would you rather have on your hamburger?"

"Thick, rich Heinz. You never run out of great taste."

Retrieved from mycommercials, July 28, 2011, "Heinz Ketchup commercial (1980)"

Crowded Cereal Aisle: Kellogg's Special K

When dozens of brands crowd into one category, the distinctions between brands become finer. It is harder to build big successful brands.

Healthy brands can be natural (close to nature, pure, simple), quasi-medicinal (get healthy, stay healthy), or sensible (take control, enhance performance).

Granola, Muesli, Grape-Nuts, All-Bran, Bran Flakes, Total, Oatmeal, Special K, Cheerios, Raisin Bran, Life, Smart Start, Shredded Wheat, and 100% Natural all have offerings.

To complicate this for cereal producers, other categories offer the same benefits and compete for the same share of the stomach—diet shakes, breakfast drinks, breakfast bars, nutritional supplements, protein bars, fiber bars, fruit roll ups, and liquid all-in-one meals.

Rather than go head-to-head with another cereal brand, Kellogg's Special K took on the diet shakes, offering the same visual end benefit with more taste and mouth-feel satisfaction.

Kellogg's Special K

http://www.youtube.com/watch?v=pOcmLBTChvc

What does this woman know about dieting that maybe you don't?

That you don't have to drink your breakfast.

Because a serving of Special K

actually has fewer calories than a glass of the leading diet shake.

In fact, the entire Special K breakfast, including fruit, skim milk, and coffee

has fewer calories than the diet shake.

So, if you're going to have something special when you are trying to lose weight,

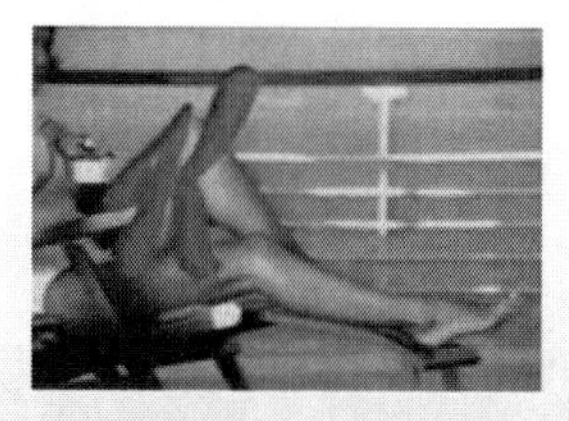

shouldn't it be something special with fewer calories?

Kellogg's Special K, lose the fat.

Retrieved from VCRchivist, Apr 1, 2010, "90s Ad Breaks Vol. 1 – Sept 1991"

Just Right vs. Total

Kellogg's Just Right was a brand created to be directly competitive in the hypercompetitive nutritional cereal aisle.

Just Right came along during the "vitamin wars." After one brand started to advertise one vitamin, another brand would offer that vitamin plus more until most healthy brands had some combination of vitamins boldly displayed on their package fronts.

General Mills came along and offered 100 percent of vitamins B6, B12, C, D, E, calcium, iron, niacin, pantothenic acid, riboflavin, and zinc. Whew, the consumer reading the side panel would have a hard time finding its core grain—ground wheat and flax.

Kellogg countered with Just Right, which matched Total on the nutritional items people actually knew about, and loaded it with fresh fruit that, for most people, made it dramatically better tasting.

Kellogg was framing the competition, taking it back to the core of the category: good taste.

Kellogg's Just Right

http://www.youtube.com/watch?v=pOcmLBTChvc

Kellogg's Just Right
vs. Total

Try Kellogg's Just Right
it's a high nutrition cereal

How about high nutrition
Total?

Kellogg's Just Right
has vitamin A, C, B6 and
B12. Same here.

and Vitamin E and Iron.
Us too.

Kellogg's Just Right has
sweet dates, lots of crunchy
almonds, juicy raisins,

Yep. And two out of three people
in America prefer the taste of
Just Right to Total.

Two out of three? Yep.

The taste makes Kellogg's
Just Right, just better."

Retrieved from VCRchivist, Apr 1, 2010, "'90s ad breaks Vol. 1 – Sept 1991"

Trusting Woolworths Supermarkets for Fresh Meat, Produce, and Deli Products

In 1980, Woolworths and Coles were battling for top position in the Australian supermarket retail business, with Coles being a strong number one.

You could take the Woolworths name out of their TV ads, and it would have looked like the advertising of hundreds of other supermarkets around the world. They were using the discounts offered by manufacturers to tell their customers they were offering fabulous deals this week, so do your weekly shopping at Woolworths.

Each week, different lost leaders were featured. They depended on their great locations, clean stores, efficient checkouts, wide-ranging products, and open parking to generate the sales they needed.

Growth was dependent on their ability to add more stores in underserved locations, and their competition was the other similar big supermarket chain in each city (Coles), but also the small mom-and-pop groceries that were being displaced by the growth of these two chains.

Woolworths

http://www.youtube.com/watch?v=SwngBIkILiM

Song, "It's the one-stop shop that's got the lot.

where you get's your dollar's worth."

"You'll really smile at the savings from Woolies this week.

From the dairy case, Woolies Orange drink. Just $1.39. Smile at the 50 cent savings.

From Woolies bakery

Sponge rolls just 49 cents. You'll smile at the 19 cents savings.

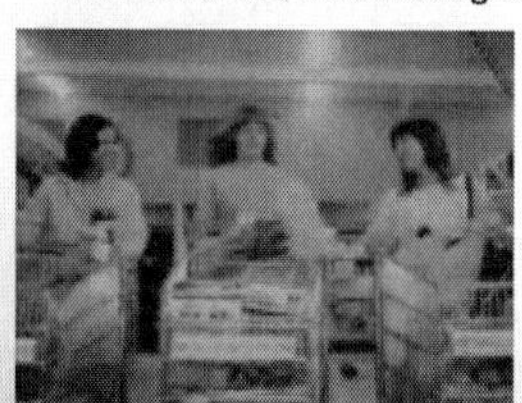

And from Woolies grocery department

Nescafe instant coffee $2.99. For a smiling 30 cent savings."

Get your dollars worth with Woolies lower prices.

Retrieved from oztvheritage,Jan 23, 2011, "Woolies"

Only women who saw themselves as need-driven price shoppers talked about specials they found in the newspapers or had really thought much about the quality of the store brands that the different chains offered. Most of them did not feel that the bigger stores, which did have better prices or cheaper but acceptable quality store brands, were worth driving out of their way for their weekly shopping. Instead, they saw themselves as willing to go once a month or less often to stock up on the really few items that seemed much lower in price.

Woolworths was so much more pleasant to shop in than those brands, and customers assumed they were paying for the wider better-stocked aisles and the better lighting and parking.

It was the exterior aisles of the stores, where brands they can trust are few, that drew the most critical examination of grocery stores from potential customers. Here the comparison was not another grocery store but their local green grocer, butcher, and baker, which could be found on every high street throughout the metropolitan areas of Sydney. These shops offered friendly personal service and a perception of better quality but were less convenient to shop at and charged higher prices. They were also not particularly child friendly.

People who mostly shopped at Woolworths had a different story. They had developed a relationship with the butcher on call at the store or the produce manager. They found these Woolworth employees as, or even more, friendly than the local butcher. They defended the quality of the products they were buying, claiming that the high volume made the products they were buying fresher than those that had been sitting out at the local stores. Plus, they really valued the ability to have shrink-wrapped half melons or a variety of prebagged vegetables.

Of course, this represented a real challenge to the budgeting process of marketing. The current practice in Australia was to use the money generated from promotional displays and discounts to fund TV ads and the weekly shopping guide placed in every mailbox surrounding each respective store. These circulars were actually a source of profits, and in an industry that typically had only a 1% or 2% profit margin, the advertising was actually not a cost but a profit center.

Similarly, discounts from manufacturers paid for both the production dollars and the media buy for TV and radio.

The fresh areas of the stores—deli, produce, meat and dairy—did not have sufficient national advertisers to fund their advertising, and so making a choice to advertise their prices was a cost, not a source of profit.

The real power of the major chains was their market dominance, so they were able to change their budgeting process and free their advertising dollars to reach potential new customers; they simply added slotting allowances to their negotiations with national manufactures and spread the discounted volume allowances over all the products they sold, not just those they sold during promotional periods.

Woolworths started to focus on better merchandising and advertising of their fresh brands, and when they got the merchandising right in their stores, they were able to stretch the depth of their purchases to become "the fresh food people."

The key was the word *people*. They were selling a buying experience as much as the food. They already had butchers, produce managers, and deli clerks in their stores who were dedicated professionals interested in helping people. These employees loved the change of focus, and as a result, their attitude spilled over to the customers. The chain also invested in the misting technology to keep their fruit moist and cool right to the moment of purchase.

Woolworths

http:/ / www.youtube.com/ watch?v=ZgMkqI_B2-U

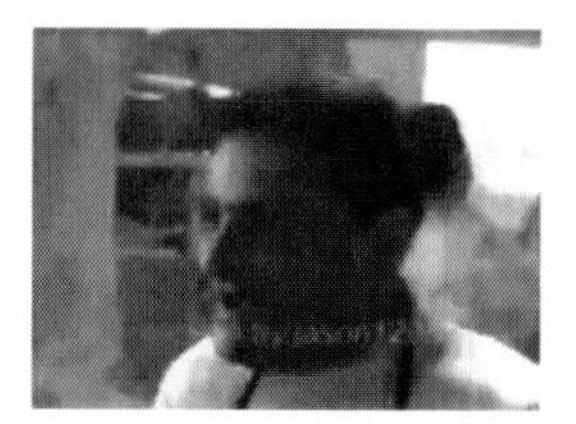

"Well I'm not just a butcher
I'm a Fresh Food butcher

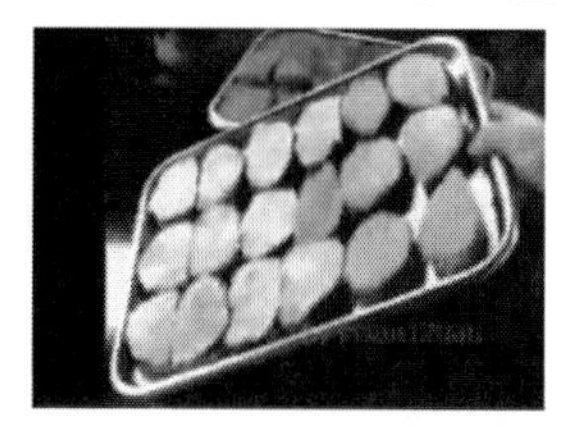

You can't get fresher than
that

Who would want to miss
a steak like this?

And you can't get fresher
than that.

We're the fresh food people.
With fresh ideas for you.

"We're not green grocers,
We're the fresh food
people.

You can't get fresher than
that.

We're Woolworths. The fresh
food people with fresh ideas
for you."

'The Fresh Food People'
WOOLWORTHS

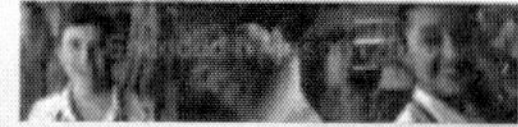

Anncr: "You want it fresh?
We've got it fresh."

Retrieved from jason120au, July 26, 2011, "Woolworths The Fresh Food People ")

Home Brand from Woolworths Supermarkets

To offer real week-after-week value in the food, beverage, and household product departments, Woolworths completely opened their horizons still further by introducing a more customer-oriented store brand called Home Brand.

It was launched with a lowest price guarantee on the package and then advertised with helpful high-quality recipe advertising.

This product now made them more competitive throughout the entire store. Home Brand appeared up and down the middle aisles—the "fresh food people" were celebrating their dairy, deli, meat, and produce departments.

In their New Zealand stores, they got a local chef celebrity to deliver recipes featuring their private label.

Home Brand

http://www.youtube.com/watch?v=iFG3qXjmO7M

One of the most important ingredients in an Australian kitchen is a can of tomatoes

We love to tip a can into casseroles, pasta sauces, or pizza.

For a tangy salsa for Mexican food,

just add a little chili, coriander, lemon and a touch of salt and sugar

For all our favorite dishes that use a can of tomatoes we want the best flavor,

and we want a bargain.

Home Brand canned tomatoes are the best for every use. And if you want them sundried, Home Brand has them, too.

There are 637 other great varieties, all with a crowd of admirers.

Shop for Home Brand in Woolworths and shop smarter.

Retrieved from TheSmartShopperNZ, July 26, 2011, "The Smart Shopper, Richard Till"

S

The result of the "fresh food people" repositing and rebranding was immediate. Woolworths grew in both sales and profitability. People responded to the improved quality and service; the margins of these products turned out to be higher, and as they grew as a percent of total store sales, overall profitability grew more than the advertising revenue lost.

Comparative Ads: Does the Brand Get Lost, Do I Lose Trust in All Brands in the Category?

The number of really good ads and the number of really successful examples are much fewer for comparative advertising. The reality in the marketplace is that when you spend precious time comparing and contrasting, you potentially take away from the ability to fully talk about the brand you want to advertise. Most brands compared themselves to the brand leaders and ended up advertising the brand leaders, not themselves.

Raising the issue of other brands can erode the trust people feel about all brands in the category. When politicians go negative, they may hurt the credibility and confidence in their opponents, but they also lower their own credibility as their profession is challenged. So too can comparative advertising remind potential customers of the problems all brands have: one bad service experience can taint ten positive uses, product defects happen to every brand, and fear of a damaged image can cause a company to avoid a general recall with potentially brand-ending risks if failures become widespread.

Chapter Nine

User Imagery

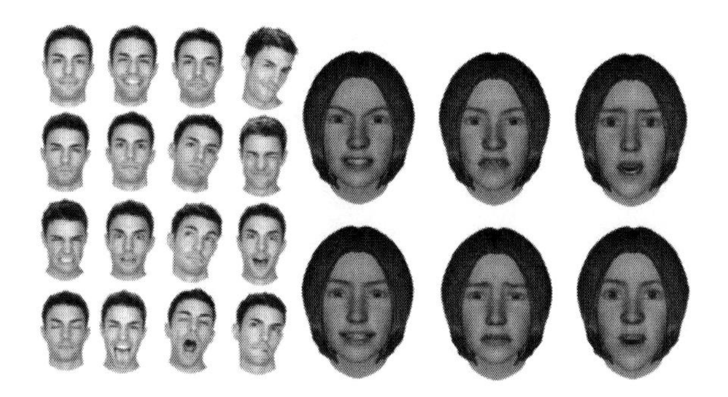

Trusting in the Emotional Connection

Ads that are primarily about the brand's users can do two things well: they can communicate a set of experiential emotional benefits, and they can inspire an understanding of how products might be used.

To the casual observer, some user ads seem to be saying "People like me use that brand." However, the world of failed ads is littered with ads that were limited to this simplistic message. All advertising that is trying to mirror people stereotypes them, no matter how artful. We do not see ourselves as primarily being young, beautiful, wealthy, male/female, or any other obvious exterior stereotype. Even what I see in my mirror seems to capture something that is not truly who I am but what I look like. Few people feel that their essence has really changed very much over time, but the image in the mirror at age twenty and then at fifty is remarkably different. Mirror advertising fails when it is just an image, not a full portrayal of people as they know themselves to be. It fails to make a satisfying emotional connection between the brand and the potential user.

To the casual observer, other user ads seem to be saying, "If you want to be like me, use this brand." This type of advertising escapes the mirror trap, but it often fails because we have too much life experience that brand ownership does not transform our lives. In a study of how brands grow, the author looked at brands that grew within a panel that allowed us to track category and brand use, both before and after the brand grew. Eighty-five percent of new brand growth came from people who had used the brand in the previous year. Thus, advertising that tries to make false promises such as "Simply use this brand and become someone else" is trying to push water uphill, against the gravity of prior brand experience.

Perhaps we should worry about the impact of user ads on the vulnerable: children, teens, or less sophisticated people. Mostly, we underestimate the amount of experience and savvy they've accumulated. In the early years, they are only worried about themselves, not who they should be. As a potential user of a brand, they are interested in how the brand will help them experience life, not the life experiences of others. Even if they are extremely peer conscious, they are balancing using this advertising to "try the brand on," as much as they are simply aping, "If I do that, I'll be like them." "That looks like fun" is different than "I have to have that, or I'll be left out."

Nonetheless, user-imagery ads can be very effective if they are used for what they do well: communicate emotional benefits and connect those to a particular brand.

Emotional Empathy Can Build Trust

One of the paradoxes of human existence is that we have a very limited active emotional vocabulary and often find it difficult to describe in words how we feel. When asked how we feel, we give vague "good," "bad," "excellent," "not very good" responses. Even as we utter them, we know internally that we are not describing the important nuances of how we feel. Often the catharsis of talk therapy is that we finally can break through and actually verbalize what we know we are feeling.

However, we have a tremendous ability to recognize and to empathize with how others apparently feel. We can recognize hundreds of different subtle emotions in the faces of others with nuances that often defy language. We now even have a "label" for the skill of people who are better at emotion recognition in others; we call it emotional intelligence.

How does a brand help you feel when you use it? Most brands do not even have the ability to articulate the emotional essence they serve, but they can *show* you the emotions of people who are using the brand. We judge advertising that shows people through the crucial filter of believability. Are the people on the screen authentic? Do we believe that is how we'll actually feel when we use the brand? Even when the emotions are obviously exaggerated to make them more interesting, does the domain of the emotion seem authentic and true?

Emotion in Advertising

Emotions have three primary characteristics: they have valence (good/bad), intensity (highly aroused, weakly aroused), and referential direction (about others, about me). All 1,200 English words and phrases that describe emotion can thus be put into one of the following eight boxes.

Valence	**Good**	**Good**	**Bad**	**Bad**
Intensity	***Aroused***	***Unaroused***	***Aroused***	***Unaroused***
Referential Direction				
About Others	Grateful	Thankful	Frightened	Hatred
About Me	Proud	Relaxed	Depressed	Sorry

In contrast to emotions are the other feeling states: moods and personality. The chief difference is that these either last for a longer time than emotion (mood) or are the quite stable types of feelings we use to color our perceptions about the world (personality).

Emotional reactions, on the other hand, tend to be moment to moment, sustained only if the situation that prompts them is sustained. Within a thirty-second ad, for instance, the average person feels several different emotions depending on the swiftness of the change within the ad. Advertising-inspired feelings are tempered by the general mood the viewer of the ad is in both before and after they see the ad. Advertising-inspired feelings are also shaped by the viewer's own idiosyncratic personality.

Critically, emotions are reactions to self-relevant events. Self-relevance is key. The same advertising can have vastly different emotional effects on people in part because the personal relevance will be dramatically different from person to person. Thus, it is really not relevant to talk about emotional advertising but rather advertising that evokes emotion in you. That emotion can be real—through empathic connection to emotions they see the actors experiencing. More commonly, it is vicarious—like the fear most people feel during a roller-coaster ride tempered by the constant knowledge that the threat is not real. Sometimes ads are compared with movies, but TV ads last only thirty seconds, and they usually follow one ad and precede another; thus, their ability to create more than fleeting emotions is severely restrained by time.

When we discern a particular emotion on the face of someone, we immediately and appropriately try to understand what is causing the emotion since emotion is a reaction. We interpret whether we believe that the event is causing "what is happing to them" or sourced internally from who they are. We can usually sense whether the person we are seeing is reliving a past experience, experiencing something fresh in the moment, or anticipating a future concern. As humans we do this unconsciously, quickly, and with amazing accuracy.

When advertising is trying to create an emotional response, it becomes an external event. Our subsequent emotional reaction may be responding to it, but it might equally be caused by a near-simultaneous memory of something in our lives that it evokes.

The self-relevant valence, intensity, and referential direction of our response is governed by our core values, what we hold to be most important to us. Since our values differ person to person, advertising that prompts an intense emotion from one person will not have the same impact, or even the same hue of emotion, for someone with different core values.

As a result, it is not very useful to type commercials by their apparent emotional content. What appears as a sad ad to some will be boring to others. What is inspiring to the few may be suspicious to the many. The importance of emotion-evoking advertising is not the emotion that is put into the ad but the emotions felt while watching the ad, and predicting viewer reactions requires understanding them, their core values, and their previous product/brand experiences.

Emotions and Brand Positioning

Advertising is just one of the ways we come to attach an emotion to a brand. Advertising can frame the usage experience, guiding what we view as an appropriate level of response to the brand. It often helps us rehearse or relive how we will feel when we use a brand. A well-communicated advertising emotional insight creates a link between the stimulus of the functional brand usage and the emotional reaction to that usage experience. Over time, the advertising can build symbolic meanings of brand use.

Since we feel good as we enjoy a coffee break, or comfort as we eat a bar of chocolate, or in control as we drive a car well, over time the brand becomes associated with enjoyment, comfort, or feelings of control. Advertising for the brand—which reflects that enjoyment, comfort, or control—is believable and creates a positive feeling, allowing us to relive those pleasant feelings and, by reliving them, deepens the connection to our unconscious and conscious components of brand judgment.

Similarly, the personality of a brand is the tendency to expect the brand to elicit consistent emotions in different situations. Consistently associating the brand with people of the same personality will communicate an expectation of how we will feel using a brand—cheerful, powerful, energetic, revitalized, optimistic, and/or thoughtful. Of course, actual brand use will either sustain these feelings or deny them, but if we expect a certain set of feelings to ensue, then they will happen more often than if we do not.

Brand-Use Rehearsal: Slice of Life

Both ultrarealistic and exaggerated portrayals of slice-of-life advertising animate the brand off the store shelf and help us understand what the brand-usage or brand-ownership experience might be. Because we are interested in people, we follow along this path willingly, interested in their stories because we are interested in people.

Casting of slice-of-life commercials is incredibly important. We have previously examined how the choice of celebrities impacts brand perceptions. Similarly, the choice of unknown actors playing “real people” in user-image ads is as important as our choice of celebrity in celebrity advertising. Usually we want the impossible: a very attractive actor, yet a person who might live next door; someone we might admire, but yet be a normal flawed human; someone who seems typical of people who might use the brand but not stereotypical; someone who does not appear to be acting but seems very natural on camera. Of course, to fulfill these objectives requires incredibly skilled actors and directors. So it is not surprising that many of today’s movie and TV celebrities started out in commercials: Brad Pitt for Pringles, Matt LeBlanc for Heinz Ketchup, Keanu Reeves for Kellogg’s Corn Flakes, Farrah Fawcett for Noxzema shaving crème, and Jodie Foster as the Coppertone girl at three, or the GAF View-Master pitch person at seven!

Much slice-of-life / user-imagery advertising follows a predictable path: it quickly sets up a situation that we have either experienced or can readily empathize with, it shows how the product “works” or “enhances” the experience, and it ends by showing the reactions of people to the product’s benefit. Redundantly, the voice-over usually tells you what the advertiser wants to communicate.

Creating a Brand Personality

Adopting a consistent brand persona allows a brand to suggest a narrower and, hopefully, inviting set of emotional-usage benefits.

This Norwegian Cruise Line ad goes one step further. Not only is this ad consistent with the mood and tone of previous ads, but it also explicitly uses the "New Constitution" to clearly share its brand persona.

The actors, while attractive, are inviting more for their vacation goals and desired experience than just their looks. The ad brings all these elements together for a campaign that increased holiday bookings.

Norwegian Cruise Line

http:/ / www.youtube.com/ watch?v=2vwkcJMnSNM

Lazy light music continues:
"A New Constitution
for the World.

Article 1. Section 3. We shall form a more perfect union.

Article 3. Section 2.

Winter will be
exiled.

Article 4. Section 7.
Work shall be abolished.

Article 6. Section 6.
We shall have adventures.

Article 10. Section 1.
There will be peace and
hope

and really good food."

It's different out here.
Norwegian Cruise Line.

Retrieved from MistyVids, Apr 17, 2011, "Norwegian Cruise Line commercial (1995)"

Creating a Unique Identity

The next ad does a remarkable job of capturing New Zealand's identity. Of course, New Zealand's landscape is sprinkled with dramatically changing, easily reached vistas.

But it is indeed "the Kiwi attitude," cleverly shown in this ad, which makes a trip to New Zealand so much fun. The people are cheerful, cheeky, helpful, and appreciative of their land.

Somehow, despite all the tourists they experience, New Zealanders seem genuinely pleased to answer the same questions about their land over and over again.

This advertisement allows you to consider a vacation to New Zealand as not just another beautiful travelogue but to anticipate a great social experience.

New Zealand

http://www.youtube.com/watch?v=nKZMMWf5x2M

Two fishermen in waders cast their flies across a river.

The fish aren't biting yet.

From the bridge above

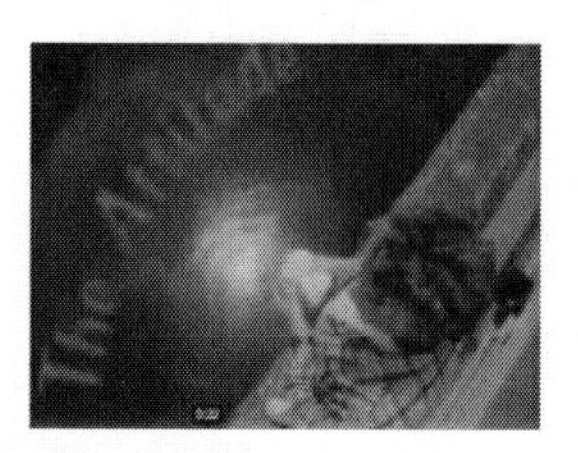

a guy throws a few slices of bread.

He dives down a bungee cord

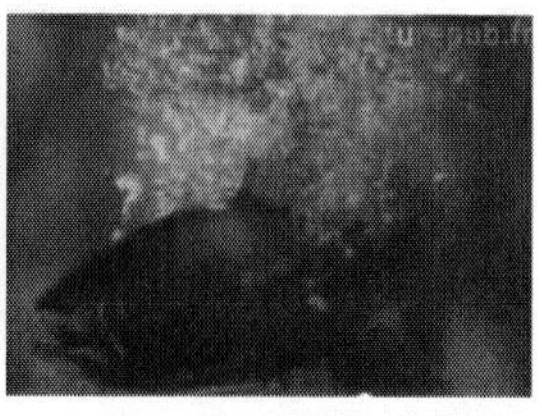

and emerges holding a huge trout.

That's the Kiwi attitude.

Have you got it?

Instant Kiwi Lotto.

Reinforcing the National Myth of "Who We Are"

One of the powerful ways to let people persuade themselves is to simply reflect how good, clever, smart, or fun they are for making the brand choice they are making (when they buy/use your brand).

Lotto Australia leveraged this reinforcement of self-esteem to dramatically build their brand at a crucial time in their lotto's game development.

Around the world, the number one driver of a lottery game is the size of the big prize. Once a game catches on, it generates enough revenue to create a really big first prize. The challenge is to capture the fancy of people in its early days before the prizes get large.

This campaign for Lotto Australia helped. When it started, the roll-over top prize was only $250,000. After the success of this campaign, they had their first million-dollar prize and grew rapidly from there.

Lotto: Australia

http://www.youtube.com/watch?v=TFH1bTvJNBM&feature=related

What is it that keeps you going, through all the troubles and strife?

A smile that says you're winning and hitting back at life.

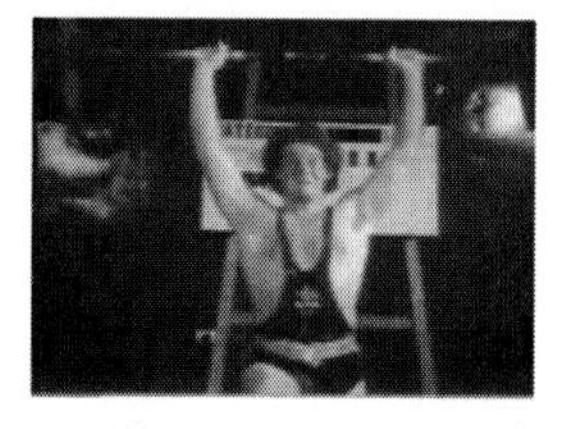

That very special moment when you come out on top.

It's winning keeps you going, winning won't let you stop.

That's why we're going Lotto, you've gotta give winning a try.

Going Lotto in the Big Smoke, and where the cockies fly.

Now Lotto is the Big Game that keeps you on the edge of your chair.

We've even got our own show, one more ball and you could be a millionaire.

Go Lotto. Go Lotto. Go Lotto. Try your luck. Go Lotto. Go Lotto. You're mad if you don't.

Retrieved from AustralianAds, July 26, 2011, "Go Lotto (Australian ad, 1979)"

Personality of Brand Vitality

Most food and drink brands want to be seen as alive, vital, and interesting.

Eating and drinking is one way we attack a negative lack of energy (boredom or depression), so brands that are felt to deliver vitality can be particularly successful.

This Pepsi ad works in two ways. Having three models all drinking the product reflects well on the brand. But the hero of the ad is you, the lifelong Pepsi drinker, with this story telling the fantasy of how Norman Pheeny became committed to Pepsi.

Pepsi

http://www.youtube.com/watch?v=rodU-UhK4qY

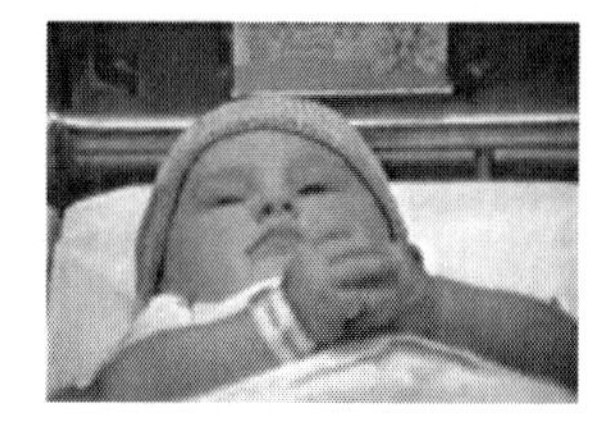

Platters 50s Song
"Can't see anyone but you."

I only have eyes

for you.

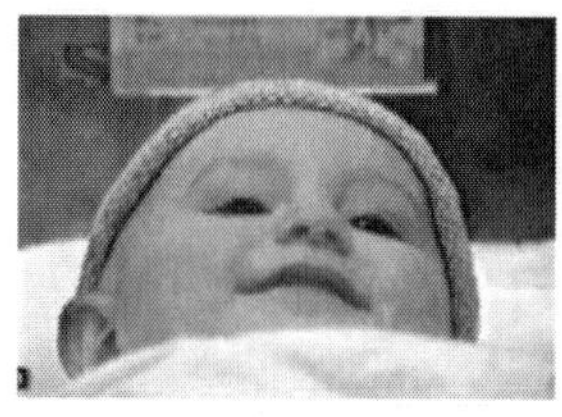

The lights are dim tonight.

I only have eyes for you, dear.

I love you.

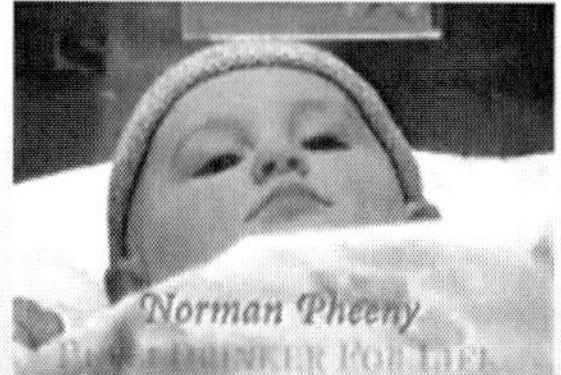

Norman Pheeny

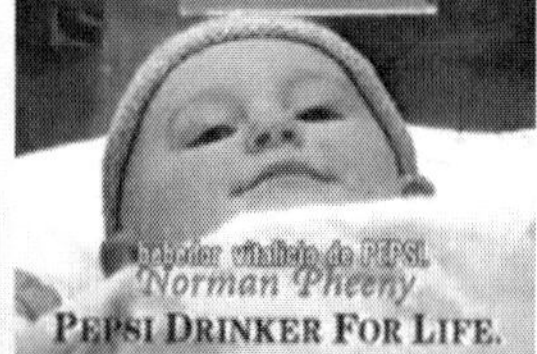

Pepsi drinker for life.

Retrieved from Joseph26mx, Feb 7, 2007, "Pepsi 1997: Cindy Crawford, Tyra Banks"

The Rebel as a Source of Vitality

This Heinz ad ran for over five years; it was all about bringing vitality to the Heinz Ketchup brand.

Heinz was also running commercials showing how much thicker and richer it was and, by implication, how much better tasting.

It also wanted to connect to young people's sense confidence, imagination, originality, mischievousness, and originality.

It took on this personality and put interesting quips on its label. But it also embodied them, via Matt LeBlanc, who would go on to a successful career as one of the original stars of *Friends*.

Rather than take an exaggerated image like the Fonz, Heinz tells the cool story of a guy who impresses the hot dog stand patrons with his imagination and wit as Heinz flowed from atop a New York brownstone to his hot dog bun below.

Heinz Ketchup

http://www.youtube.com/watch?v=N_vssdys8Ik&NR=1

Music: Light, electronic music.

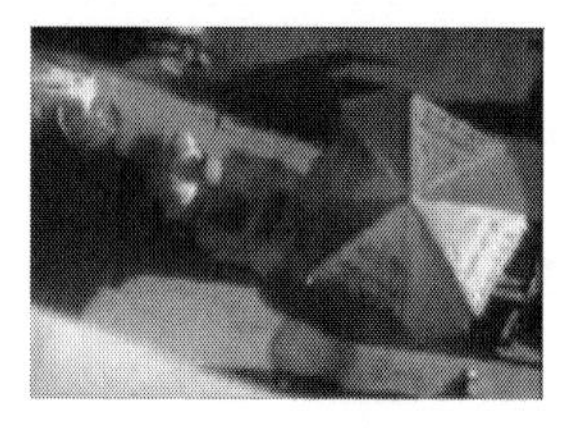

Music: Light, electronic music.

Music: Light, electronic music.

Matt, "Hot dog, please."

"Mustard on that, or what?"

"No thanks, I've got that covered."

Heinz Ketchup. It's so rich,

so thick. Why waste time on anything else?

Heinz. The best things come to those who wait.

Retrieved from xlogold, July 26, 2011, "Matt Le Blanc – Heinz"

Losing Your Customers' Trust: the Demise of Schlitz Beer

This is the inside story of the very first campaign on which I was a junior member of a team. It's a painful one of how literally interpreting research can aid and abet a brand that is on the path to self-destruction.

In 1974, Schlitz was the number two brand in the United States, second to Budweiser and with a substantial lead over Miller High Life and Coors. Miller was beginning to gain share as it consolidated its national business, and Coors was growing fast without expanding beyond where its trucks could easily reach its Colorado brewing facility. Schlitz made the decision to change its formula to a faster high-temperature fermentation process and change to less expensive malt and hops extracts. They changed gradually, and each new change was tested against the last among a sample of beer drinkers. Unfortunately, the tests did not pick up any significant differences from recipe-process 1 to recipe-process 2, or recipe-process 2 to recipe-process 3, or recipe-process 3 to recipe-process 4, but the differences between the original and where they ended up was substantial. These recipe and process changes enabled the beer to increase profits, which funded the addition of new plants, lower prices, and initially increased volume. A new plant in Baldwinsville, New York, was created around the new formula (Bamforth, Charlie, *Cool Stuff*, Brewer's Guardian: December 2007-January 2008, http://www.brewersguardian.com/industry/articles).

These changes alone may have doomed Schlitz, but this case history is about the simultaneous advertising changes that accelerated the loss of trust in the beer.

In 1973, Schlitz was in the fourth year of one of the better campaigns in the history of beer, the so-called "Men of the Sea" gusto campaign. Earlier advertising for Schlitz had been using two well-known taglines: "When you're out of Schlitz, you're out of beer" and "The beer that made Milwaukee famous." That advertising had shown humorous in-bar situations in which someone went to incredible lengths to drink Schlitz when they found that either the bar did not carry Schlitz or had run out. The on-premise bars tended to be nice tavern settings with patrons wearing business-casual clothing.

A new campaign was launched called "Go for the Gusto." In it, international sailors are shown looking for and finding Schlitz around the world. There was always the camaraderie of "real men drinking real beer" with the song "Once around life, once around living, once around life, taste the gusto of Schlitz." And then a very masculine voice said, "You only go around once, so you have to grab for all the gusto you can . . . the gusto of Schlitz." As the following ad shows, these men were no longer upscale-drinkers but blue-collar guys enjoying life and each other's company. They were having adventures, working their way around the world, and finding solace and joy in their beer.

At the same time, beer drinkers were finding Schlitz was often on sale, and the combination increased their volume in many cities. Schlitz was rarely the number one beer in a city, but a consistent two or three made it a clear top brand.

Its share allowed it to afford the right to be the exclusive beer in the Summer Olympics in 1968, 1972, and 1976 in Mexico, Berlin, and Montreal. The real reason the "men of the sea" could find Schlitz in all the exotic ports of call was that Schlitz was carried on American military bases and thus had beer volume in every country shown in the commercials.

Schlitz Beer 1974

http://www.youtube.com/watch?v=Lk3hX2ig484

It took you three weeks to get to Hong Kong and now there's no place to dock.

But when you only go around once,

you don't sit and wait for gusto,
you go out and get it.

Song, "Once around life, once around living ...

Once around beer, and you'll keep around Schlitz.

Come around taste the gusto life's giving,

come around taste

the Gusto of Schlitz."

Retrieved from OldTimeSportsFan, July 26, 2011, "Schlitz, 1974, Hong Kong"

In 1974, sales growth began to slow, and so focus groups around the country were set up to discover what had gone wrong with the advertising. While Schlitz was strongest in the rural counties of Alabama, Mississippi, and Georgia, the groups were held in New Orleans, Los Angeles, San Francisco, and Miami—much more enjoyable places to visit and listen to beer drinkers talk about beer. These groups of "sometimes" Schlitz drinkers (which quantitative lifestyle research had said were club fellows) were drinkers who enjoyed and drank a lot of beer but equally preferred hard liquor and wine.

What the brand managers and researchers behind the glass heard was an earful: "Why don't they show beer drinkers in America?" "They are so gritty, the people I know who drink Schlitz can afford to dress nicer." Then the beer drinkers then went off on all that was wrong with America—a typical lament during the Vietnam War era, which was also a time of high inflation and high unemployment.

So new advertising was developed in 1975 that brought Schlitz home—modern cowboys herding buffalos, rafters riding the rolling thunder of white water, and firemen playing tug-of-war with a beer barrel propelled by their hoses. The same music, the same tagline—there was even the same voice-over announcer. No one in the agency was as proud of this advertising. Somehow it felt smaller and more common, but it met the brief from the client of having America-based beer drinkers enjoying Schlitz.

Schlitz Beer 1975

http://www.youtube.com/watch?v=j7_rJv_zw7k

Once there were thousands

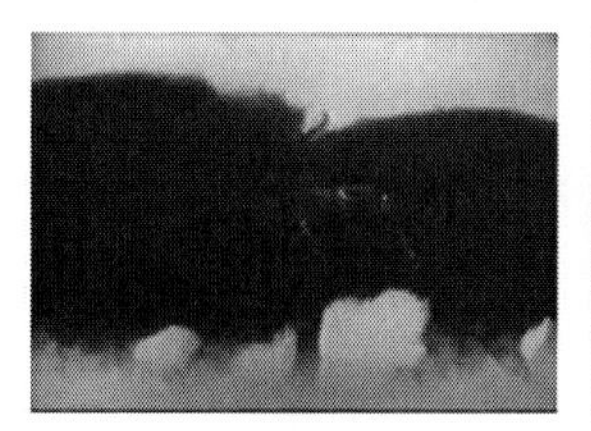

and thousands
and thousands.

And now there are again. The Buffalo are coming back

because someone cared. Hey, isn't that what life is all about? Caring?

The people at Schlitz believe it.

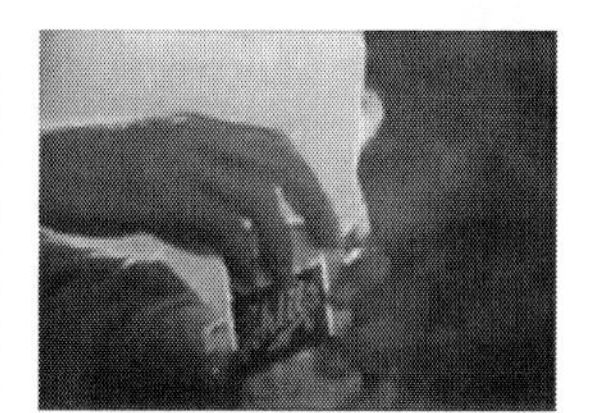

They brew their beer only one way,

with Gusto. Brewed to be the very best.

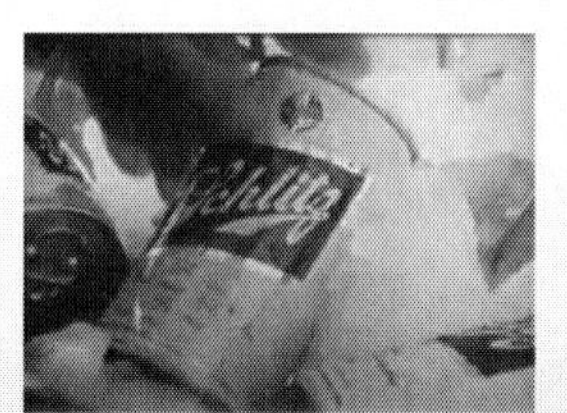

And you can taste it. Hey, life is too short to settle for less.

Go for the Gusto or don't go at all.

Retrieved from OldTimeSportsFan, July 26, 2011, "Schlitz, 1975 01 12, Buffalo herding"

Sales growth continued to slow, and so more research was commissioned with the same moderator, using the same cities, and with the same brief: "What's wrong with our advertising? We are not growing as fast as we were two years ago." The finding was that Schlitz no longer reflected real life.

Most beer was consumed in cities, and increasingly, Schlitz was consumed by suburban young men and women who bought it in bulk for parties from supermarkets and liquor stores. It was not purchased to drink after a hard day's work.

The agency was instructed to find a new campaign that reflected beer-drinking reality. The result was a "just as, so too" logic. So whether it was finding clams in New England or tag football from Berkeley to Boston, preppy folks were finding out "When it's right, you know it." No one got dirty before drinking Schlitz, men and women were equal beer drinking partners, and every group was carefully balanced for gender, age, and race.

Schlitz Beer 1976

http://www.youtube.com/watch?v=wAHAvrUp7ac

"Nope. No clams. It's not right."

"Hey man. We're running out of island."

Song, "When it's right you know it." This is the place. Clams.

Song, "When it's good you feel it."

Anncr: A clam bake. Good food and the right beer.

Anncr: Schlitz. Because you never lose your taste for quality.

Woman, "How did you know where they were?"

Man, "When one coughs, it gives them all away!" She laughs. "I'm totally serious."

Song, "There's just one word for beer. And you know it."

Retrieved OldTimeSportsFan, July 26, 2011, "Schlitz, 1976, Friends on Beach"

Sales now dipped from slow growth to absolute losses. The agency was in trouble because it seemed obviously to be a marketing problem. After all, advertising folks had taken credit for the earlier growth of the brand. Focus groups revealed that few people liked the new ads.

The new brief was simple: gain awareness—make Schlitz the beer everyone would talk about in the bar. The new Miller Lite advertising, "Tastes great, less filling," was what people were talking about in focus groups.

The Clydesdale Budweiser campaign seemed to be casting Schlitz as a poorer quality beer. So the agency tried again to fulfill these goals. A quality campaign celebrated the new brewing process: ABF (agitated beer fermentation). The main advertising campaign sought to return to the growth years of "When you're out of Schlitz " . . ." Only the new line was "You want to take away my Schlitz, my gusto?"

Schlitz Beer 1977

http://www.youtube.com/watch?v=f_baloTGt5M

Anncr (timidly). "Excuse me sir, we'd like to take away your Schlitz and have you try our beer."

"Shuttup. Down baby. I'll handle this.

You wanna take away my Schlitz? You wanna take away my Gusto?

You're the first person that ever made me laugh.

You want to take away my Schlitz, my Gusto?

Say hello to your lunch.

Take away my gusto."

Anncr: "If you don't have Schlitz, you don't have gusto."

"You don't have beer."

Retrieved from OldTimeSportsFan, July 26, 2011, "Wilderness man and cougar"

The campaign was a disaster. Many did start talking about it, but as the butt of Johnny Carson's jokes.

Of course, by this time the beer-drinking public had soured on the new beer formula. In bars, the Budweiser, Pabst, and Coors salesmen were whispering about "protein wisps" that could be seen floating in Schlitz, and sure enough, if you filled two or three glass pitchers, you could see some unfermented beer floating. No health danger, but not very appetizing. And the "cool, crisp taste of Schlitz" was negatively translated as "less taste, more filling."

The lessons from this disaster were many. From a researcher's perspective, literal playback of the wrong people in the wrong markets who were asked the wrong questions can lead to the type of insights that may be true for them but dead wrong for the brand.

From the brand's standpoint, honesty in understanding the total marketing array: product, price, promotion, packaging, and people was needed. The growth and decline of the brand was never just about advertising/promotion but needed a better understanding of the product, pricing, distribution, brand usage, and brand-satisfaction dynamics.

Unfortunately, there was not a good attempt at understanding the essence of why Schlitz had become number two in the nation. The on-premise environment and "blue-collar no-nonsense beer drinker" focus turned out to be one of the few strengths of the brand. The core southern-market strength was ignored, and the attempt to mirror the user was wrong for a twofold reason: it did not truly reflect their users, and it gave no "reason to believe" for beer drinkers to stay with Schlitz.

The original "Men of the Sea" gusto campaign did a great job of reflecting why people drink beer. Beer is a social lubricant. When you drink a beer, even in private at night in your own home, there is comfort in being one of the guys—a common-sense, straightforward man and proud of it. The campaign communicated that emotion: the ads were not mirrors of current drinkers (far from it), nor were they aspirational in a literal way. But the way the actors were living their lives and drinking their beer truly captured "the gusto of life," a phrase that in its heyday meant much more than just good taste.

Leo Burnett was fired, and the new agency produced advertising featuring Frank Sellinger, the chief executive officer of Schlitz: "Behind every Schlitz is a man who knows his beer." Clean-cut beer drinkers came up to him aboard a tourist riverboat in St. Louis and said, "I'm a Budweiser drinker, but now I prefer Schlitz." Apparently, the lesson of actually understanding beer motivations was not internalized before they briefed the new agency.

In 1981, Schlitz suffered a major labor strike in Milwaukee. Its workers at the new factories were making more and more beer with fewer and fewer union workers. Sales continued to fall, unused factories were shuttered, and beer formulation did not return to the beer that had made Milwaukee famous. Schlitz sold their company to the Detroit-based Stroh Brewery Company.

Chapter Ten

Benefit Stories

Stories Communicate Experiential Benefits

People buy things and use services not because of the features companies put into those products but because of the benefits those features provide. There are two types of benefits: tangible benefits that you can judge before you buy and experiential benefits that become obvious only as you use a brand. Trust in a brand dictates how closely people check the tangible features before they buy and is crucial as they gauge the potential value of experiential benefits.

A good example is men's casual clothes. When people buy them in a department store, they can tangibly judge these clothes by how they fit on their bodies, their current fashion, and how they complement what buyers already have in their closets. However, when these clothes are bought in a discount store, the judgment shifts to experiential concerns about durability, and the questions are different. Will it shrink after the first wash? Will the colors fade? Will the buttons come loose? Advertising informs and reassures the potential user about these experiential questions.

Of course, many, if not most, products are bought primarily for experiential benefits. Will this new piece of technology be more intuitive, and will it actually fit into my life? Will this cosmetic fit into my beauty regime, and will it truly enhance how others see me and how I feel about myself? Will the total quality of the ownership experience make the price I pay a good value?

Five Reasons Benefit Stories Work

Human stories that bring these experiential benefits to life can be truly helpful in purchasing decisions. Stories work in five different ways. First, they facilitate visualization of the product in use. In thirty seconds, they can help you vicariously know more about what the ownership experience with this brand will be like.

Second, they help you test the personal relevance of the ownership experience by allowing you to compare your unique needs to those depicted in the advertising.

Third, they help you test not only whether you should care about the brand but also whether the brand cares about you. Increasingly, service is a major component of the usage experience—the qualities and attitudes of those who serve you, both when you buy and as you use the brand, is critical. American Express discovered that their advertising was turning away customers, not because the brand's features were irrelevant to potential cardholders, but because their advertising made it seem that Amex was likely to not value prospective customers; it made American Express seem haughty, opinionated, and judgmental.

Fourth, stories can create a persona for the brand, as if the brand was a person. Our ability to judge other people is one of our most developed capabilities. When a brand fits into a well-recognized type and is consistent in the way it presents itself, we imbue the brand with a holistic set of expectations that match how we have experienced people with similar traits. Disney, Hallmark, McDonald's, Google, Facebook, and Toyota all have personalities that advertising can either leverage or, at their peril, disrupt.

Fifth, we recognize and remember stories better than facts, and so even brief exposures to the brand story will last and build on themselves over time. For many years, Kodak staged their brand in classic "taking family snapshots" moments. These ministories seemed so familiar, so parallel with our own choice of times to pick up a camera, that long before the familiar gold-and-red Kodak logo came up, we knew it was a Kodak commercial and we were seeing Kodak moments. Kodak's hope was that when we were in a drugstore or discount store and presented with several brands, all the feelings we wanted from the total experience would be connected to the Kodak logo, and we would pay the additional premium for Kodak quality. The challenge for Kodak was that the products they offered and the stories they told did not evolve to include the camera in the smartphone, the digital world of sharing photographs, or world of e-books and electronic photo albums.

Platform for Launching Brand Varieties

Well-told advertising stories assume a voice of the author that makes each new commercial like another chapter in a continuing series. This voice communicates the broader narrative of the brand that includes new varieties, new products, and additional benefits that fit naturally into the continuing story. It was Hal Riney who provided a rich narrative as we considered a second term for President Ronald Reagan.

Whether it was "Morning in America" or "Some think there is a bear out there," Riney defined the first four years in a way that united Americans and gave Reagan one of the largest reelection victories in history. Hallmark and McDonald's each tell stories about different products and different features, and speak to different audiences with the same brand voice, and keep their consistent persona across different product introductions.

Most successful stories are really tracks from an album, not singles. The classic albums of all time make you want to buy and listen to the entire album, not just download and own the most popular single song; like a movement in a symphony, distinct yet essential parts of the whole. So too does successful advertising harmonize all the ways people come into contact with the brand's advertising across diverse executions in various media. If the stories they tell are jarringly dissimilar, the potential synergy of time and seeing the brand in different complementary media is lost, and the story's power is dissipated.

Is the Story a Good Story?

Our criteria for judging a story are well formed. Does it have a hook that draws me in? Is it timely, something worth remembering? Does it have a visceral impact and human interest? Does it resolve a conflict and reach a memorable conclusion? These are the same criteria that we use when we decide to read and reread a particular novelist. Benefit storytellers must therefore be creative artists and effective merchants.

Hyperbole in Stories

While the Green Giant may be one of the most famous myths portrayed in advertising, many commercials use hyperbole to talk about the experiential values of their brand. Like verbal puffery, the purpose is to communicate a richness of experience while maximizing the viewer reward for taking the time to see the ad.

Axe-Deo, the French brand sold in many countries by Unilever, takes an oversized dose of male fantasy and brings it to life in this commercial. The story is all about the benefits and expectations the user might have, and the story would fall apart with a different brand. Fun.

Axe-Deo

http://www.youtube.com/watch?v=fIPu94TiJH4&playnext=1&list=PL617D6D2748DEBD90

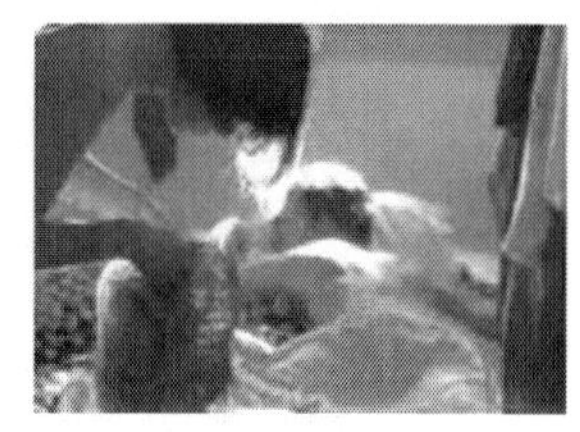

Jazzy song under.
A young woman is running late and can't find her perfume.

So she uses her boyfriend's Axe instead.

We see the responses of other women as she passes.

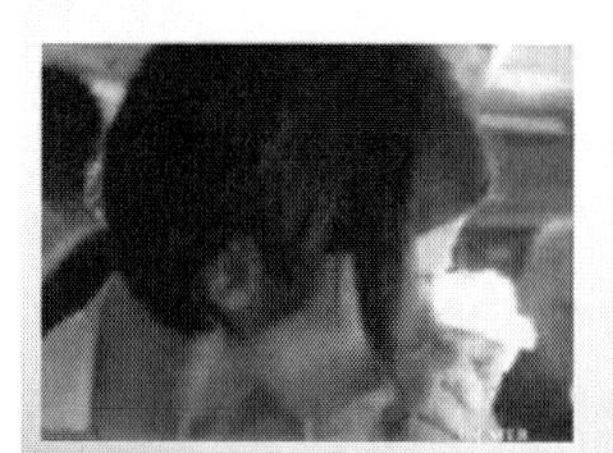

The scent is something of a revelation to her.

She comes back to the apartment and finds her boyfriend's Axe-Deo and throws it.

Axe: For Men!

Retrieved from whoyknows, Apr 25, 2007, "AXE commercial, jealous girlfriend"

Braathens Safe Airlines in Norway produced this ad with the exact same thought in mind: how to take a promotion to bring your relatives to Oslo for half-price.

The story is all about the benefit (although perhaps it is a stretch to say the hero deems it a benefit to have his in-laws come in at half-price), and only this unusually low fare would result in his in-laws arriving with so little notice.

The delight is that the tone of voice of the ad transfers to the airline as being distinctly Norwegian. It would be difficult to imagine a similar ad for a Swiss, German, or English airline.

Braathens Safe

http:/ / www.youtube.com/ watch?v=yQ8hdM9IR8I

A chap comes home

planning a lunchtime surprise for his wife.

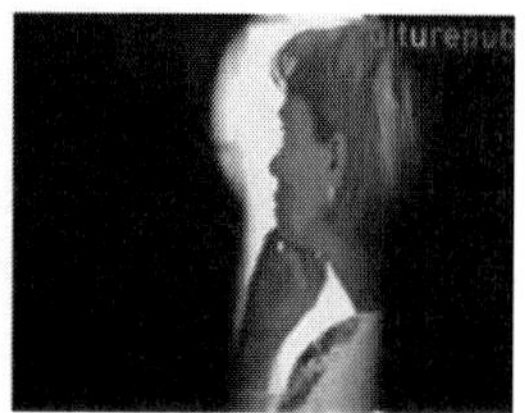

All because Braathens Safe have a promotion to fly your in-laws at half price.

Retrieved from CulturePub, Oct 9, 2010, August 1, 2011, "Tea for two"

Creating a Brand Persona

It is easier to trust a brand persona if it flows directly from the benefits that the brand provides.

Focus groups among Cadbury Whole Nut users reveal that each one ate the bar in slightly different ways. Some would look at the bar and make sure they had a whole nut in the piece they broke off to eat, find it with their tongue, and then bite down, crunching it into the warm melted slurry of nutty milk chocolate. Others would carefully suck off all the Cadbury's Milk Chocolate before they ate the now-unadorned whole hazelnut.

It was the unique combination of the small whole hazelnuts and the thick Cadbury's Milk Chocolate that gave the bar its play value, which enhanced the eating experience. The advertising took that playful nature and told deliciously funny stories in their ad series.

Cadbury's Whole Nut

http://www.youtube.com/watch?v=KJ7QxKuB4gg

Man in rowboat in middle of the ocean humming to himself.

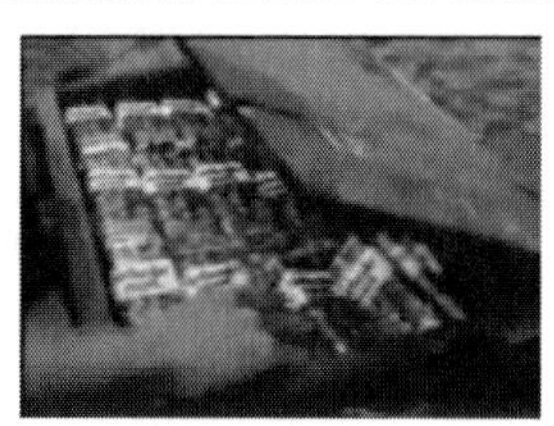

Man opens box full of Cadbury Whole Nuts.

Submarine periscope pops up next to life raft.

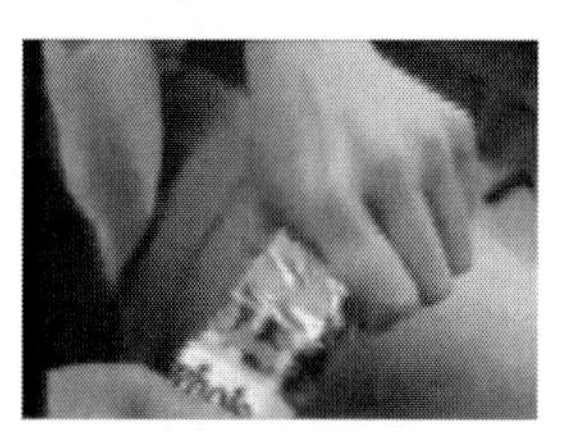

Man picks up the golden foil of Cadbury's Whole Nuts.

From nowhere comes shouts of "Nuts. Whole Hazel Nuts."

(CU of periscope) Cadbury takes them and covers them with chocolate.

Man covers scope, "Shut up or everyone will want a bit."

Sound of down periscope.

Empty sea.

Cadbury's Whole Nut. Whole hazelnuts in thick milk chocolate.

Retrieved from NinaOPerez, July 26, 2011, "Cadbury's Whole Nut Submarine-UK

Visualizing the Brand in Use

The before-and-after story sets up the product-as-hero story.

After World War II, Lucozade became a household staple. It was an era during which sick children were not rushed to the doctor for antibiotics, and so they had to be nursed as their fever raged and their hunger vanished.

Lucozade is a slightly carbonated glucose drink, which, like 7UP in the United States during this period, was used by mothers to comfort their children.

The brand monitored the number of reported cases of flu nationwide, and when flu numbers started their annual uptick, this campaign was run. It reminded last year's users and potential new users of oncoming illness and made the expectation of getting better part of the value of the purchase. Its theme and tagline was "Lucozade aids recovery."

Lucozade

http://www.youtube.com/watch?v=a8GjM_Pmubl

"A day at the Zoo.

A holiday treat that last week I'd thought she would have to miss

because she was still recovering from tonsillitis.

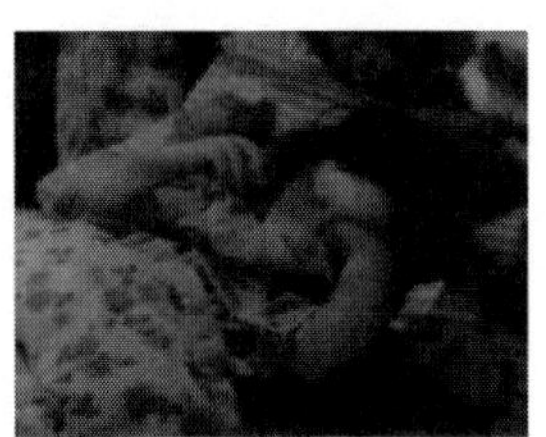

She was so listless. She couldn't take solid foods,

but she did take lots of Lucozade.

I'm sure it made the difference and gave her the energy to get better.

To say nothing of what it did to keep me a busy, happy mum.

Anncr: When you are her mother and her nurse, remember Lucozade.

Lucozade aids recovery.

Retrieved from welle550, July 26, 2011, "Marlboro Werbung-1-.wmv"

Visualizing "Me" Using the Brand

In the 1980s, Lucozade broadened its reach trying to appeal to housewives who needed a little energy boost during the day. Perhaps they were feeling a bit under the weather or needing more energy than a rest and a cup of tea could provide.

The story they told leveraged their past advertising with a reference to "When Johnny was ill." However, the story was simply a slice of life with Lucozade's benefit of "aiding energy recovery" becoming the vehicle through which a newly energized mother could be ready to greet her Johnny at the end of the day.

Interestingly, after success with this effort, the brand was able to transition into the energy drink market in the UK via the endorsement of the Olympic decathlete champion, Daley Thompson.

Lucozade

http:/ / www.youtube.com/ watch?v=Vq9ewRHzaVU

Mom, "Whew.
(picking up bear) Come on
Mr. B…what a morning

What I need is some
Lucozade.

I bought an extra bottle
when Johnny was ill.

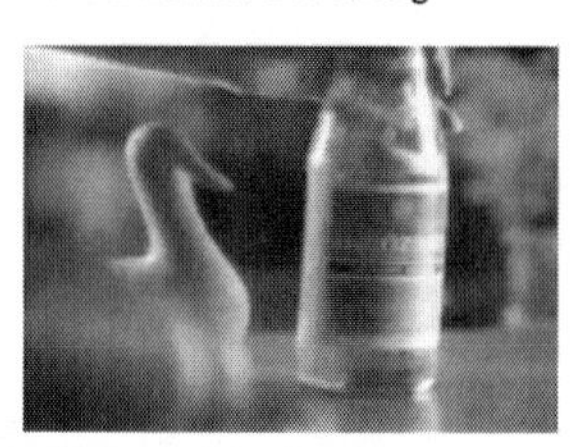

I'm sure the glucose energy
in Lucozade will help me."

Lucozade provides glucose
energy in the form that the
body can rapidly absorb.

So have some Lucozade.

before you get up and
go again.

"Hey Johnny, did you win?"
Boy, "Yes, we beat them."

Lucozade aids energy
recovery.

Retrieved from GrubcoTV3, July 26, 2011, "Lucozade commercial [1980s]"

Trusting in the Intangible Benefits of a Brand

Some products' benefits make more sense when they are shown in a story than when they are logically described.

Coffee is one of those products. Most brands of coffee focus on the particular flavor promise. Instant coffee often promises the taste of drip coffee, like Taster's Choice did with "Looks, smells, and tastes just like ground roast," Sanka's "Real perked coffee in a jar," and Starbuck's Via "Take the taste challenge."

In Australia, Bushell's Instant Coffee went one step further. It created a story around the seemingly mutually exclusive benefits: relaxing you (the ritual of putting on the kettle and settling down for a cup) and getting you going again (the caffeine) with a "fresher roast."

Bushell's Instant Coffee

http://www.youtube.com/watch?v=TFH1bTvJNBM&feature=related

There are times when those little everyday obstacles

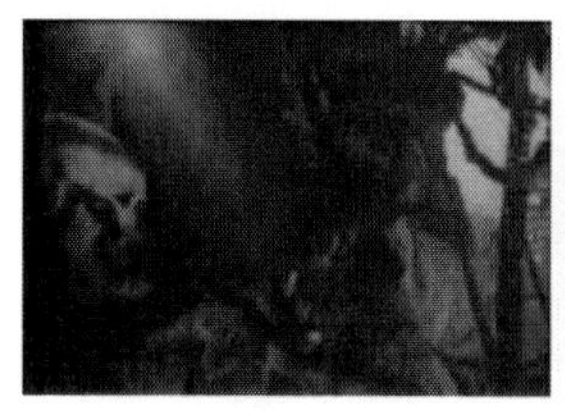

become impenetrable barriers

and you can't see the forest for the trees.

So you have to get into the swing of things,
because there is one sure way to get out of the woods.

When you get home,

Bushell's instant coffee, a blend of fresher roast beans with all the flavor and

satisfaction you need in a coffee.

Bushell's Instant Coffee.

A fresher roast when you need it most.

Retrieved from smscmaster, July 26, 2011, "Australian Bushell's Instant Coffee com"

How Do You Visualize *Easy*?

Often, the very act of explaining that something is easy raises the specter that it might be complicated.

Rice Krispies Treats, made from Rice Krispies, is relatively easy (though not as easy as buying the treats from every corner convenience store), but for most people, cooking skills are rarely practiced in this era of prepared foods.

This commercial does a delightful job of providing mom the reward she seeks, preparing the dessert she know her family will enjoy, and getting credited with home cooking.

The dab of flour on her nose might have been over the top, but it is a story after all.

Rice Krispies Recipe

http://www.youtube.com/watch?v=MWZXoGZijH4

"Mom, are they ready yet?"

"I'm working on it."

Rice Crispies Treats are so easy to make,

they take no time at all.

Mom, "These things take time."

"But they taste so good."

Your family will think you slaved over them all afternoon.

And if that's what they think, then what they don't know won't hurt them.

Rice Krispies Treats.
So good. So easy.

Retrieved from elithecast, Dec 7, 2007, "Rice Krispies Treats"

Ensuring Product Integration into the Story

Kellogg's Raisin Bran is an insight story about the transition from product attributes to product benefits.

The following ad was one of the first after the "raisin war." During this time, each brand with raisins declared they had more than the other brand.

All the bran cereals were coming out of the era of first claiming the most fiber, and then claiming better taste because of all the stuff they combined in the cereal with the bran.

Kellogg's Raisin Bran was doing well in that comparison with its "two scoops of raisins in every Kellogg's pack" claim.

However, these ads feature ministories in which the combination of raisins both provides the burst of high energy the hero of the ad portrays in the activity selected and the reason to "charge back" for the great taste of those two scoops.

These dual benefits stand out only because of the engaging story when all the other bran cereals are simply claiming the same product features.

Kellogg's Raisin Bran

http://www.youtube.com/watch?v=nN3vUh4Kkrw

James is a racing man, but more than bikes

what game he likes is two scoops

in every Kellogg's pack, keeps him coming back

for two scoops of plump juicy raisins.

Riding as hard as he can,

he leads the pack.

But now he's thinking back

to those two scoops and lovely flakes of bran

in Kellogg's Raisin Brand. part of this complete breakfast.

Retrieved from Libmanmusic, July 29, 2011, "Racing' Man" 1984 Commercial

Stories That Provide a "Reason to Believe"

As United, American, and Pan Am glamorized the image of the stewardess, the worry to the airline promoting their friendly skies was that many average fliers might feel intimidated by that very glamour.

Elegant, stylish, well-dressed, chic, and refined can potentially clash with friendly, cooperative, caring, and ready to lend a hand.

This United spot bridges the gap between caring and classy.

Everyone can empathize with the rite of passage graduation from United Airlines' stewardess school. The tearful images, the John Denver song, and the proud father all combine to retain the image of the stewardess, implying that they can and will be a natural part of the friendly skies.

United Airlines

http://www.youtube.com/watch?v=YPWTcu0yPGs

Song: (female singer)
All my bags are
packed, I'm ready to go ...

Anncr: Graduation Day
at United's stewardess
College.

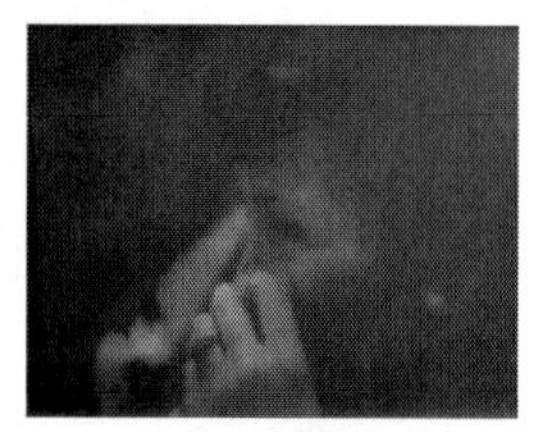

Song: I hate to wake
you up to say goodbye.

Song: But the dawn is
breaking. It's time to go.

Anncr: It's a happy day
for the girls and their
families.

Song: I'm so excited.
Just can't wait to go.

Anncr: Above all. It's when
the Friendly Skies become
even friendlier.

Song: I'm leaving on a
jet plane. And soon I will
be back again.

Song; Fly the Friendly
Skies of United.

Retrieved jetluvr2000, July 26, 2011, "United Airlines Commercial – Graduation Day"

Motivational Cues about the Category: Hallmark Cards

Greeting cards are huge in the United States. More than six billion cards are purchased every year, and it is estimated that over 90 percent of households buy at least one card a year with an average of thirty individual cards a year. Women buy 80 percent of the cards. The market is large enough to enable sections in most large groceries and drugstores as well as specialty card shops on main streets and malls across America.

At a superficial level, the benefits seem to be for the recipient. Getting a card brightens your day, is a sign of how much someone values a particular type of relationship, and gives the recipient warm feelings of friendship or kinship.

However, the benefits are equally balanced. The sender gets just as many benefits as does the recipient. There is a pleasure in choosing just the right card for someone, a confidence that you really know what they will like, and a sense that you are making a statement both about the type of person you are and how much you respect them.

Brand trust flows both ways. The giver trusts the card to be high quality ("When you care enough to give the very best") and knows that the recipient may very well flip the card over to check out the brand, and if they find the Hallmark logo, it means that they are valued enough to be sent a quality card.

Thus, one strong dimension that a story must convey is getting the balance right between being from me to you. From presenting yourself in the best possible light, to a positive reflection of you in building a relationship with someone else, to providing support, to maintaining ties, or to reconnecting.

There is another dynamic tension that has to be in balance: a desire to convey a unique meaning about a unique relationship and fitting into your culture's accepted pattern of acknowledging events and holidays.

The card shows how well you know and understand the recipient, helps you celebrate what you and the receiver have in common, portrays your sense of humor, captures just the emotional tone, and either celebrates fond memories or takes pleasure in surprise and delight.

But it can also simply be an acknowledgement of an occasion, a part of a tradition of sending cards at a particular season, being polite and courteous, showing respect for traditions and customs, or as an act of generosity.

Thus, giving cards provides the benefits of self-expression, making meaningful connections, doing the right thing at the right time, and/or providing assurance that a relationship is continuing.

Hallmark conveys this breadth of benefits across a number of efforts. They develop TV movies that embrace sentimentality and heartfelt emotions. They sponsor a TV channel that features shows that embody the type of quality, values, and emotional connections they want to represent. They run successful retail stores that embrace each different card-giving season with all the seasonal "extras" that go with Valentine's Day, Mother's Day, Father's Day, birthdays, American holidays, and religious celebrations.

Consistent in their efforts is an attention to detail and a concern about the total effect. The card stock needs to match the sentiment of the card. The movie needs fewer commercial interruptions. The channel needs to become an important destination for potential viewers.

The Challenge for Hallmark Advertising

A person who buys forty cards a year is not buying them for only one benefit. Sometimes they are strictly a spontaneous self-expression you want to share with a friend or loved one. Sometimes they are an even more personal attempt at making a meaningful connection. Sometimes they are bought in bulk for the spirit of the season. Some are just the polite thing to do, like sending a thank-you card to your child's teacher at the end of the term—nothing to be gained, no relationship to be maintained, but a pleasant feeling for both giver and recipient. The student in this ad wanted her teacher to know that her gift was heartfelt.

Hallmark Cards

http://www.youtube.com/watch?v=tu5vgtEMyvM

"Mrs. Elliott, has he finished his tea yet?"
"He should be just about done."

She rushes through the music building as the sound of tuning echoes.

Song (her voice) Oh I knew it was your birthday and that you didn't know I knew.

And I wanted to find the right surprise for you.

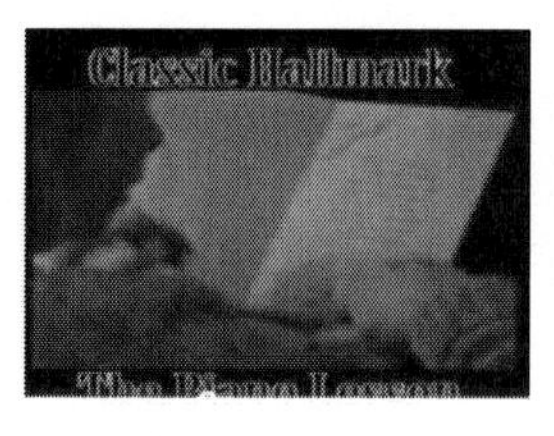

"Good afternoon, Lisa."
"Good afternoon."
"Are we prepared?" "Yes."

"Mmm. Let's see what Mr. Beethoven thinks."

So I'm giving you this Hall-mark so that I hope that you will see,

what I'm really giving you is a part of me.

Anncr: "Make someone's day special. Give a Hallmark.
When you care enough to give the very best."

Retrieved from schnelman Dec 25, 2009, August 11, 2011, "The Music Professor"

Building Trust in an "Outsider" Brand Image

The stories of this brief campaign for RC Cola came in the middle of the cola wars.

This campaign tried to take the outsider regional persona of a Southern brand and make it work nationally.

RC adopted the traditional stories of country music, visualized them, put a country lyric and tune together, and made the individual choice of drinking RC Cola a benefit, a personal statement about the kind of person you were.

The brand never made very large inroads and eventually was relegated to a small regional player. Whether it would have worked in a world where the firepower of major campaigns was not being waged, we'll never know.

RC Cola

http:/ / www.youtube.com/ watch?v=Wm_LmIFeNnM

I get my kicks on summer nights on a beat-up quarter-mile.

I'm happy just to win 3rd place and give my girl a smile.

I put my foot right on the floor and won the second race.

Then downed an RC Cola, and gave my thirst the chase.

Me and my RC.
Me and my RC.

Now the final race this dude shows up with 20 coats of paint.

I took a look at Wanda and she looked like she'd faint.

I said, "Honey, just hang loose, don't be afraid of all that dough. It's knowing how to take the turn and not how fast you go."

Me and my RC.
Me and my RC.
'Cause what's good enough for other folks, ain't good enough for me.

Retrieved from CarolosEmelectrico, August 1, 2011, "Me and My RC"

Chapter Eleven

Use of a Symbol, Analogy, or Exaggerated Graphic of the Benefit to Link a Brand to a Range of Benefits

Greek Gods of Strength, Beauty, and Wisdom

Greek Gods of Strength, Beauty, and Wisdom

Visually Branding the Benefit

One of the major tasks of advertising is to bring experiential benefits of a brand to life—the advantages that only can be experienced once the brand is bought and used. Symbols can embody those benefits in a unique and powerful way. In the same way that the Greeks sought to embody strength, beauty, and wisdom in their portraiture of Atlas, Venus, and Athena, so too have advertisers sought to convey strength, vitality, and good taste in the symbols they create for their brand.

Many times we choose brands based on the level of trust we have accumulated for them, but not always. Sometimes we buy a terrible brand of coffee at the train station, trading off quality for convenience. Sometimes we try a brand we expect we might not like, but someone else liked it, and so we are willing to give it a go. Sometimes we simply make an aesthetic decision—we like the way it looks, feels, or is displayed. Symbols can be transferred from the advertising to the packaging, so when we are at a tire dealership and see Mighty Atlas, we may transfer all we aesthetically know about lasting strength and protection of the mythical figure of Atlas to a brand of tires.

Most times we seek the middle ground. The best value is usually somewhere between the highest quality and lowest price. Fun is balanced by sensible, traditional is balanced by new, and sweet is balanced by eating healthy. Part of balance is contained across the breadth of our actions: a balanced diet allows one to eat meat and chocolate cake as long as there are vegetables; a balanced portfolio allows one the safety of treasury bonds and the risk of growth stocks. Symbols permit the ultimate extreme benefit to be visualized while the advertising can surround that benefit with the necessary elements to reduce the inherent tension. The leaping figure of the jaguar is "frozen" in stately silver; the curving swoosh of Nike is balanced by the thick typeface spelling out NIKE.

Choosing a symbol for the brand that communicates a benefit is like choosing a brand name that connotes a benefit. The risk is that someday the brand will want to sell a product in which the benefit is quite different than the name. The short-term competitive advantage is the incremental number of people who try the brand because of the benefit promise. You can buy Bulmers Cider or

Frosty Jack's Cider. You can buy Life Savers or Jawbreakers. You can buy Campbell's or Cup-a-Soup. Long-term Bulmer's, Life Savers, and Campbell's have been successful at extending their brand into many categories, but their direct competitors, with a benefit in their brand name, have not been able to expand. Bakers Square is an example of a company having to rebrand their stores when their original benefit name, Poppin' Fresh Pies, proved too limiting.

One of the advantages of an advertising symbol is that the total brand can evolve into more products that do not feature the symbol, while the core brand has the option of retaining the symbol. Thus, many people have been introduced to McDonald's restaurants when they were children through a combination of the golden arches and Ronald McDonald. The arches remain, but both teenagers and retirees rarely come into contact with the Ronald, either in the advertising they see or the products they buy from McDonald's.

Building Trust Based on Specific Benefits

Much of advertising is directed not to all people but a subset of potential people who are dramatically more likely to buy a brand. This is called segmentation, and sometimes this is based on age, income, or gender. These are the characteristics that most potential media use to create environments in which their shows, articles, or information will be more relevant. In this way, advertisers can synch the brand's message to the potential people who will view it.

The ads that appear on E! Entertainment are for products with much younger potential users than the ads that appear on Retro Television, home of *Bonanza*, *Route 66*, and *Perry Mason*.

Sometimes segmentation is based on actual behavior; Google synchs the ads that are displayed online with the type of information the computer user has been viewing up to that moment.

Benefit segmentation is not aimed at different classes of people but at the different benefits someone is seeking within a category. For instance, in cereal some brands are bought because they are primarily fun and indulgent—a treat, comfort food, something to satisfy the sweet tooth or to feel childlike. Other brands are bought because they are linked to health and vitality—wholesome, nourishing, a solid way to start the day. There is little confusion about which brand does what, so they are segmented along the dimension of health or indulgence. Few would buy Frosted Flakes or Total for the same reason. However, the same household often buys both, either for different members of the family or different "moods" in the morning.

Similarly, cereal brands may appeal to tradition. These brands keep the same typeface and packaging design year after year. Other brands appeal to a desire for novelty and change the associated imagery to fads and trends. Chex Cereals and Buzz Blasts, with a cereal box designed around *Toy Story*'s Buzz Lightyear, could hardly be more different.

Personifying the Benefit

Tango in the UK has adopted the Orange Man as a personification of the fresh, invigorating taste of its drink. It is a highly involving visual that makes watching the commercial very rewarding. The Orange Slap translates directly to the taste impact they are trying to tie to their brand in the especially difficult competitive world of the omnipresent Coke and Pepsi. The rude, rebellious personality of the brand helps Tango escape the association of the orange taste as a young child's drink.

Orange soda is one of the first carbonated drinks that UK moms give their children, believing it to be a more acceptable product for their young children than caffeinated Coke or Pepsi. However, this might become a liability for those brands when those same young children become rebellious teens, hence, the Orange Man.

Tango

http:/ / www.youtube.com/ watch?v=I1jywIZG74o

"Hello, Charlie, I think we might use a video replay here."

"OK, Ralph, let's do that."

"Oh yes. We could be in for a quintessential orange sensation here."

"Why yes. Charlie, let's look again."

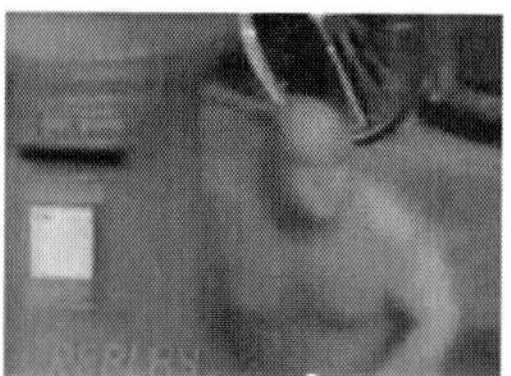

"Yes, Ralph." The big orange guy runs in from the left

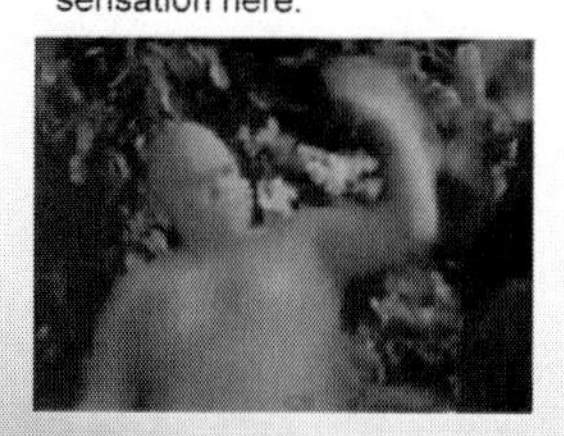

and gives him a right good slapping.

"It just illustrates the bite of real oranges in Tango."
"That's right, Ralph. Super taste sensation. Lovely."

You know when you've been Tango'd.

Retrieved from Comrade71, May 3, 2006, August 9, 2011, "Advert – Tamgo Orange Man"

Vitality as a Brand Symbol

There are two experiential benefits of Life Savers candy that have proven valuable: the small lift-of-energy/mouth refreshment from its sweet flavors and the shareable form of its roll.

This Life Savers ad, developed in Australia, takes these two and literally explodes them into a vital symbol for the brand.

The Life Savers' blow-up tube became a wintertime (snow tubing) and summertime (white water tubing) sensation, both as a promotion and as an advertising campaign. The sight of these giant colorful tubes cascading down the mountain was captivating and energized the brand sales from the moment they were launched.

Life Savers

http://www.youtube.com/watch?v=YkjUdPCHbhA

Everywhere you go you're feeling all right.

Getting out into the sun.

Going to hit the runs, going to give them a hiding.

Feeling good.

Life Savers.
Life Savers.

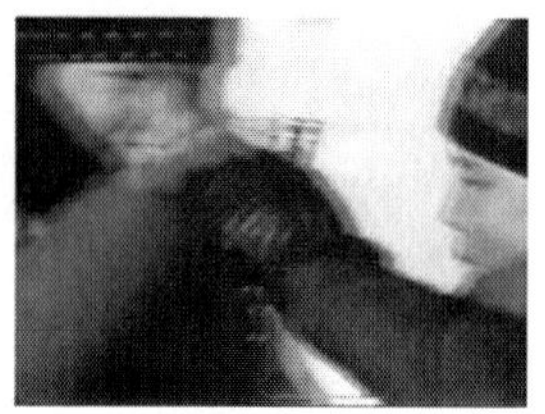

Hand them around.

Life Savers.
Life Savers.

Hand them around.

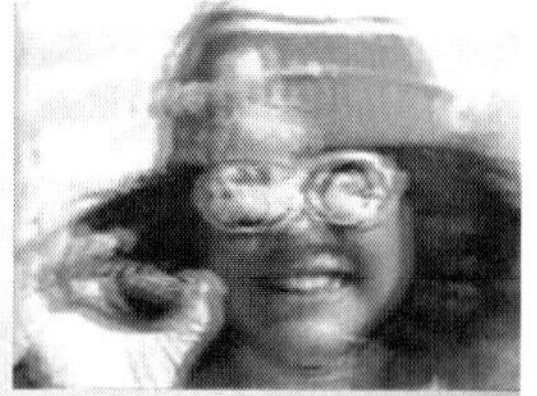

Life Savers. Life Savers.
Hand them around.

Retrieved from retrooldcommercials, July 26, 2011, "Life Savers (Australian ad) 1980"

The Schlitz Malt Liquor Bull

If there was ever a symbol that signaled a brand's vitality and potency, it was the bull for Schlitz Malt Liquor.

The bull came into the scene at the end of every commercial, breaking through the wall, tearing through the house or bar, and causing general mayhem. Eventually the brand symbol migrated to the can, and users began asking for "the bull."

African Americans consumed the majority of all malt liquor brands long before advertising was created with these users in mind.

Schlitz followed along with each musical trend of the African American market, featuring reggae, R&B, rap, and hip-hop long before other commercials used similar music.

Although the commercials rapidly changed to catch the wave of urban popular music, the brand continuity became the bull's signature entry.

Schlitz Malt Liquor

http://www.youtube.com/watch?v=ZCm07WceaQw

(All music and break dancing)

When you're up and down,

all around, look for the Schlitz Malt Liquor.

When you're looking around, you better look out for the bull.

Look out. Look out for the Schlitz Malt Liquor Bull.

Look out for the bull. The Schlitz Malt Liquor Bull.

Nobody makes Malt Liquor like Schlitz. Look out, look out, Schlitz coming through. Pop the top and let it pour.

Nobody. Look out for the bull.

Nobody makes Malt Liquor like Schlitz. Nobody!

Retrieved from drinkschlitz, July 26, 2011, "Schlitz Malt Liquor Commercial"

Kellogg's Critters

The Kellogg Company has launched quite a number of animated characters to represent the appeal to the five senses of their cereals.

Toucan Sam's nose led him to the aroma of fruity tastes, and his colors matched the visual appeal of the cereal. Snap, Crackle, and Pop communicated the unique sounds of Rice Krispies in milk. For Apple Jacks, they animated an apple and cinnamon stick to race to the bowl and communicate the specific taste. And Sugar Pops Pete introduced the brand with his whip, transforming a rough corncob to crunchy corn pops.

Tony the Tiger has been the most versatile and successful symbol for a Kellogg cereal. Constantly updated with modern graphic treatments, he has remained the energetic fun mascot for Frosted Flakes.

Kellogg's Frosted Flakes

http://www.youtube.com/watch?v=QqD2iM8o9Hc&feature=feedrec_grec_index

"Are you going to brave the rapids?

"Sure,

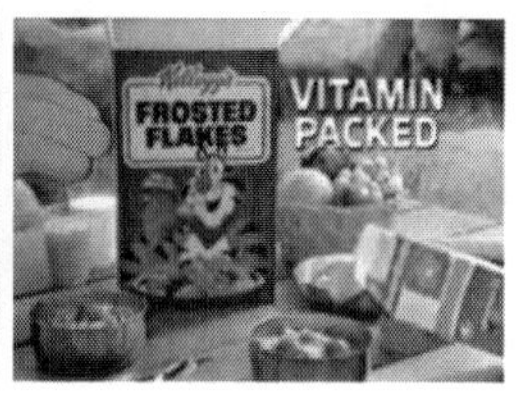

after this complete breakfast including my Frost Flakes.

They bring out the Tiger in you."

"Good you'll need it."

"Good?
They're GREAT!"

Song.
You'll show us you're a Tiger.

Show 'em what you can do.
The taste of Frosted Flakes

brings out the Tiger in you.

Retrieved from 80sCommercialVault, Apr 22, 2009, "80s Commercials Vol. 54"

Snap, Crackle, and Pop have been used in many ways over the years. For several years they told the story for the brand, literally coming out of the cereal bowl to interact with the children who were eating it.

They were carefully crafted to complement each other as a family trio.

From time to time, as in this commercial, their individual sounds were used as the dramatic punctuation of a music video.

Extremely unique and powerful symbols that had two uses, they not only introduced each new generation to the unique aural qualities of the cereal but also lent continuity, which gave Rice Krispies a strong traditional appeal that transcends age.

Kellogg's Rice Krispies

http://www.youtube.com/watch?v=0ELu6ciGsJE

Only Rice Krispies have

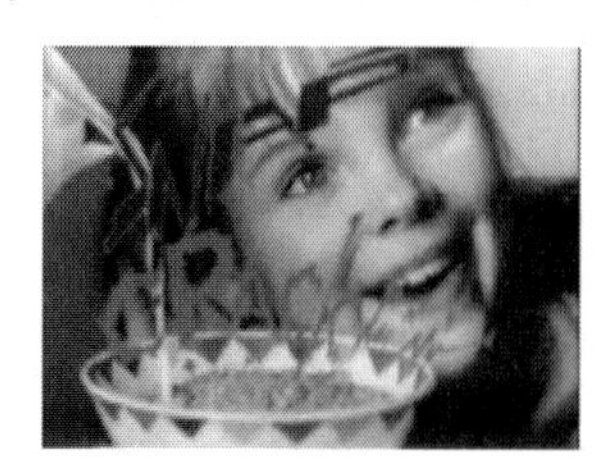

Snap. Crackle. Pop.

Snap. Crackle. Pop.

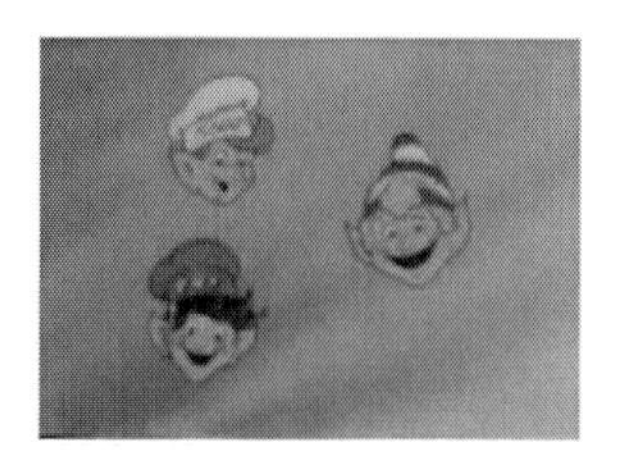

Snap. Crackle. Pop.

Snap. Crackle. Pop.

Snap. Crackle. Pop.

Snap. Crackle. Pop.

Snap. Crackle. Pop.

Kellogg's Rice Krispies. Have you heard how good they are?

Retrieved RetroWinnipe, July 29, 2011, "Kellogg's Rice Krispies commercial"

1 Hollow Tree Lane

The Keebler Elves have so permeated the Keebler Company that their corporate headquarters has the address 1 Hollow Tree Lane, Elmhurst, Illinois.

Keebler became one of the dominant cookie companies by buying a series of regional bakeries in the late fifties and sixties.

The brilliance of the Keebler Elves is that they served as an umbrella for all the different taste and texture benefits of each separate cookie.

Nabisco put all its resources behind the megabrand Oreo and fared well.

However, Keebler could tell the different product stories behind Pecan Sandies, Vanilla Wafers, Country Style Oatmeal Cookies, Fudge Shoppe, E.L. Fudge, and Chips Deluxe all under the umbrella of one campaign.

Keebler Cookies

http:/ / www.youtube.com/ watch?v=oUs2IxOxpMQ

"Hey!

Careful with that fudge."

"Sorry, Ernie, it's the rookie first time covering cookies.

"Do I have to use so much fudge?"

"We're Elves, we always use a lot."

"Lots of creamy fudge makes our Keebler cookies taste even more uncommonly goo

"Keep your eye on the cookie kid."

"Making Keebler fudge-covered cookies takes lots of fudge. And lots of practice."

Fudge Sticks, Fudge Stripes, Fudge Marshmallow and Deluxe Grahams from Keebler.

Retrieved from FuzzyMemoriesTV, Apr 27, 2008 Keebler Cookies – "Oh, Fudge!"

Brand Persona: Ronald McDonald

McDonald's has been a family friendly, quick-service experience from its creation. With affordable meals that the whole family liked, McDonald's proved a good value for families; all their children at every age would be interested in getting away from home. The food matched all the criteria that a child likes: simple, easy to handle, and with an interesting variety of tastes within each meal.

With the creation of Happy Meals and Ronald McDonald, McDonald's had the opportunity to truly understand the unique needs and desires of children and provide a total experience that they would look forward to eating time after time.

The McDonald's experience starts with the crew. Their ability to stay cheerful, helpful, and speedily serve meals was an essential component. Everyone has seen and recalls the lack of patience of children, especially when they are tired and hungry. The squirming at a table for food, the immediate gratification, and the "lack of surprises" in product delivery all enhance the preteen experience. Repetition gives children a sense of mastery and adequacy that they enjoy, as can be attested to when they are seen watching their favorite movie for the tenth time.

McDonald's strives for operational efficiency, trying to be the fastest, easiest play to use. Their site location dedication ensures that they find the most convenient places to be. Just as Coke became successful being "an arm's length away from desire," so too has the frequent, multiple locations actually increased usage per store rather than diluted sales. Perhaps less well-noticed is a commitment to their communities, sponsoring local sports teams, giving vouchers for educational fund-raisers, and becoming a hub for after-school playgroups in their colorful toy parks. In practice, all these efforts demonstrate that McDonald's cares for kids.

Their menu offers choice and variety so that every child in the family can have their favorite item. They are also aware that absolute price matters. When their average price per meal has drifted above the competition, their overall sales and profits have suffered. The price would not be good value if they did not offer high-quality food in a clean, safe, and welcoming environment. All these factors are designed to create a sense of joy in their cheerful, youthful spirit that is intended to make everyone feel special.

The challenge that the clown, Ronald McDonald, faces is how to appeal to children of all ages. Children's intellectual capacity increases dramatically across childhood. What is funny at one age is ridiculous at another age. Children's perceptions, values, beliefs, and expectations about events become increasingly more sophisticated as their social understanding becomes more involved and complex.

In the earliest years (ages one to three), they are seeking mastery of their sensory and motor development. Pratfalls and body noises are hilarious to them. Being a clown, with the occasional physical overstatement, can be done quickly with a smile and is noticed far more readily by the youngest of those watching their commercials.

The preschool years (ages four to six) are all about play and action. Almost all of Ronald McDonald's actions are centered on play with different combinations of sexes and ages, making the nature of the action more involving to this group, who not only enjoy watching but are also busy internalizing the rules of the game.

Increasingly, in the elementary years (ages seven to eleven), skills of concrete thinking take over. It is here that Ronald's extended use of puns and wordplay are noticed and appreciated.

Teenagers are peer focused, and Ronald is dramatically less relevant. Different advertising has been developed, which focuses on these crucial swing years, when the food is still important but would be ignored if it were portrayed as too babyish.

The motivations of children are as multidimensional as adults, only simpler in language to describe. Adults are looking to grow through self-interested striving that involves learning leadership skills, embracing change, experiencing moments of personal achievement, risking adventures, seeking freedom, and being self-indulgent. For children, all these different motivations can be summed into one word—fun. Fun is not being bored; it is about smiling, not getting frustrated, and experiencing things that give children a sense of mastery and amusement. Ronald is dedicated to fun, with outlandish costumes and gravity-defying and time-shifting high jinks that always revolve around Ronald and his friends having a good time.

Children and adults are also motivated by externalizing the love and respect they have for other people. For adults, this focus on others is quite complex; it relates to being loving, broad-minded, honest, sociable, philanthropic, unselfish, empathetic, kind, and caring. For kids, all these different motivations can be summed by being nice. Being nice is about taking turns, sharing toys, noticing others, and sharing fun.

Balancing the two motivations of being nice and having fun are being brave and serious. For adults, this can be about power and wealth, stature, inner direction, following traditions, and being responsible. For kids, it can be as simple as not crying when things don't go their way or focusing on taking one activity to its completion. These are separate skills, but when exhibited, they open the gates for them to have more fun.

Watch a Ronald McDonald ad, and you will see Ronald having fun, being nice to everyone who is in the commercial, and yet braving new adventures and completing a game. As a clown role model, Ronald is showing the youngest "how to do it," and for the oldest of those, he is appealing to the rewards of his skillful navigation. At times Ronald may seem like a friend, at other times a loving brother or a caring father figure, but he is always the mythical magician. For children, these role models morph as each adult they know who fulfills these roles may at times be fun and childish, stern and directing, loving and kind, and capable of introducing sudden change without explanation.

Ronald McDonald: The Prankster

In the following commercial, Ronald exemplifies many of the motivations we have just described. He begins as the friendly loving dad, instructing his son to throw him the ball and encouraging his efforts. He quickly morphs into the magician as the ball shatters into thousands of playground balls. As he helps the kids navigate the balls, he is the big brother, lovingly tending their fun. He flops into the balls (hopefully the young kids laugh); he absurdly shouts “Play ball!” in a sea of balls (hopefully the preteens laugh). Keeping similar formats makes each more enjoyable, but the variety of jokes, roles, and food offered keeps it all fun.

McDonald's Happy Meal

http://www.youtube.com/watch?v=o9C-v7R14v8

Ronald, "Give me a fast one."

"Thatta boy."

Music: Pops and shatters.

Postman, "Mmmm."

Ronald, "Play ball."

"Anybody seen first base?"

"There's one new toy in every Happy Meal

celebrating Disney's new Animal Kingdom."

"Did somebody say McDonalds?"

Retrieved from OptimumPx, July 30, 2011, "'90s Copmmercials"

Symbols Have Distinctive Voices

If you've been watching the YouTube examples of these ads, you probably will have noted that each character or critter has a distinctive voice-over actor who communicates much about the intended benefit of the product and to whom the product might appeal.

Cadbury's Caramel is a very distinctive product; it has luscious liquid caramel enrobed in thick Cadbury's Chocolate. These two ingredients literally melt and blend in the mouth, providing an indulgent eating experience.

The voice of the rabbit in this commercial communicates 90 percent of the benefit. The voice is sensual, seductive, unhurried, and hypnotic. It certainly captures the floating pink heart of the squirrel!

If only Cadbury could find a way to play the rabbit's siren voice in the corner sweetshop.

Cadbury's Caramel

http://www.youtube.com/watch?v=EjQ5Yw72xtA&playnext=1&list=PL9C409A11AA46AF8C

"Hey Mr. Beaver,

why are you beavering around?"

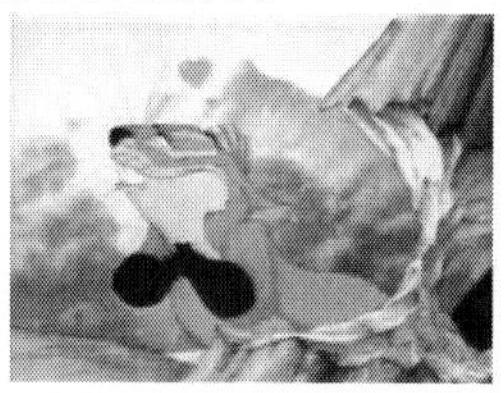

(Hearts popping)

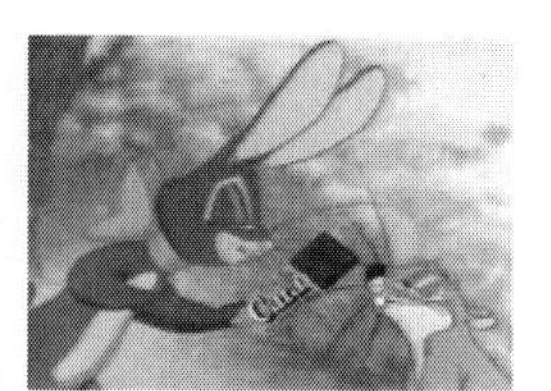

"Haven't you heard of Cadbury's Caramel?

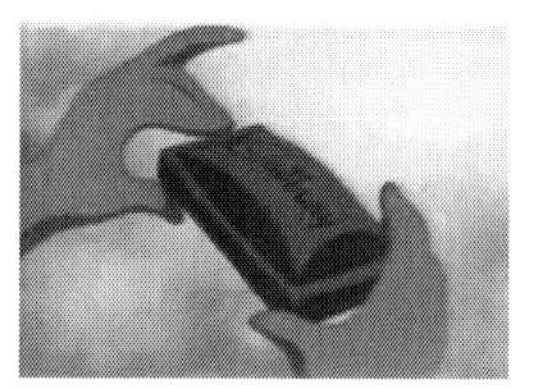

The thick Cadbury's chocolate melts

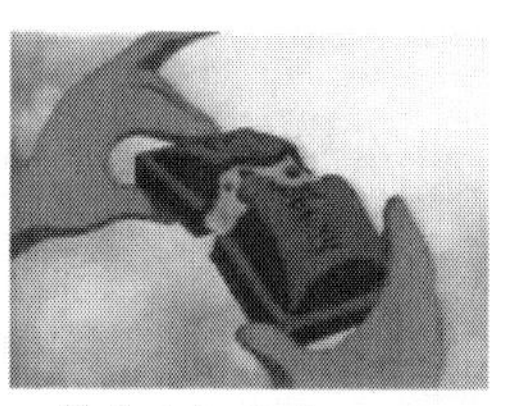

with that dreamy caramel.

You just have to take things really easy."

"Looks like someone else could do with some."

Take it easy with Cadbury's Caramel

Retrieved from FibonacciPrower, July 26, 2011, "Cadbury's Caramel 1980 ad"

Sorry, Charlie

Certainly using a tuna as a symbol for StarKist Tuna might not seem very original, but for twenty years, Charlie the Tuna has been trying to convince StarKist to pick him because of his good taste, only to find out that StarKist wants tuna that tastes good.

This advertising series exemplifies the best of benefit advertising: an involving memorable figure who not only can tell stories but who also personifies the benefit of the brand.

Charlie's image is brought to point-of-sale, his distinctive voice is used on the radio, and the tagline has made a generation of kids named Charles rue the day that their moms didn't name them Robert or William.

StarKist Tuna

http://www.youtube.com/watch?v=VaU5I_UQbXQ

"Charlie?"
"What's that?"
"Art."

"See, guys with good taste dig this stuff."

"How come?"
"Who knows?"

"I think all that good taste confuses them. Now, wait until StarKist sees this!"

"But Charlie, StarKist don't want tuna with good taste. They want tunas that taste good."

"Sorry, Charlie."

"Only good tasting tuna gets to be StarKist. Good tasting 100% Prime Filet."

"Boy, this is good-tasting tuna."

"Get StarKist"
"Note the name, StarKist."

Retrieved from michen2003, July 30, 2011, "'80s Starkist Tuna Commercial"

Launching Brand Varieties: Symbolizing the Brand Benefit

Symbols have been used to provide energy to a brand and as a platform to launch energetic varieties. Tango, Life Savers, and Schlitz Malt Liquor are good examples of products that gained competitive leverage by attaching a symbol of energy and vitality to their brands.

The retail atmosphere changed in the 1990s. Major retailers wanted fewer better-known brands that nonetheless covered the breadth of benefits shoppers desired. This allowed their logistical supply-side focus to ensure minimal out of stocks, maximum pressure on manufacturers ("in or out" puts pressure on keeping prices low), and yet provide the customer with the brands that signal good value. Brand manufacturers responded to this pressure, even going so far as to create centralized retailer-focused managers that threatened the focus on brand management.

Crest and Colgate expanded across tooth care, taking over the benefits that once were associated with single-benefit brands like Ultra Brite, Gleem, Aquafresh, and even mouthwashes and mouth rinse brands. Advil and Tylenol became megabrands that offered a variety of products for a wide range of pain, head cold, and sleep problems.

Keebler faced the challenge of Nabisco's Oreo. Oreo had become the megabrand with the most microvarieties in cookies. You could buy an Oreo with white or dark cookie, white or dark filling, and regular or double-stuffing-sized crème filling. Keebler's advertising symbol of the elves of the hollow tree gave them the platform to offer a variety of different cookies across an even wider range of flavors and textures. Similarly, Charlie the Tuna allowed StarKist to expand across the range of tuna products and expand into tuna lunch products to compete with the strong Kraft brand, Lunchables.

Ronald McDonald gave McDonald's the ability to provide younger McDonald's patrons with a wide assortment of products across a variety of different mealtime offerings.

Chapter Twelve

Brand Stories with a Distinctive Voice

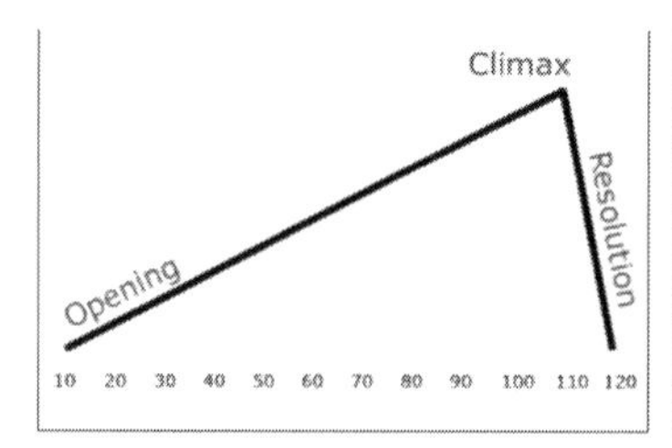

Making Sense of the World

If an advertising insight is going to help someone trust a brand, the person needs to have a rich sense of that brand. This becomes especially important as a brand with many varieties within a category expands to other categories where they may have less perceived competence.

Each person has a larger context in which they put a brand that is tied to the broader needs and wants they have as a person: personal indulgence, obtaining control, providing care, creative outlets, authority figures, comfort, compensation for life's less pleasant requirements, and part of habitual rituals. The brand is not trying to teach but rather acknowledge the broader and more personal trust of where a brand fits into life and fits its symbolic role through consistency of portrayal.

A brand is a bundle of qualities that link to rich associations of deeply felt beliefs. These beliefs have links to the broader culture, connections to social peer groups, truths acted upon in their family, and consistency across time in their lives. A brand has a heritage—a story of where it was created and why and how it has lived. A brand has a personality—a bundle of traits that are epitomized by many people and the celebrities they know. A brand has a distinctive appearance—an outward expectation of consistent looks. A brand is associated with activities that are part of peoples' lives; these events have rich contexts and textures. In net, a brand has a reputation that it has earned, and like any reputation, it has depth, strengths, and limitations. A brand's reputation is a key element of brand trust.

Stories have the advantage of building on familiar traditions and unwritten rules that allow us to place the brand in narrative contexts that give the brand a deeper sense of heritage, personality, and reputation. They serve as extended metaphors and analogies, tools we use in our everyday conversation to help people understand what we mean.

The Brand's Essence

Every commercial would love to share with the potential buyer the brand's essence—the most important feature, the identifying nature of the brand, the one element in all of what a person could know about the brand that would be most important to retain. The essence must be consistent with the entire brand. However, boiling it down into one slogan, one tagline, or one vision often minimizes rather than illuminates the essence. A story, on the other hand, that communicates the brand's essence can be both more simply and more powerfully stated than taglines or set of mission words.

Involving Stories

Like celebrities, a well-told story has the potential to overwhelm the presence of the brand. Could you tell the story without mentioning the category? If the answer is yes, that's a problem. For instance, there is this great commercial of returning veterans walking down a large airport terminal in full combat fatigues. As they walk, someone stands and starts to clap, then others do. Soon the entire group of waiting passengers is applauding. In slow motion, we see the faces of the young soldiers—surprised, proud, pleased, and resolute. The army doesn't sponsor the ad, but as the story is told by one person to another, it's hard to recall what the category was about—memorable, but a problem for the sponsor of the commercial.

Could you tell the story without mentioning the brand? One of the potential problems for involving narratives is that the storyteller does not want to interrupt the flow to show or mention the brand. One charming commercial has a driver going down a back road in a rain shower. Ahead, a clumsy beaver is making his way across the road with a branch. At the last moment, the driver sees the beaver and makes a fast stop, just missing the animal. We see the scene again. This time it is really storming, and just as the driver approaches the same place, a tree falls across the road. He gets out and sees that the water has swamped the road, and as he looks back, the same beaver gives him a nod as if to say, "Back at cha." Great story, but which tires—Firestone, Goodrich, Bridgestone, or Michelin?

The two tests of whether a story can build trust for a specific brand are if it capture your involvement, and if it is personally relevant to the way you use brands in categories in which it completes. The ads that follow show how stories can do both quickly and deliver a deeper, richer, and broader context for the brand.

Involving Stories that the Brand Made Possible

Is the story involving?

Involvement is one of the two essential elements of effective advertising, setting the stage for the personally relevant message.

In this BASF story, the advertiser mixes *M*A*S*H*, the eleven-year TV series, with the appeal of a classic country music genre—a Dear John letter from the girlfriend who is now dating his brother.

Since the story is told on tape, BASF is hoping its message of clear reproduction sings through.

BASF Tapes

http://www.youtube.com/watch?v=CD6S8DZHpG4

Sergeant: "Pierce, Bronchoski, Brown, and Gallager."

Private says as he open cassette in the letter. "From my girl, Shirley. "We're going to be married."

BASF Tape goes into cassette player, beautiful country voice, "Dear John."

Loretta Lynn like voice sings, "How I hate to write..." Shots of patrol enjoying song.

"Dear John,
I must let you know tonight

that my love for you ...

is gone. So I'm sending you this song. Tonight I'm with another. You'll like him, he's your brother.

So goodbye to you forever. Dear John."
BASF Even the bad times sound good

"Play it again, John."

Retrieved from Klwidealz, Nov 5, 2006, "BASF WW2 Dear John TV commercial"

Stories That Charm through Empathy with the Brand Playing a Central Role

One use of a story is to attempt to transfer to a brand a persona that could fit and would enhance the brand but probably does not yet.

United Airlines told wonderful stories about their flight attendants being part of the friendly skies at a time when they were not as friendly as customers hoped they would be. These stories influenced flight attendants to live up to expectations.

The following ad tells the charming story of J. R. Hartley, who first tries to contact many different bookstores himself before using the Yellow Pages to help him with his task.

The burly Yellow Pages catalog that is dropped on your doorstep is not necessarily the friendliest book in your house, but when you recall your personal experiences of saving time, the feeling of it being a true helper increases.

Yellow Pages "J.R. Hartley"

http://www.youtube.com/watch?v=abt6wGtWVX8

"I don't suppose you have a copy of "Fly Fishing" by J.R. Hartley?"

"I'm sorry,
it is rather old,

it's by J.R. Hartley."

Book seller shakes her head and points down the street.

We see a man saying, "No."

"No luck, Jack. Never mind. Why don't you call around?"

Anncr: We don't just help with the nasty things in life like blocked drains. We help with the nice things as well.

"You do! Oh, that's wonderfu
Oh, my name?
It's J.R. Hartley."

Retrieved from shaunokeefe, Sept 13, 2006, "Yellow Pages advert"

Stories That Realistically Have the Brand Inspire a Fading Truth

A story that takes what should be and makes it so can be powerful.

The images of Steve Jobs and Sam Walton being involved in all aspects of their business, ensuring everything rises to their standards, are images we want to believe.

We want to believe in a magical Disney experience, our babies comforted by Huggies, the Germanic excellence of BMW, and the precision of Toyota. Why? Because the stories that have happy endings are the ones we choose to read to our children.

The businessman in this ad speaks about a core set of values we believe in—forthrightness, honesty, a desire to serve, and a responsibility to customers. Because we want it to be true and it is so realistically portrayed, it is a natural next step to transfer our core values to the airline that apparently shares our beliefs.

United Airlines "Speech"

http://www.youtube.com/watch?v=mU2rpcAABbA

"I got a phone call this morning from one of our oldest customers.

He fired us. After 20 years,

said he didn't know us any more. I think I know Why.

We used to do business with a handshake, face to face. Now it's a phone call, a fax.

Well folks. Things have to change. That's why we're going to set out

for a little face to face chat with every customer we have."

"But Ben, that has to be over 200 cities."
"I don't care."

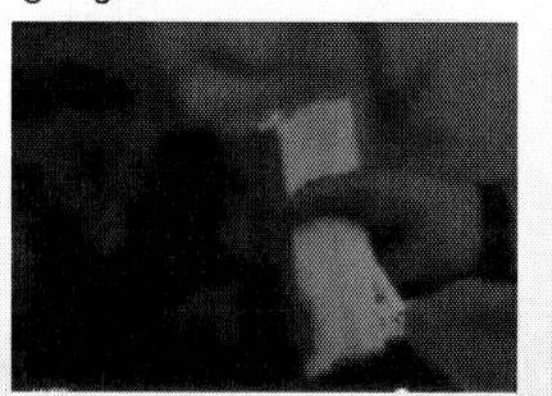

If you are the kind of business that still believes personal deserves more than lip service,

welcome to United. That's the way we've been doing business for over 60 years.

Retrieved from 7LtV, Aug 16, 2010, "7L: United Airlines Commercial 1990 Speech"

McDonald's: Storytelling at Its Best

McDonald's is an iconic brand that illustrates both the richness of a brand and conscious attempts to capture the essence of the brand in reputational advertising that builds trust. The vast majority of impressions by sheer viewings are of specific aspects of McDonald's: the different varieties of hamburgers, fries, breakfast foods, and drinks or the promotions that run for short periods of time featuring both low prices for particular items and "collect for a chance to win" offers. But McDonald's also sponsors ads that are focused on the brand's reputation. In the sixties, they kicked off with the memorable "You Deserve a Break Today."

From 1985 through 1995, a series of McDonald's stories were created. The ad that follows is one from that series. All in the series shared commonalties: music to set up a nostalgic fun background and a timeless scene that "could have happened," which not only uses the McDonald's product and store range as props but also sought to mirror the very essence of the brand.

At McDonald's core are the people who serve you. Their managers are taught how to give respect and recognition so that they pass along that same feeling to their customers. The young crews are constantly learning, developing, and growing personally. This constant progress reflects a different tone than a restaurant that expects its people to do one job at one pay grade and be bossed. One McDonald's ad delightfully showed a sixtyish senior citizen on their first day on the job, an ad that was both sincerely trying to get older people to apply for jobs as it publicly shared their service goals.

Connected to their training goals is a desire to be the fastest, easiest to use, most convenient restaurant that offers choice, variety, and personalization and genuinely cares for kids. In addition, to fulfill their mission, they must be affordable, clean, safe, and inviting. The chain sets the standards for operational excellence and consistency. As people drive across their town or across the country, they are assured they will know and feel comfortable in every McDonald's franchise they visit.

Part of branding are the visual icons that remain a rock upon which to offer different foods, different eating experiences, and appeal to different members of the family. The golden arches and red roof call out their stores, while the bright red-and-yellow packaging of their fries and Happy Meals highlights the food, and the red-striped shirt and yellow jumpsuit outfitting Ronald McDonald shouts fun.

Their ubiquitous locations permit McDonald's to attract half of all quick-service restaurant users every week. It is crucial to have a wide variety on their menu—something for everyone. For a while, McDonald's was so focused on children and teens that it forgot their parents. Offering fresh salads, Starbucks-variety coffees, and desserts helped them recapture the entire family's desire to eat at McDonald's.

Convenience is the necessary, but not sufficient, reason to eat at McDonald's. They have to be fast. Over half their visits are drive-through, so a double-drive through with two ordering monitors was an investment, ensuring their continued speed. Quality has two components: the place (clean, safe, consistent, and dependable) and the food (hot, appetizing, high in both great "mouth feel" and enough protein to satisfy). Value comes both from having some products offered at really low price points, and all products as inexpensive as you could buy, cook, and serve at home.

The key point of differentiation for McDonald's turns out to be the complex blend of heritage, personality, appearance, and activities they support. Other restaurants have made a run at them by framing their differences: Burger King focusing on their made-to-order process and flame broiling, Wendy's nostalgic square meal, KFC "doing chicken right," Taco Bell's cuisine and longer hours of operation.

The essence portrayed in these two ads is the same despite showing two different age groups, different products, using different taglines, and different movies.

McDonald's

http://www.youtube.com/watch?v=OkyxNidbW9w

Dear Mom and Dad,

I'm having a great time here at Camp Nippersing. There is lots to do.

Song, "What I really want to say, it's raining every day.

Maybe I should come on home.

"Nippersingers, we're going to town, for lunch.

Song, "McDonalds and you."

McDonald's and you. Just like old times.

Girl, "Yes the cooking's fine."

Want to learn a song
Duck, duck wantta little,
Duck duck wantta little

Retrieved from VintageTVCommercials, July 30, 2011, "Camp Nippersing Commercial"

In both of these ads, McDonald's shows they know the real life of kids: rainy days at camp and the first day of high school.

In each, the food is the permission to be together, whether it's five rain-coated campers or five goober freshmen. The safe, clean, familiar, welcoming format can be demonstrated rather than claimed; the sharing of the food, the happy bites, and the smiles of the kids ring true rather than forced.

The taglines shift over time as well as the music and the age of the cast, but the essence captured in the story, that it could only be McDonald's, rings true and puts the brand in the most favorable light.

You trust McDonald's to deliver an experience that makes these stories seem like they could happen and feel like they probably do many times a day.

McDonald's

http:/ / www.youtube.com/ watch?v=fZBpKp6r95c&feature=feedrec_grec_index

Welcome to Mt. Clair high school. This year is special because this year this class is challenged.

"Oh. Great."

Song, How come it's so big. Are you going to be late? Why does everyone look older than you?

Where's your pass?
I'm looking for my homeroom.
You need a pass.

How do you go in the right direction. How come you don't know what to do.

"Welcome to Astronomy 2."
"Woops."

By the end of the day you're finding you way. Time to get away to our place.

For the good times, great taste of McDonald's.

"Tomorrow will be better."
"You mean we have to go back?"
Good time, great taste of McDonald's.

Retrieved from garion21, Jan 16, 2007, "McDonalds First Day 1980s Commercial"

Stories You Wish Could Happen

The Twix story that follows shows that you do not have to be literal when the brand is wrapped within a story that carries the drama.

The frequent eaters of Twix are not active old-timers. The appetite appeal of the brand is not reinforced by the "bite and smile" of traditional food ads. Eating a Twix does not cause the actual story or the level of exuberance; the magical ending is in the story.

Rather, the product's personality (quirky, fun, a quick eat) is communicated along with enough product information to let those who have never eaten a Twix know what it would be like.

The story is strong enough that it will be engaging the next few times it is watched, allowing the essence of the brand to have more chances of being connected to the viewer.

Twix

http://www.youtube.com/watch?v=TkscCMUhQq8

Song: You can keep on moving with Twix.

Old Timer "You can zip it high"

"O.K. You can kiss this good-bye."

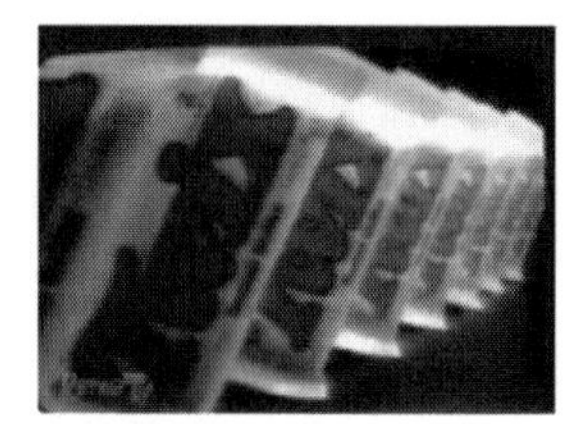

Rounding the bases. Those whipper-snapper bases.

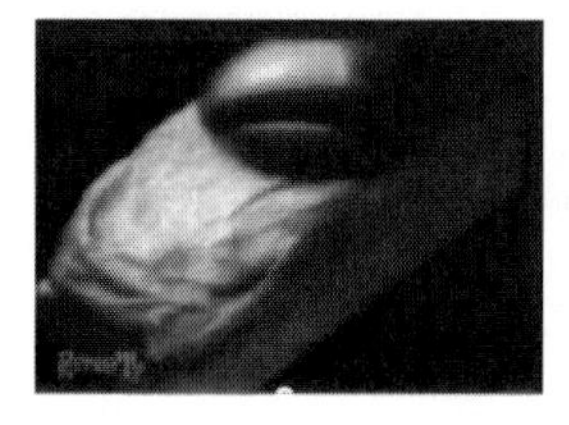

Chocolate peanut-butter satisfaction.

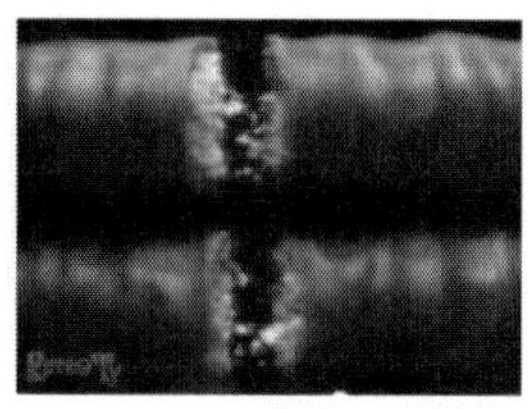

Light crispy cookie lets you stay in the action.

Won't slow you down when you gotta get around.

Trotting on home!

Keep on movin' with Twix.

Retrieved from RetroTy7, July 30, 2011, "1987 – Twix: Old Timers Baseball"

Capturing Heritage, Personality, and Reputation in a Story

This final story is short and sweet, telling about the new generation of Smucker's who will be taking over the family business in Orrville, Ohio.

Smucker's has had the same simple graphics, high quality, and sweet flavors of jam and jellies since everyone who might buy the brand was a child.

Casting the next generation in their small town as kids connects them to their heritage and is an honest portrayal of their different personalities while being consistent with the nostalgic feeling of the brand's reputation.

Most "owners of the company" advertising feels forced. The advertising insight for this ad was that a truthful slice of life from the past would be relevant today and consistent for all that is Smucker's.

Smucker's Jams

http://www.youtube.com/watch?v=o9C-v7R14v8

Music, up and under.

"Better eat your crust, Richard."

"Why?"
"It gives you curly hair"

"If crust would let me hit the ball 50 yards, then I'd eat it."

Kevin and Richard love strawberry jam spread on warm toast.

Now they are the fourth generation of Smuckers making it.

"Now if crust got me As in school, then maybe."

"Nope, curly hair."
"Here, have my curls, Kevin"

For over a hundred years, with a name like Smucker's it has to be good.

Retrieved from OptimumPx, July 26, 2011, "90s Commercials – CBS 1998 Part 2"

Chapter Thirteen

Using Celebrities Wisely

When you wish upon a star, your dreams come true.

—*Pinocchio*, 1940 Disney movie

For many brands, it was a dream come true—an opportunity to back the best golfer of his generation and launch a range of golfing products. After winning three consecutive US amateur titles, at the age of twenty, Tiger Woods left college and entered the pro ranks with a $40-million-dollar contract with Nike. General Motors, American Express, Gillette, Electronic Arts, and Gatorade all piled on with over $100 million a year in fees to buy his endorsement, and all except Nike left quickly when his marriage floundered and his career faltered.

Nike always focused on one aspect of Tiger: his fierce, competitive drive would not allow him to use anything but the brand that would best further his goal of becoming the greatest golfer ever. And through his personal trials, his operations, his change of swing, it was hard to doubt his competitive drive, and that was a halo that Nike could share.

Creating Brand Buzz

When a brand partners with a celebrity, it hopes to quickly create brand buzz among three types of people. First are broadcasters, people who follow, write, and talk about the celebrity: journalists, bloggers, and ultra fans who will share the news of the brand-celebrity connection. Next are the category influentials, people who have source authority; they might be excellent practitioners or knowledgeable, infectious enthusiasts. The ideas of broadcasters and category influentials are picked up by the conversationalists, a mass of people who are interested enough in the category to include it in conversations with their family, friends, and colleagues.

Not all categories have equal amounts of these people in the general population to spread the celebrity buzz. Automobiles, computers, clothing, household appliances, electronics, airlines, music, and telephone companies have armies of people interested in the category who seek out information to share or happily include news in their conversations. On the other hand, most food staples, household products, general types of retailers, tools, and over-the-counter drug products do not have nearly so many, or the expectations that other people will find information about these products interesting. Men and women tend to have quite different categories for which they share information, as do those who are young and those who are older.

Transfer of Affinity for the Celebrity to the Brand

Brand affinity is a combination of acceptance, empathy, respect, understanding, appreciation, and commitment. Outstanding celebrities bring more than just brand buzz; if they are creatively used well, they bring the dimensions of affinity that you feel toward them to the brand. Foremost is trust. Tiger Woods was such a brilliant choice for Nike because you trusted that this intense talented superstar would not trust his career to using inferior clubs. When he boomed 300+ yard drives, you believed, in some small way, that his Nike wood helped make a difference.

Understanding, forgiveness, and appreciation undergird trust. Because we have often seen celebrities in many different roles, a sense is created that we know them, understand they are human with character flaws just like ours, and appreciate the joy, amusement, or feelings we associate with their professional roles. Brands attempt to transfer this depth to their own brand persona.

Whenever a brand uses a celebrity, we all cast ourselves as judge of both the celebrity and the brand's motive. Do we respect their mutual choice to work together? Was the celebrity "bought," or did they choose to work with the brand? Did the brand simply use its economic power to lure the celebrity, or is it making a statement of "whom the brand really is"?

When we trust, appreciate, and respect the brand-celebrity connection, then we can feel empathy and acceptance of the brand. In a real sense, if the celebrity we know is willing to put their good name on the line for the brand, perhaps we should do so too.

Celebrity "Role" Transferred to a Brand

Some ads use the celebrity in their most famous role to tell their brand story. In the early days of television, the celebrity would talk about the product within the show's context (Jack Benny stopping at a Texaco station or Milton Berle talking about a Kraft product). Later, ad campaigns would feature the celebrity in their costume or in a theme centered on their character. For instance, Toshiba sold its television sets around the theme "logically entertaining" with Leonard Nimoy dressed as Spock. Lucille Ball appeared with Desi Arnez to advertise a new Ford convertible with the tagline "Even a woman can drive it."

Barclaycard in the UK not only hired Rowan Atkinson but also gave each ad a mini-movie feel around his cinema personality.

Barclaycard "Rowan Atkinson"

http:/ / www.youtube.com/ watch?v=vsHMGYNhHtI

"Still no answer boss."
"Right, we're going in.

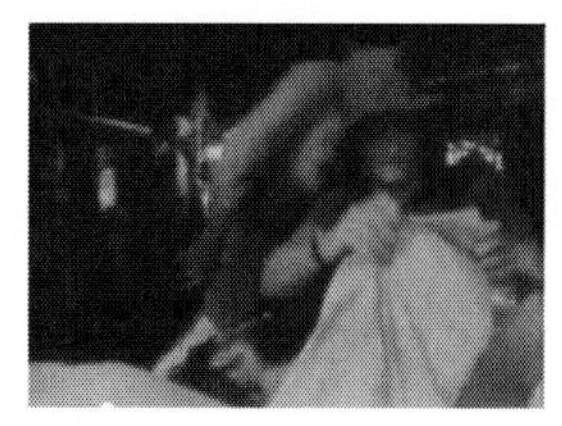

Peter!"
Patient: "Snake bites"

"You loosen his clothing,
I'll get the local doctor.

Blast. Apparently he is
the local doctor.

"That's enough looking.
I'm looking for his Barclaycard."

"His Barclaycard? This
man is in no shape to
go shopping!"

"I'm going to phone them up
For medical advice. Barclay-
Card international rescue.
they can send doctors ..."

"We don't have time, I'm going
to have to locate the wound
and suck out the poison."

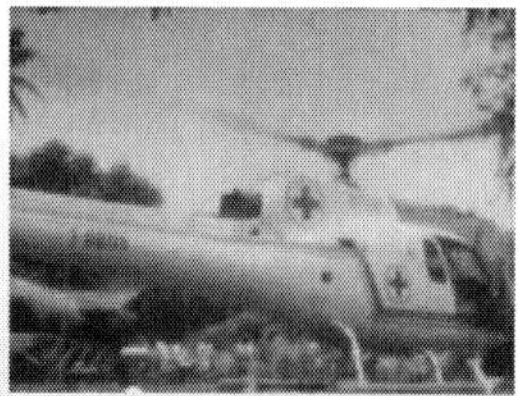

"Ah, maybe your right.
Thank goodness, I guess
my tongue isn't what it used
to be, eh what?"

Retrieved from Soopytwist,April 1, 2008, August 9, 2011,
"Barclaycard ad – Rowan Atkinson the spy"

Celebrity Advertising the Product Because "I Believe in It"

Often the celebrity featured makes a point of explicitly saying that "it's not the money" but the product that led them to advertise it. In the early days of TV, cigarette companies paid movie studios a promotional fee to get their famous stars to grace print ads so that the celebrity in the ad could claim they were not being paid to advertise.

The celebrity/studio would then turn around and influence when the ads would appear, timing them to coincide with the next movie featuring the star.

In this ad for Portland GE Power, Frank Zappa uses his intense personal distrust of all things commercial to promote the brand!

Portland G.E. Power "Frank Zappa"

http://www.youtube.com/watchv=J02NJ6ga4MM&playnext=1&list=PL9BE7E7242F90EB9D

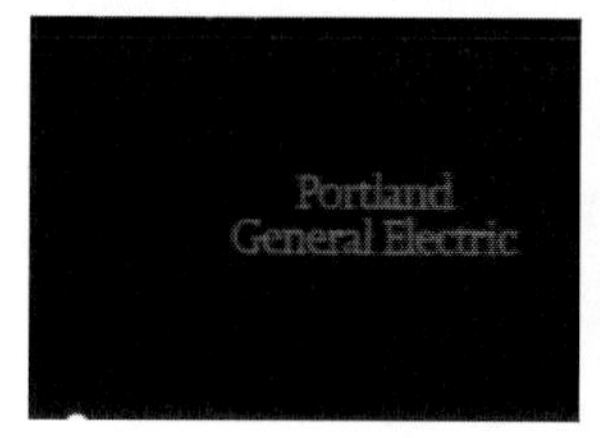

Portland General Electric

offered to pay.

I told them,
"I refuse to sell your product"

They said,
"Great."

In fact, I told them I would tell people to use less of it.

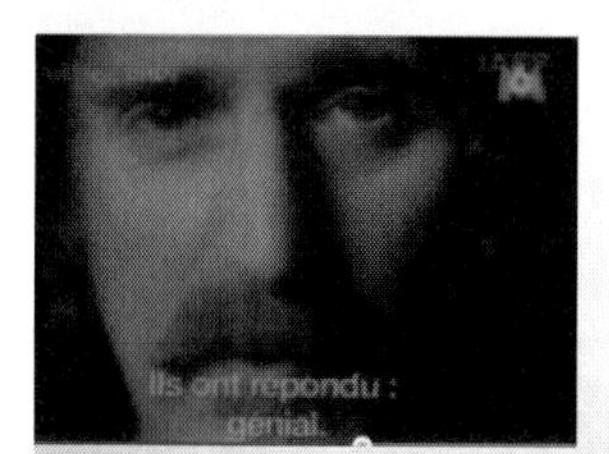

And they said,

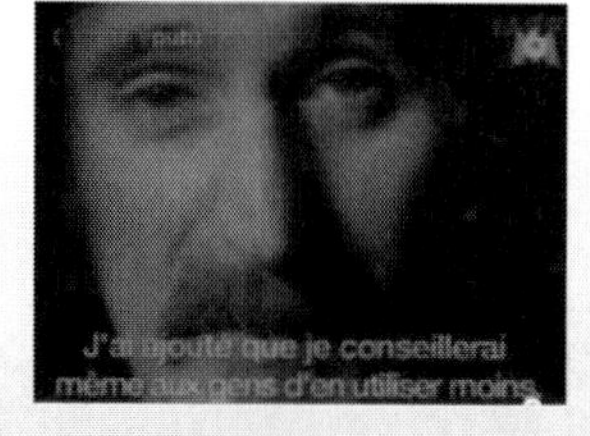

"Perfect."

Retrieved from colonelslog, March 8, 2007, "Frank Zappa Commercial for Portland GE"

Megawatt Endorsements

Like Tiger Woods for Nike, other advertisers used endorsements in a powerful way.

The NFL Super Bowl spot for McDonald's Big Mac was such a pairing. Larry Bird and Michael Jordan were at the peak of their careers, team captains leading their teams to division and world championships in the NBA.

Their on-court rivalry and their friendly off-court personas led to this remarkable spot.

In 2010 when this YouTube spot was put online, it got over one million hits fifteen years after first appearing.

It also sparked a series of similar commercials for McDonald's featuring Charles Barkley, Kobe Bryant, Dwight Howard, LeBron James, and even a Gatorade ad that showed Jordan playing himself one-on-one.

McDonald's: 1994

http:/ / www.youtube.com/ watch?v=ZrUA-BB6Kd8

The Showdown
Larry Bird, "What's in the bag?"

Michael Jordon, "Big Mac, fries."
Larry Bird "Play you for it"

Jordan "You and me for my Big Mac?

"First one to miss watches the other one eat … no dunking."

"One knee."

"Other knee."

"Off the floor, off the scoreboard, no rim."

"Off the 2nd rafter, off the floor, nothing but net."

"Through the window, off the wall, nothing but net."

Retrieved from creamsugar82, July 30, 2011, "Larry Bird vs. Michael Jordon"

Oldsmobile's Failure to Manage in a Changing Automobile Landscape

George Burns, at the tender age of ninety-one, was featured in a 1987 ad praising the ninety-year-old Oldsmobile. Oldsmobile celebrated its ninetieth anniversary at the Michigan State Fairgrounds with a look back as well as a look ahead. The showground was filled with antique Oldsmobiles that had featured innovative engineering firsts: chrome-plated trim, a fully automatic transmission, front-wheel drive, turbo-charged engine, and Rocket V8. Also for special viewing was a look ahead: the first clay model of the ultimate Infinity-Lexus fighter, the Aurora, which was set to be introduced in 1994.

There are two types of change that transform brands and categories. The first is based on innovation that either your company or a rival develops through R&D or worldwide sourcing. Apple's constant product and selling innovations have changed personal computing, music recording, and telephones so far, and dozens of companies—which were not as nimble, capable, and equally innovative—have already failed. Walmart's mastery of logistics changed the look of small town USA first and then devastated mom-and-pop shops that sold food, toys, clothes, and housewares as well as giant retailers like Sears and Kmart.

The second is when the people who buy your products change. Their needs and wants transform; their buying styles and priorities are different. This change is hard to manage in part because it happens unequally. The spurt of national brand consolidation after World War II had been associated with standardization of the buying public: one-income families with union men and newly GI Bill-educated vets having three children and living in the suburbs. As this baby boom moved through the population like a pig in a python, the major brands focused on each new set of products in demand; companies that could efficiently produce these brands thrived. But this changed, and by the early eighties, companies had planning groups that were charting "future shock" type changes: many different household types, segmentation of needs among quite different subgroups in each category, outside shocks of price—oil embargos and foreign wheat shortages driving US food prices higher, technology changes that required constant investment in offices and plants.

GM saw these changes coming. In Europe and Asia, they were competing with companies whose home markets had changed before the United States and had adopted practices of design and engineering that gave them faster time to market, higher quality, lower-priced "cost of change," and a culture that demanded and facilitated exporting to larger world markets.

In 1988, Oldsmobile charged its agency with completely transforming its image. At its peak in 1985, Oldsmobile had sold one million vehicles but had been shifting from unique cars to small modifications of the GM body styles. Oldsmobile's top-selling Cutlass became almost exactly the Chevrolet Monte Carlo, and the Calais was almost exactly the Pontiac Grand Am. You could buy the Chevy or Pontiac or pay $1,500 more and have an Oldsmobile of exactly the same fit, finish, engine, and on-road nonreliability. Sales dropped to 750,000 units.

The agency was tasked with shifting the buyers from those over sixty to the boomers who were flocking in record numbers to the Honda Accord and the Toyota Camry. The "new" Oldsmobile would be positioned to compete with the 1986 opening of Acura, Honda's upscale division, and the 1989 introduction of Lexus, Toyota's upscale division. To do this, in 1990 the initial wave of high-tech electronics was going to be introduced into the Oldsmobile line first—the electronic touchpad information center, higher fidelity sound systems, and computer-controlled fuel injection. However, the bodies of the car would match those of GM sister divisions until 1994.

The following commercial to launch this effort was well received by GM and Oldsmobile. The earthquake that had created the tsunami of change had already happened in Europe and Japan; the tide of new-world cars was literally on drawing boards and in container ships headed for our shores. The saying often heard was "When a steamroller is coming down the road, you have two choices—become the steamroller or be the road."

Oldsmobile Anthem

http:/ / www.youtube.com/ watch?v=-qcsUWMaQAE

Song,
"There's a new wind blowing.

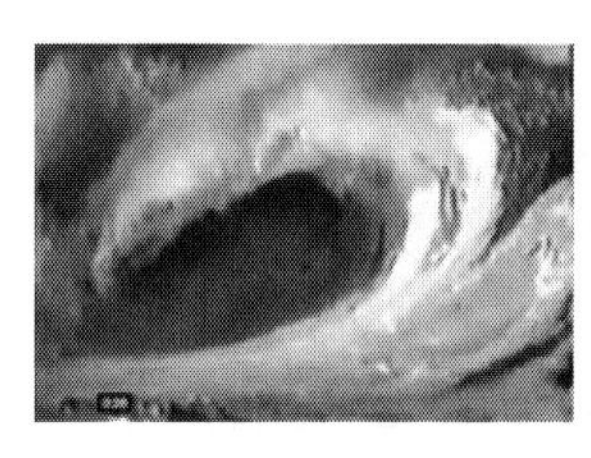

A change is on the way.

Like the sound of distant thunder

bringing on a brand new day.

A free-wheeling feeling

coming down the track.

We aren't waiting till tomorrow and there's no looking back.

This is the new generation of Olds. This is you, this is hot.

This is not your Father's Oldsmobile, this is the new generation of Olds."

Retrieved from bajabusta, August 3, 2011, "Not Your Father's Oldsmobile Launch"

The strategic debate was whether to focus on the only truly new car in 1990, the Oldsmobile Toronado Trofeo, or the entire line with its minor refits. The strategic insight was that like other examples in car history, it would take years to change Olds' image, and therefore, every advertising dollar should be spent on the new image aimed at the new audience: younger import buyers who had never owned an Oldsmobile and, in many cases, never owned a GM car. Chevrolet was tasked with enticing the entry car buyers focused on price and preserving the older base that really wanted to buy an American car.

In fact, this strategic wisdom was not consumer based. GM did not sell to drivers; GM sold to dealers. They did not design their cars based on car clinics of what drivers wanted; GM conducted car clinics to find out what customers liked about the cars GM would sell them. GM did not predict how many customers would buy each model based on customer satisfaction; GM negotiated car line goals with the divisions, car plants, and dealers. The agencies of GM were tasked with selling what GM knew their dealers wanted to sell and focusing on the new features that made the new model somewhat different than the model it replaced.

This Is not Your Father's Oldsmobile; This is the New Generation of Olds

To fulfill this brief, Leo Burnett created one of the most infamous campaigns of all time, a campaign that accelerated the collapse of the brand. Sales went down 20% in the year it was launched and 20% per year for the next three years.

GM initially loved the campaign. They cheerled it as they presented it to their unhappy dealers. They told them to "hang in there," the new line of cars was coming. The Silhouette Mini-Van would finally match the Chrysler and Ford Mini-Vans. The Bravada would be the first sport-utility vehicle with upscale interiors. They were urged to wait for the Aurora, the car with BMW-Mercedes specifications at lower-than-Lexus prices that was only four years away. But the dealers were savvy businessmen and would be hard to convince. Their showrooms were attracting few potential new buyers, and while sales declined, the average age of the Oldsmobile purchaser had advanced to sixty-two. The chances of finding someone aged seventy-five in the showroom were much greater than someone aged forty-five. But many of these dealers now also owned a Japanese or European car dealership. They had sent their hippest best salesmen to those import brands because they knew firsthand that they had created a group wanting the next new Toyota or Volkswagen, not the next GM car.

Celebrity Power

Enter the power of celebrities to excite a dealer community. Each car line would feature a different celebrity and their son or daughter. A new jingle launched the two-minute teaser campaign that ran in late 1989. Typically, every dealer probably saw the full two-minute ad more than any consumer since that lengthy ad was rarely used on TV over the more cost-efficient one-minute or forty-five-second cut down.

For the signature Oldsmobile Cutlass, William Shatner's twenty-six-year-old daughter, Melanie, was one spokeswoman. As an aspiring actress in her own right (she later performed in several sci-fi and horror made-for-TV shows), she was an engaging presence. She said that since her father drove the starship *Enterprise* on *Star Trek*, it was only natural that she drove around in something space-age totally redesigned for the future.

In another spot, to the *Twilight Zone* music intro, Rod Serling's daughter, Jodi, told the audience that the new Cutlass was leaving all the costly imports "here in the *Twilight Zone*." Lee Starr also said the Cutlass Supreme was "a real scream," and its "Fab Four doors" made it a real family car, and it even had her dad, Ringo, singing, "This is the new generation of Olds."

The following ad is for the Toronado Trofeo. The two-door, front-wheel-drive car featured all the new electronic attributes, plus was the first GM car to have the new FE-3 suspension, which tuned the car to a European feel. It featured the daughter of James Bond star, Roger Moore.

Toronado Trofeo: 1990

http://www.youtube.com/watch?v=Wnb2rxrJ35U&feature=related

Villain, "Do what you want with the girl ... I want the car."

"My father's Moore, Roger Moore.

Dad is not the only one that would like to get their hands on my new Olds Trofeo

It's precisely the kind of sophisticated technology

he's always relied upon.

A visual information center,

anti-lock brakes, FE-3 suspension.

It's everything he's dreamed a car could be."

This is not your father's Oldsmobile.
This is the new generation of Olds.

Retrieved from bajabusta, May 20, 2010, "1989 Oldsmobile Toronado Trofeo Ad"

Each subbrand picked celebrities they thought would best represent their image. The Silhouette van featured Josh Saviano, the nerdy sidekick of Fred Savage in the then popular TV show *Wonder Years*. The "awkward teen in the backseat" persona of Josh was used in the ad.

The Cutlass Calais chose a slightly different way to feature "Not Your Father's Oldsmobile." Pop Eddon, 102 years young, worried about what his son, Joe Junior, would be doing in such a sporty car. Then "Junior" is shown skidding through a turn at the spunky age of seventy-four.

Buzz for the Campaign: Irony Magnified

The campaign theme instantly entered the public's lingo, becoming one of the one hundred most memorable advertising lines in history, according to Buzzle.com (along with "All the news that's fit to print," "Because you're worth it," "Good to the last drop," "Let your fingers do the walking," and "Do you . . . Yahoo?").

However, it was instantly the butt of comedy jokes. One said "Ads always tell you exactly the opposite of what they are really thinking. If the ad says, 'This is not your father's Oldsmobile,' the advertiser is desperately concerned that it appeals primarily to old farts like your father." In explaining the opening of the new Chevy plant to make the Chevy Sonic with 40 percent fewer factory workers per car, the plant manager said, "This is not your father's Oldsmobile plant."

European and Japanese import aficionados did go to the Oldsmobile showroom in record numbers. In the first six months of the campaign, total visits to the showroom climbed dramatically but, seeing Buick, Chevrolet, and Pontiac look-alikes, walked away without buying. Their trust in Oldsmobile was low, and their doubts were confirmed by their showroom visits.

Older people who had bought GM cars all their lives had their trust for the Oldsmobile brand shaken. They believed the brand and their type of large comfortable cars was gone. They did not venture into the showrooms to see that the Oldsmobile 88 still delivered the room, soft ride, and comfort they desired. Sales dropped.

A new campaign was developed, which focused on the virtues of the cars Oldsmobile was actually trying to sell, but it was too late. GM brutally learned that trying to change products, meet new consumer needs, and compete with new competition in the middle of a stream is incredibly difficult.

George Burns, who had created such an interesting commercial for Oldsmobile at age ninety-one, lived to be a hundred, but the Oldsmobile brand died in 1994 at the age of ninety-six—a victim of the loss of brand trust.

Matching the Personality of the Brand to the Personality of the Celebrity

Cadbury Dairy Milk's signature chocolate bar comes in a two-hundred-gram bar of thick milk chocolate that is primarily bought in the UK by mums.

Research indicated that they only sometimes shared the bar with their kids—that in fact it was a lovely indulgence that often stayed in their bedroom to be enjoyed privately.

However, the image of Cilla Black merrily singing on a Blackpool bus to students and young women fit the brand perfectly.

When the harried housewife added the bar to her groceries at the small corner market, she and her neighbor in the checkout line could share the joys of self-sacrificial motherhood. That glow would stay until the thick chocolate coated her mouth and sweetly satisfied her cravings.

Cadbury Dairy Milk: UK 1978

Kids, "Hello Cilla."

Cilla sings, "Oh no sir, nothing taste nicer than Cadbury Dairy Milk."

Cilla, "Lovely isn't it."
Girl "Mmmm"

Cilla sings, "As anyone can see

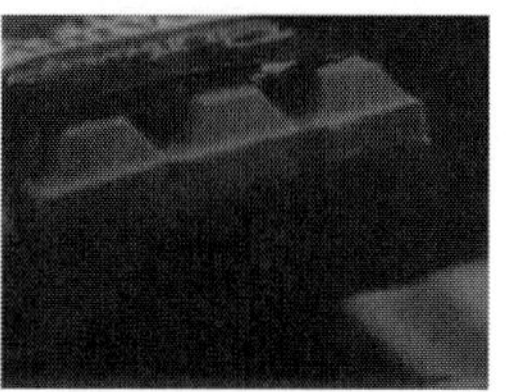

every bar is chunky."

Teen, "Magic."
Teen, "Yeah."

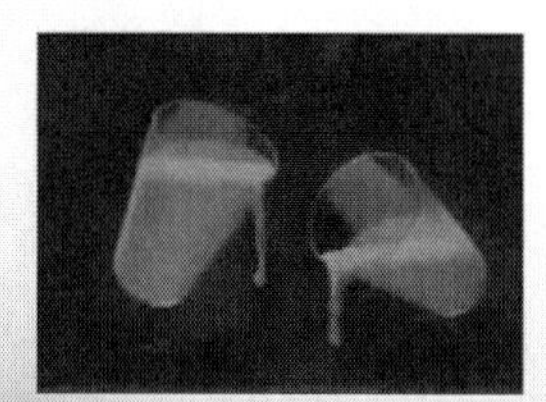

Anncr: That's because there is a glass and a half of full cream milk in every half pound.

Cilla sings, "That's why sir, nothing tastes nicer than Cadbury Dairy Milk."

All sing, "Than Cadbury Dairy Milk."

http://www.youtube.com/watch?v=UAoyeb2dXPs
Retrieved NinaOPerez, July 26, 2011, "Cadbury Dairy Milk Cilla Black, 1978-UK Advert")

Relevance and Involvement When the Right Celebrity Only has to Be Who They Are

British Paints successfully wed themselves to a perfect personality when Rolf Harris came aboard.

Rolf was known as a successful painter, musician, and composer when he began advertising for the British Paints line of household interior and exterior paints. He starred in British TV programs on which he drew the characters in his distinctive style. He wrote and performed the famous song “Tie Me Kangaroo Down, Sport.”

On the serious side, he painted an official portrait of Queen Elizabeth II.

His commercials for British Paints always allowed him to make exaggerated puns, show off the latest British Paints innovation, and entertain the audience. Behind this marketing, British Paints became the number one brand of paints in Australia.

British Paints, Rolf Harris

http://www.youtube.com/watch?v=S-qbdxaADhQ

It's worth going to a bit trouble to give your house year round protection

with British Paints, 4-Seasons, of course.

It stands out as a shining example.

In the conditions you get here, a paint has to be tough to survive.

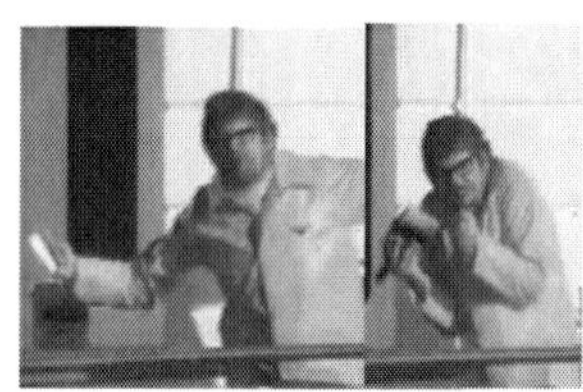

And because 4-Seasons expands in the heat and shrinks in the cold.

it hangs on in weather that would leave most exterior paints all at sea.

Brushes and rollers just wash out in water.

4-Seasons All Seasons. When it comes to out-weathering weather, it really shines.

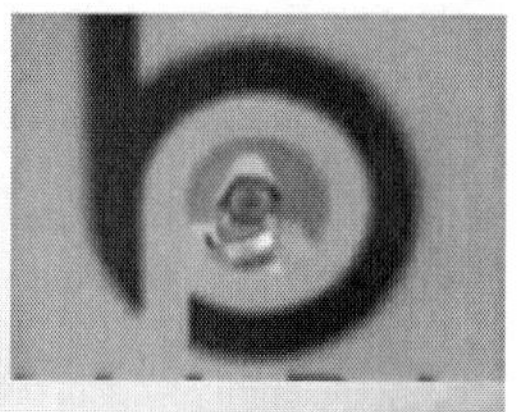

"Trust British Paints?" (Drums on top of can.) "Sure can!"

Retrieved from tramman82mk2, July 26, 2011, "British Paints 1984")

"It Was Twenty Years Ago Today": The Mini and Twiggy

Twiggy and the Austin Mini had two things that matched: both became famous during the rockin' sixties, and both were still looking pretty good in 1980.

This artful campaign was part of a major effort that continued to reinvent the Mini, giving it one last shot before it was scrapped by Austin-Rover in early 1980.

The campaign was a tremendous success. The distinct brand ethos, without being substantially changed, survived, thrived, and was updated by BMW when they bought Leyland.

Austin Mini: UK 1980

http://www.youtube.com/watch?v=ApZLK7Xi5R4&playnext=1&list=PL4E6FFD85CC1CC8EB

60s song under.
Scene of 1980 Twiggy coming out of restaurant

Mature Twiggy sees 60s Mini at the curb.

Picture of 60's Twiggy in black and white standing next to same mini

Mature Twiggy comes wandering down to look at the Mini.

Cut back to 60s ad with Twiggy in "roomy" back seat!

Pictures of Carnaby St., Beatles.

Still in black and white, Peter Sellers, cut of Mini inside train station and Twiggy on model runway.

Twiggy gets in Town Car and looks back at Mini parked by the road.

Drives by billboard featuring new Mini Campaign.

Retrieved from CilkTV1, July 26, 2011, "Twiggy in ad of Mini"

Creating a Brand Around a Celebrity

In 1984, Kellogg was the dominant brand in cereal in Australia, except in the growing area of health brands. No Kellogg health brand held a significant share. The company's image was good taste but not good health.

Rather than invent a healthy brand name to launch a new product, Kellogg built a brand around the celebrity status of the Australian Institute of Sports.

The agency contacted Richard Telford, the director of sports sciences, and asked if he could help design a product he could offer to his Olympic-caliber athletes as a healthy choice. He did; Sustain was the result.

The Australian Institute of Sports athletes starred in the ad, including Andrew Gaze (five-time Olympic basketball competitor) and Robert de Castella (Commonwealth Games marathon champion).

The brand succeeded both in sales and in changing Kellogg's nutritional image.

Kellogg's Sustain: Australia 1985

http://www.youtube.com/watch?v=rfb7nmJiQAk

Performance like this takes the sustained energy

that only one cereal was created to give,

Kellogg's Sustain.

Made for the Australian Institute of Sport,

this delicious blend of grains, fruits, nuts, complex carbohydrates,

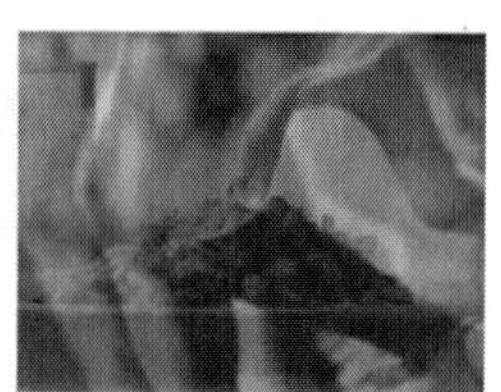

controlled sugar with low salt and fats,

gives you the essential fuel for lasting energy

and better performance. A fact that champions like these, prove every day.

Kellogg's Sustain. Keeps the energy in your day longer.

Retrieved from tapesalvage, July 26, 2011, "Kellogg's Sustain with Robert DeCastella"

Chapter Fourteen

Borrowed Format / Parody
Adopting a Tone and Manner

Tone and Manner

A common requirement of an advertising strategy is tone and manner. This requires the team to consciously consider the desired brand persona, the heritage of the brand, the style of the previous manner, and the sensibilities of the parent company. The desired style influences the color palate of the advertising, the pace of images, and the modernity of the hairstyles and clothes. If the style and manner are not agreed up front, much advertising is rejected—not because of its ability to communicate or embody the strategy or because it will simply disappear in the barrage of images with which it competes; it is rejected because it does not feel appropriate for the brand.

One shortcut has been to use the language of modern culture, dominant TV, and motion picture themes. *Mother Knows Best*, *Miami Vice*, *Star Trek*, *The Sopranos*, and MTV had dramatically more impact on TV advertising than their share of the TV audience would warrant. Secret agents, *Star Wars*, Marilyn Monroe, and Peter Sellers movies equally had huge impact on the styles adopted by advertising. These formats not only instantly communicated the tone and manner of the brand to the audience but also to the brand team.

Some brands simply try to keep current by following "what's hot" trends. Others see in a popular format the opportunity to adopt a persona that fits with their brand and maintain it even after the original series or movie's popularity surges and fades.

The danger for this is the same as for celebrity advertising—that the popularity of the format will dominate the brand, which will be missed or ignored. Not to mention that many of the commercials that try to imitate a particular format do so at their peril with a fraction of the budget and end up looking second best. The other option is to play with the format, to wittily parody or vary the main elements. If the brand's message can be seen as the clever reason for the change, this can work well.

WWII Dramatic Moment

One of the most dramatic movies to come out of WWII was *The Dam Busters*, the true story of an RAF squadron sent on a near-suicide mission to destroy key dams by flying at sixty feet above the water and dropping round bombs that "skip" into the dam, destroying it at its base.

The ad for Carling Black Label takes this tension and relieves it with the watchman on the dam making brilliant and preposterous goalie saves. In the same "stiff upper lip" humor of a Monty Python skit, it is wonderfully entertaining.

The goal of the ad was undoubtedly to get guys in the bar to laugh and order a round. In Britain, perhaps even more than the United States, a tradition of carefully crafted TV ads is appreciated as part of a brand's image of quality.

Carling Black Label

http://www.youtube.com/watch?v=iVSBtivbUs4

World War II bomber, in-flight sounds.

Lone German sentry eats his sandwich and walks along an important dam.

Bombardier focuses on upcoming dam.

He releases the round bomb that skips along the lake ready to crash into dam.

Sentry takes a goalie position and makes a great save.

Bomber releases several more bouncing bombs.

Sentry makes outstanding saves.

English bomber, "I bet he drinks Carling Black Label."

Anncr: "Your best bet for fuller flavor."

Retrieved from john23582, May 18, 2008, "Carling Black Label Dambusters"

Parody of parody

After two decades as a character actor in dramatic films and TV shows, Leslie Nielsen starred in parodies of various movie formats. His trademark was a deadpan reaction to chaos happening around him and verbal puns.

Red Rock Cider used this parody style to parody parody movies.

In beer advertising, there is a whole suite of campaigns that attempt to gain talk value. This ad goes straight for the funny bone and yet also allows the actor, in character, to deliver their *permission to believe*—"less gassy and no aftertaste."

Red Rock Cider "Fraud Squad"

hhttp:/ / www.youtube.com/ watch?
v=TmhwTxosYU4&playnext=1&list=PLE185CB356D9B7AFF

Fraud Squad

Tonight's episode.

The Secret Assignment.

Leslie Nielsen, "I'm going to the bar, All. Cover me."

The man playing pool misses his shot and falls in the pool.

"What can I get you?"
"Screwdriver."
He tightens up his chair.

"Anything to drink?"
"Cider."
"What's that?"
"Just cider."

"This isn't just cider, it's Red Rock Cider. You see it's less gassy, with no aftertaste. It's a different type of cider."

"Book her, Al."

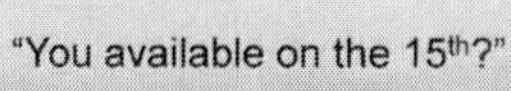

"You available on the 15th?"

Red Rock Cider.
It's not red and there's no rocks in it.

Retrieved from dante314159, Feb 18 2007,, "Red Rock Cider – Fraud Squad!"

In the Style of the Director

Not only the movies but also the styles of famous film directors are often imitated in advertisements. In this commercial, Australian Gas Light parody Alfred Hitchcock and his famous *Psycho* shower scene.

This commercial attempts to work at several levels. Of course, being an ad for installing instant hot shower water systems makes the connection obvious and perhaps even relevant.

AGL has the task of getting potential customers to install heating and hot water systems in the summer before their very short winter season. It is akin to getting people to buy flu medicine before the flu season starts—challenging.

Therefore, they were ready to experiment with usual formats to not only grab attention but also invite action.

AGL: Australia

http://www.youtube.com/watch?v=8izgEXFd-BE&playnext=1&list=PL6ADB580F08D81721

Hitchcock looking man under umbrella, "Good evening. Tonight a little tale about heading into hot water.

Our heroine, Evelyn, in all other aspects an admirable woman,

had one little weakness, hot showers.

Long, languishing hot showers.

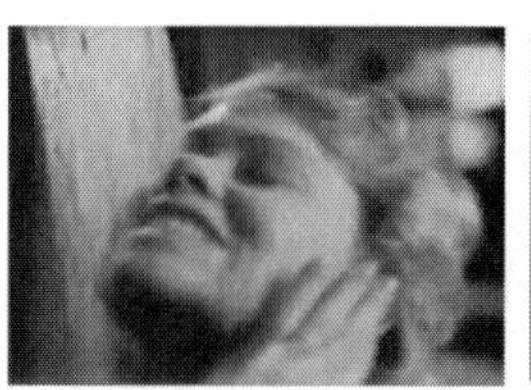

And before she had gas hot water, there were times when she couldn't help feeling her energy bills were creeping up

on her."
Husband, "Another long shower, is it?"
"Tony!" Husband "Sorry."

Tony, "Anyway, now that we have gas hot water our bills are a lot more reasonable."

Hitchcock, "If you have the gas on and install gas storage hot water, you qualify for bulk rates."

Wife: "That's a relief. The one before was murder!" Anncr, "Bulk rate gas. The more you use, the less you pay."

Retrieved from GrubcoTV3, July 26, 2011, Natural Gas (AGL) commercial {1982}

Adopting a Format That Becomes the Image of the Brand

When the man in black "all because the lady loves Milk Tray" series started, James Bond was the very popular novel and movie sensation. The lavish production values on what was a commonly priced box of chocolates set the brand apart.

The actors playing James Bond changed every few years, and the movies became less popular, but the man in black still raced ahead of snow avalanches, parachuted off swinging ski gondolas, dived off cliffs into shark-infested waters, and "all because the lady loves Milk Tray."

Cadbury's Milk Tray

http:/ / www.youtube.com/ watch?v=n1pg1zpNgB0

Man in shadows on a cliff overlooking the bay. James Bond music swells.

Long shot of yacht.

Man dives into sea next to the anchored yacht.

Patrolling white shark swims menacingly close.

Man scampers on board and enters the bedroom down below.

He takes a box of Milk Tray out of the briefcase and lays it on the bed.

Lays a card on the box, all white with a picture of the man in black.

Man sees the shark, and puts a knife between his teeth as he jumps.

Anncr "And all because the lady loves Milk Tray."

Retrieved allads, July 26, 2011, "Milk Tray"

Imitate Almost Anything That's Familiar

This final borrowed format shows the breadth of what is possible to imitate.

Here it is not a particular movie or TV series that is copied but a whole gamut of Broadway-Las Vegas-Paris nightclub song-and-dance lines. From Jackie Gleason's June Taylor dancers, to Esther Williams's aqua-musicals, to the actual shows in major European cities, these dancers are familiar to most.

Austin takes advantage of the full scope—lively music and dancing, clever lyrics, and using the entire chorus line sitting inside the "roomy" car—to convey its message of spaciousness and power.

Austin Morris Allegro

http://www.youtube.com/watch?v=IO_6Ive0kt4

Women Singers & Dancers

"Allegro's got room,

lots and lots of room.

Room for long legs,
plenty of room for fun."

Male Singers & Dancers
"Allegro's got vroom,

Lots and lots of
vroom. Miles and
miles of vrrrooom."

"Change up to top, Allegro's
got room to spare.

Allegro has room to spare."

Allegro

Retrieved from haribokey, July 26, 2011, "Austin Morris Allegro"

Chapter Fifteen

Summary: Building Brand Trust
Discovering the Advertising Insights behind Great Brands

Volkswagen
Advertising Insights Linking Great Products and Advertising Campaigns

Volkswagen: From the Ruined Factories of WWII Germany, Continuing Today

As the aftermath of Japan's terrible tsunami ravaged the ability of Toyota to supply cars in 2011 and GM continued to stumble after returning from bankruptcy, Volkswagen sales surged ahead to overtake both and become the number one car company in the world. The namesake core brand, VW, was the largest part of this surge. Sales grew on every continent: 18% in North America, 7% in Western Europe (when total sales of cars declined 3%), 32% in Central and Eastern Europe, 3% in South America, 43% in Australia and Southeast Asia, and 23% in China. Volkswagen became the number one-selling car in China.

Over the years of growth, Volkswagen has inspired its agency to take risks, starting at the beginning with "Think small" and continuing on to Gold Cannes Lions winners in each of the past five years. According to the Gunn Report, Volkswagen was the number one performing company in the past five years for winning advertising awards.

I am using the sweep of this worldwide campaign to summarize this book for I've found, in both Volkswagen's company story and their advertising campaigns, the truth of what I have tried to shared: that by illuminating insights, VW has enabled people to trust the brand across time and across international boundaries.

Brand Trust Is the Foundation of Brand Growth

Brands grow by helping people trust in a newly identified need. In 1956 when the "Think small" campaign originated, the need that VW identified was not "inexpensive basic transportation," a need that did not fit the tenor of those times. Rather, it was that a small parking space, a small set of repair bills, and a small insurance bill made big sense.

Brands grow by having each difference in the car be truly perceived as a personal benefit. Volkswagen survived in the era of big cars and big chrome. Every September, the new styles were introduced by dramatizing each feature of the car, one at a time, whether it was the air-cooled engine that did not need antifreeze and could power up after three months under a snow drift or being so dependable that the snowplow guy drives to work in a VW.

Brands grow by trusting that the brand, which offered one benefit in one form, may still be trusted in distinctively different forms. Volkswagen was able to expand beyond the Beetle into four-door cars and vans by retaining the distinctive features of their first model: efficient, great use of space, solidly made, better gas mileage, and high trade-in value. The new Beetle, Golf/Rabbit, Jetta, Passat, and Touareg (crossover SUV) have all been able to remain Volkswagen and successively expand what a VW vehicle can be.

Brands grow by defining their essence. By permitting their agencies to violate the category stereotype of car advertising, Volkswagen has remained consistent, allowing itself to stand outside the norm of all other car communication. They innovated the use of white space and grabbed attention at a time when Detroit filled every printable inch with more and more information about features. While Volkswagen told stories, allowing customers to star in their ads, Detroit pitched cars, remaining focused on chrome flashing in the blazing sun. While Detroit had different agencies develop their print ads, websites, and iPod apps, VW allowed their core agency to expand into each of these specialty advertising areas and literally had them interact with each other.

Brands grow by building the trust to expand into new categories; for Volkswagen, there was one area of the car market that was inconsistent with the VW brand, specifically the luxury segment. Of course, for a car company founded by the Porsche family, the luxury arena is not one that is unattainable, so they have fully developed the ultra-expensive range. People who can afford these brands are certainly aware of the backstage connection. Volkswagen owns Audi, Bentley, Bugatti, Lamborghini, and Porsche. In the case of Porsche, they have such a complex ownership relationship that it has been unclear at times whether Porsche owns VW or vice versa. Like Lexus for Toyota and Infiniti for Nissan, Volkswagen luxury car lines have been very successful for gaining share in the niche of high luxury, high margin, though comparatively smaller volume, vehicles.

Brand Trust Is Built by Resting on Recognizable Truths Connecting People and Brands

Advertising insights need to be revealed in the context of the advertising that offers them. When offered up as statements, advertising insights get nods of agreement. However, when embedded in an advertisement, insights allow the totality of the ad to be registered, and the truth offered about the brand gets filed in the brain with the brand, but in a richer sense than just another brand statement. People are very smart about advertising language and images, and they know they are self-serving. It is advertising insights that link to readily accepted truths, which enable the ad to bypass the cynicism filter and register as relevant to the people who see them.

I'll be sharing a range of insights about Volkswagen in the context of their award-winning advertisements. These insights helped VW build an ongoing brand relationship with the car-buying public, which helped build brand trust. Volkswagen did not violate the trust they built; they did not have quality problems that weren't corrected. VW made the safety of their passengers an important part of car design. They sought to maximize gas and ownership economy. They avoided changes in the car design that might have gotten them short-term sales while forsaking the lifetime value of their car. Trust was a quality that they had to earn and must continue to earn as they do business.

Brand Trust Is about the Integrity of an Honest, Realistic Voice

VW broke into people's consciousness as a brand in 1959 when they introduced the "Think small" campaign. Visually, the campaign was completely different than the feature-filled ads of its era.

Lemon.

This Volkswagen missed the boat.

The chrome strip on the glove compartment is blemished and must be replaced. Chances are you wouldn't have noticed it; Inspector Kurt Kroner did.

There are 3,389 men at our Wolfsburg factory with only one job: to inspect Volkswagens at each stage of production. (3000 Volkswagens are produced daily; there are more inspectors than cars.)

Every shock absorber is tested (spot checking won't do), every windshield is scanned. VWs have been rejected for surface scratches barely visible to the eye.

Final inspection is really something! VW inspectors run each car off the line onto the Funktionsprüfstand (car test stand), tote up 189 check points, gun ahead to the automatic brake stand, and say "no" to one VW out of fifty.

This preoccupation with detail means the VW lasts longer and requires less maintenance, by and large, than other cars. (It also means a used VW depreciates less than any other car.)

We pluck the lemons; you get the plums.

Think small.

Our little car isn't so much of a novelty any more.

A couple of dozen college kids don't try to squeeze inside it.

The guy at the gas station doesn't ask where the gas goes.

Nobody even stares at our shape.

In fact, some people who drive our little flivver don't even think 32 miles to the gallon is going any great guns.

Or using five pints of oil instead of five quarts.

Or never needing anti-freeze.

Or racking up 40,000 miles on a set of tires.

That's because once you get used to some of our economies, you don't even think about them any more.

Except when you squeeze into a small parking spot. Or renew your small insurance. Or pay a small repair bill. Or trade in your old VW for a new one.

Think it over.

The tone of voice of the Volkswagen campaign was as distinctive as the visual.

> Our little car isn't so much of a novelty anymore. A couple of dozen college kids don't try to squeeze inside it. The guy at the gas station doesn't ask where the gas goes. In fact, some people who drive our little flivver don't even think 32 miles to the gallon is going any great guns. Or using five pints of oil instead of five quarts. Or never needing antifreeze.

It wasn't "aw, shucks," but it wasn't hyperbole either. Compare it to the language of the typical car ad of that era. The following was edited from one Chevrolet ad:

> Spanking quintet of wagons to choose from! Beautifully styled inside and out with space to spare, from the luxurious to the rugged. A pleasure to look at—a joy to drive. The rakish dash combines with utility in this sleek model. Only Chevrolet gives you Sweep-Sight vision. Rugged and handsome in *every* detail. Your choice of two new "Blue Flame" 6s or the new "Turbo-Fire" V8. Glide-Ride suspension and outrigger rear springs give new driving ease.

As important as tone of voice is consistency of voice. The copy in the seventies for VW is shown below:

> You need a scorecard to tell the '70 from other years. Or any year from any other year. We still use old-fashioned words like "nifty" and "swell." And we stick to old-fashioned ideas like craftsmanship and dedication and skill. So, for $1839, our thing becomes your thing. And what happens is wild. People treat VWs like something else. They polish them,

> stripe them, and flower them in very far-out ways? Why? We think it's affection, pure and simple. Maybe you thought we were in a rut, maybe we were really in the groove.

And when they introduced the Jetta to the United States, they made it look old and reliable in 1985:

> What good is a car that could make it to the next century, if you can't get past the first payment? It's sporty, roomy and reliable as a VW. We tested it through 3.7 million miles of hell and high water. Jetta. Because a car can't get you to the next city, let alone the next century, if you can't afford the car.

The same tone of voice extends to all their vehicles. Here's copy from the Volkswagen Van in 2009.

> It's unusual to drive the vehicle you were conceived in. Love was everywhere the year you were born. Love on sheepskins, now moth-eaten. Love on thick pink polyester runs, now burned to ashes. Love on beaches, now washed away in countries with new names. Following gurus now turned realtors. Come to think of it, apart from you and the Volkswagen Van, there isn't much left of those years. The Van is 60.

In 2006, when the price of gas in the United States suddenly made gas-efficient cars the rage, VW was able to run this ad—with a straight face.

Volkswagen "Think Small"

http://www.youtube.com/watch?v=qw2rRSLvlO0

This year

just about everyone will
be coming up with
a brand new small car.

So this year

just about everyone will
be telling you about this

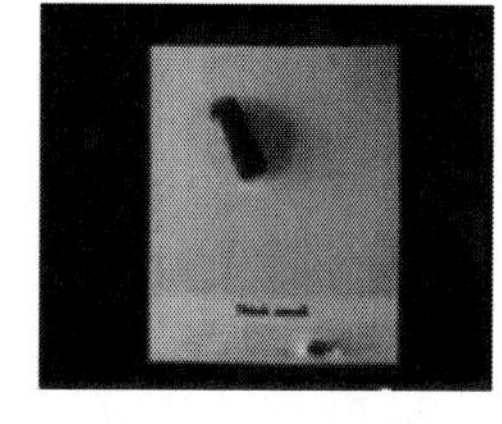

great new idea…to
think small.

It is a great idea.

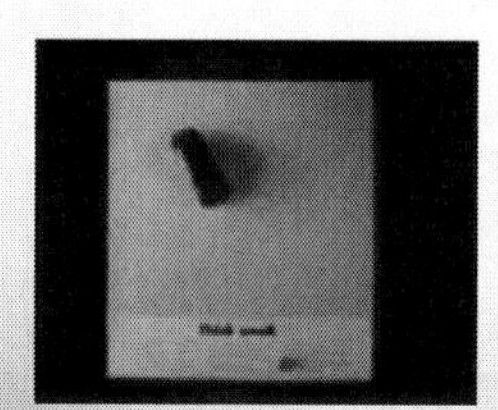

We, at Volkswagen,

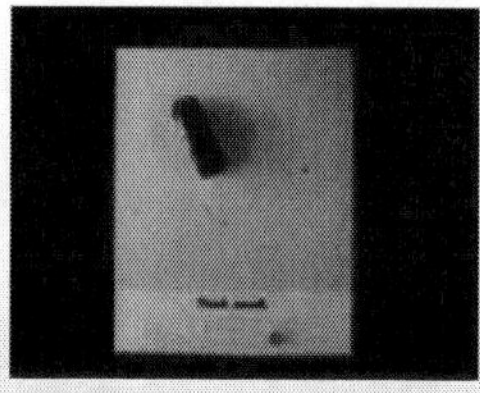

have been working on it

for 21 years.

Retrieved from bettlejuice150, Dec 11, 2006, "Think Small"

By being realistic, VW has set a tone that allows it to morph through the years to be in step with its times yet consistent. One of the challenges of brands that get caught up in the excitement of advertising hyperbole is that the ads quickly become dated, and more importantly, they feel hard to trust.

Building Brand Reputation Builds Brand Trust

VW has not had success with every model it has brought to the United States or with every commercial format it has used. But even when their ads were less successful, their tone of voice and creative instincts were high.

This presenter format ad ran in 1967 for the Volkswagen Fastback Sedan, which did not do well. The look and feel of it seems like so many other car ads—a presenter crawling around the car, showing off the features, using words like *jazzy*, *wall to wall carpeting*, with weasel word comparisons like "most powerful engine *we've* ever made." But that unknown spokesperson is Dustin Hoffman, who would star in the 1967 megahit *The Graduate*. And the tone of voice is pure VW—showing the trunk in the front as well as the back and asking you to seek out the engine.

Volkswagen "Dustin Hoffman"

http://www.youtube.com/watch?v=L3RD-hG4nbc

"If you've never bought a Volkswagen because it wasn't big enough,

Okay. Here's a Volkswagen that's big enough.

The new VW Fastback Sedan. It seats four,

with more room for elbows and legs.

It's pretty jazzy, too. It has an electric clock and wall to wall carpeting.

The fastback also has the most powerful engine we've ever made.

It's air-cooled and goes 27 miles per gallon and that's pretty good for a car whose top speed is 84 miles per hour.

Since we made a VW that's a little roomier on the inside, it's got a trunk where most cars have their motor.

And in the back, where most cars have their trunk, we have... a, er roomy trunk." Come into your VW dealer, he'll show you where the engine is.

Retrieved from delddrive, Sept 13, 2010, "Dustin Hoffman sells a Volkswagen"

This celebrity format ad ran in 1973 at a time when Jimmy Durante was viewed as a national treasure for his wit, vitality, and charm.

So the halo he cast on the VW Beetle was in keeping with its developing brand reputation. In the same manner, having a Vegas star like Durante appear with the Beetle was a way for Jimmy to connect with the youthful fans of the car.

These types of mutually beneficial links are essential to making celebrity endorsements work.

The product story of the surprising amount of room inside the Beetle is played with via Durante's famous "snozolla" and his equally surprising charisma with glamorous Vegas-style women.

Volkswagen "Jimmy Durante"

http://www.youtube.com/watch?v=fwm4DtOr-es

"They finally made a car big enough for Durante.

You know folks, when you are built like me, you can't just get any new car.

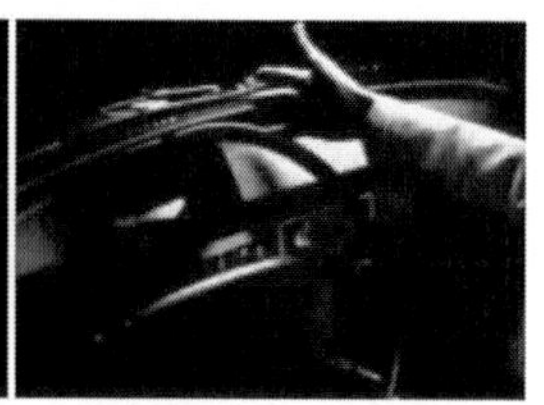

You have to get one with all kinds of extra room,

especially extra breathing room.

for the old snozolla. And plenty of head room, and lots of leg room.

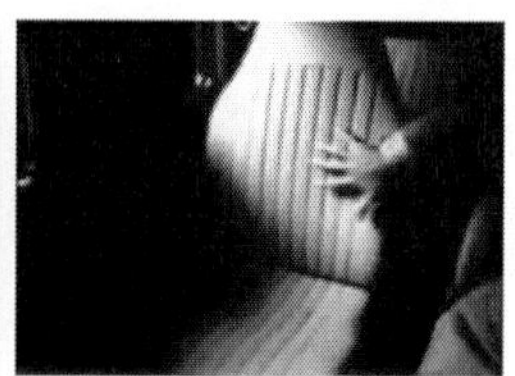

This car also has big bucket seats.

And folks, when I say this car is big enough for Durante,

that also means its big enough for a little companionship. Good night folks. Inka dinka do.

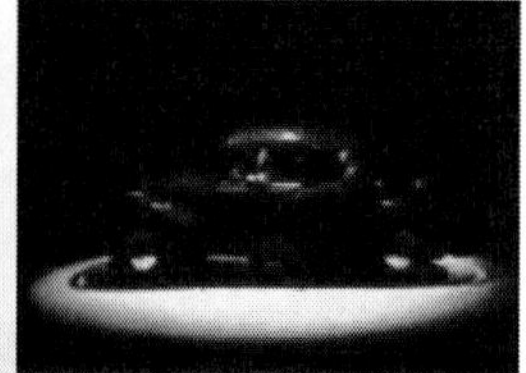

Introducing the all new 1973 Super Beetle. It's so big and comfortable inside, you won't know it's a Volkswagen.

Retrieved from bettlejuice150, Dec 11, 2006, "Classic Beetle with Jimmy Durante"

At the heart of brand reputation has to be a solid product truth that can be linked to brand trust.

In cars, safety is such a truth. Except for Volvo from the seventies through the nineties, no car really owns safety. However, as Volvo became more and more like its corporate owner, Ford, in body styles and safety stance, Volkswagen stepped in for many as the safest car to buy a young driver.

In this ad, Volkswagen uses a benefit story told with sudden and dramatic impact. Two people are discussing a TV ad they saw that showed two guys in an accident and the safety features of their VW, which allowed them to walk away from the crash. Then—*bang*—it happens to them!

Part of brand reputation is an honest voice. Even going so far as having the potential victim talk about seeing the other Volkswagen ad might just have been for shock value, but it gives an authenticity to their message.

Volkswagen "VW Safe Happens"

http://www.youtube.com/watch?v=Jqcdt6A8A54&feature=related

"So they're just driving along, talking about whatever

when "Wham."
"I know, I saw it."

"I think, maybe they went too far."
"I think where they went was real."

"It's just shocking for the sake of shocking."
"Don't you think an accident is always a shock?"

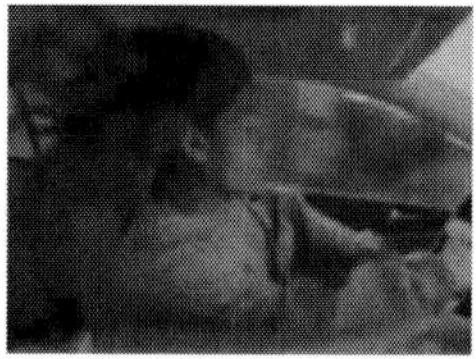

"That's why they call it an accident."
"Yea, well, you're watching TV and the commercial

comes on..."
Sounds of breaks, shattering glass.

Sounds of smash, and skid.

"Oh." Muffled cry of exasperation.

Safe happens.
4 Star side impact.
5 Star front impact.
Consumer Reports

Retrieved from Czechzenski, Feb 9, 2009, "Safe Happens – 2006 Passat Commercial"

Reliable Brands Are Brands You Can Trust

At the heart of brand trust is the promise of brand reliability.

Even in an era of products that you buy today being usurped by the constant pace of innovation, people need the promise that over time, if they want to keep a brand, it will continue to provide the benefits they bought.

Volkswagen has understood this throughout its years of building brand trust. Their ad about the man who drives the snowplow getting to work in a VW was run in every country that snows.

Simple, honest, dramatic—it made for great TV. Not only that, it communicated a story we wanted to tell others about the car we own—a car that starts even in the coldest weather—the air-cooled, "no antifreeze required" VW Beetle.

Volkswagen "Snow Plow"

http://www.youtube.com/watch?v=cUnEbNgHFco

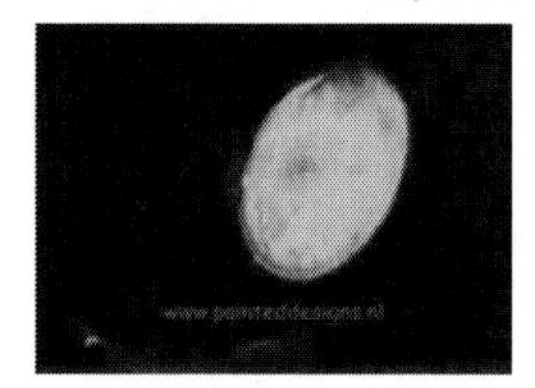

Sound effect: Car starting

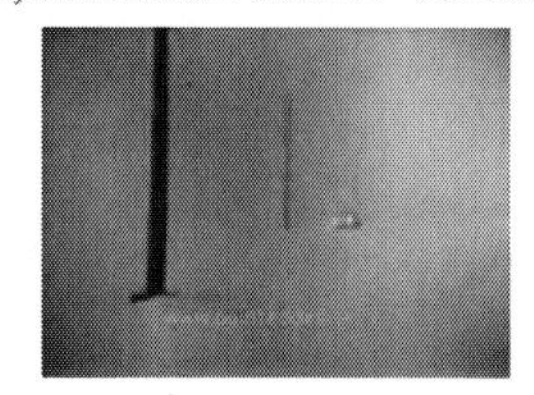

Car driving sounds

Snow crunching sounds

Car driving sounds

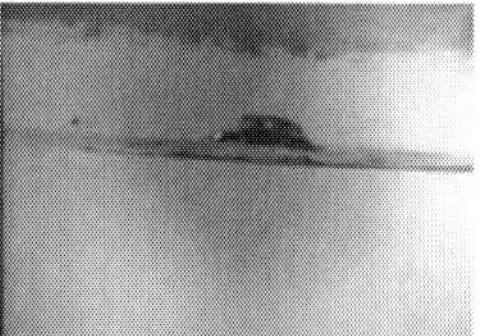

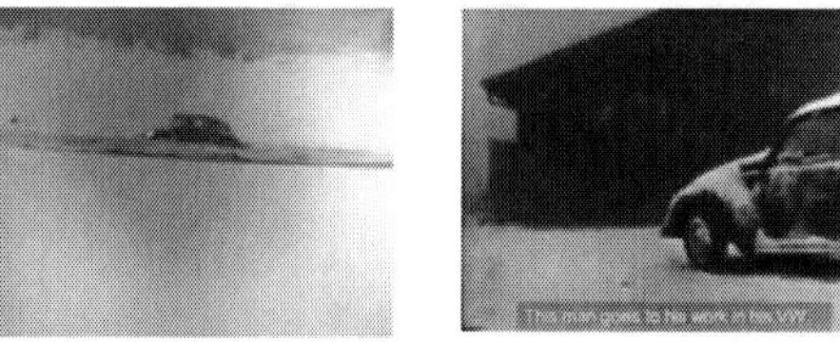

This man goes to his work in his VW.

His work is driving a snow plow.

Next time you go to your work,

why don't you try it using a Volkswagen?"

Retrieved from bettlejuice150, Dec 11, 2006, "Famous VW snow plow"

The same product features that enabled the snowplow story also allowed another even more explicit benefit story called True Story.

This is about the VW Beetle that was abandoned in a snowstorm, found, and driven off by the emergency crews that discovered the car.

Reliability is such a crucial part of brand trust. Reliability is synonymous with consistency, steadfastness, uniformity, stability, and balance.

We have observed that most benefits represent a dynamic balance between extremes of mutually desirable but also mutually exclusive benefits: affordable luxury, sweet and sour, pluck and luck, thoroughly clean but gentle.

Reliability in an era of constant change and world sourcing is incredibly important to brand trust.

Volkswagen "True Story"

http://www.youtube.com/watch?v=mAbGaqSJZrE&feature=related

This is a dramatization of a true story.

On Nov. 28, 1970 a storm developed in the Sierra Nevadas

that was termed the worst ever.

Six months later, when emergency crews were finally able to clear the road,

something strange happened.

A car was found. A Volkswagen buried beneath tons of snow and ice.

But stranger than that. When the crew chief turned the ignition key,

the engine started and he was able to drive away."

The 1974 Volkswagen. Covered by the VW Owner's Security Blanket.

Retrieved from bettlejuice150, Dec 11, 2006, "Vintage VW: a true story!"

One way to build trust is to create powerful demonstrations that show new features in ways that truly communicate the benefit.

This is particularly important when the feature is, in and of itself, quite new and potentially "hard to believe."

In this ad for its new Park Assist feature, you see that the onscreen person in the inset is hand signing what you are hearing.

You might focus on the features, the camera, the side sensors, or the onboard computer, but all the while you see the person in the lower corner signing the message. When the car stops and you realize that the man who was signing was, in fact, the same person who was parking the car, it is one of those extremely effective "aha!" moments.

Volkswagen Tiguan "Translator"

http://www.youtube.com/watch?v=y7GtQ_itsyM

"The Tiguan has always stood out among off-road cars.

And is now the first car in the country to feature park-assist

and a built-in camera.

A revolutionary way to park.

Side-sensors calculate the space,

and the onboard computer manipulated the car so

you can park it like this."

The translator in the insert box unclicks, and you realize that he was the driver, all along.

"Without touching the steering wheel."

Retrieved from nognogueira, July 20, 2011, "Volkswagen Tiguan Commercial"

Continuing on this theme, how do you dramatize that the combination of a large gas tank and incredibly good gas mileage allows you to drive the new Passat Diesel 795 miles between gas station stops?

Of course, you might want to slide over the fact that not every gas station has diesel fuel, so not having to stop too often is not only a benefit but also a necessity.

In this commercial, two guys set off on a great road trip with all the stunning scenic diversity that the west affords—ocean, mountains, and desert grandeur.

But the payoff is when they decide to put a "Learn Spanish" CD into the audio system and arrive at their destination speaking Spanish.

Volkswagen “Vamonos”

http://www.youtube.com/watch?v=SsTqGa2gd0E

“Road trip.”
“Let’s put some music on.”

“Welcome to learning Spanish in the car.”
“You’ve gotta be kidding me.”

“Yea, this is good.”
Driver turns up the radio.

“Dominos”
Both men echo, “Dominos.”

“Gracias.”
Both men echo, “Gracias.”

Background road sounds.

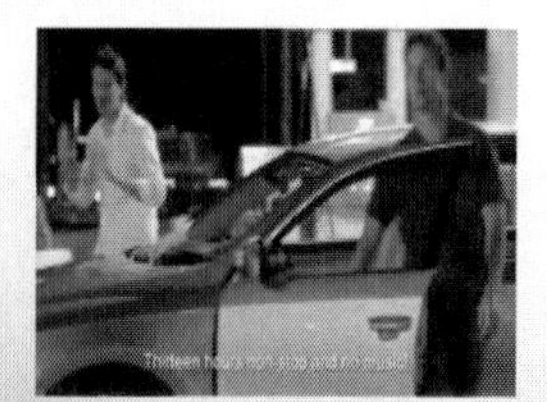

“Trece horas sin parar y sin musica!”
Screen subtitle:
Thirteen hours non-stop and no music!”

“Me compre algunos chips mientras estas alli.”
Screen subtitle:
Buy me some chips while you’re in there.

Get up to 795 miles per tank in the all new Passat TDI Diesel.

Retrieved from Volkswagen, Sep 15, 2011, “2012 Passat Commercial: Vamonos!”

Volkswagen has become remarkably adept at looking at the lives of its customers and understanding how they use and appreciate their car.

The search for real insights about how their products fit into the lives of their owners has given VW advertising, based on these insights, a sense of trusted reliability.

In this ad, people are singing to Elton John's "Rocket Man." To all of us who have done this, whether in the shower, publicly in a karaoke bar, or just singing along in our heads, we have to admit to not *really* knowing the words to familiar songs.

But that has never stopped any of us from barreling ahead, joining in, and singing the wrong words. VW's audio system promises to be so clear that we might actually learn the real words to the songs we love.

Volkswagen “That’s What He Says?”

http://www.youtube.com/watch?v=bWy-LCGDsd8&NR=1

Singing along with Elton John’s “Rocket Man.” “I’m burning up this useless telephone.”

“My hammer’s gone.”

“All alone.”

“Burning up the room with my cheap cologne.”

“…in my musty motorhome.”

“I’m a Rocket man”

“burning out his fuse up here alone.”
“Burning up his fuse up here alone. Ah, I get it.”
“I told you it wasn’t provolone.”

Crystal clear Finder Audio. One of the new premium features

on the all-new Volkswagen Passat.

Retrieved Volkswagon, Sep 15, 2011, “That’s what he says?’

The Brand Values of Volkswagen Have Always Been Unmistakable to and Shared with Like-Minded People

Beginning with the youthful Dustin Hoffman, Volkswagen has maintained an urban, contemporary, jazzy persona that reflected onto its users as cool, nonmaterialistic, and youthful.

This commercial focuses on the double-Dutch urban jump rope song sung by a voice of a young woman. As the young man drives around a city that might well be Milan, London, or New York, a variety of sources spontaneously give him a "clap clap"—a passenger in an expensive sedan, a pedestrian at a crosswalk, an older model Beetle, a policeman on horseback, a retro pimped-up car, a Hell's Angel, and most memorably, a black-and-white dog. Few other cars would evoke this warm, fun, universal approval.

Volkswagen "High Five"

http://www.youtube.com/watch?v=aPiuKjw4Bis

Song, "Three, six, nine
the goose drank wine
the monkey came back
on the street car line.

The line broke,
the monkey got choke,
and they all went to heaven
in the little row boat,

Clap, clap.
Clap, clap.
Clap, clap.
Clap, (pause) clap.

Clap your hands,
pat in on your partner's hands,

Right hand.
Clap clap.
Left thumb. Pat your

partner's left thumb.
Clap clap.

Clap clap.
Left thumb.
Pat your partner's
left thumb, clap clap."

"The all new Beetle.

It's back."
Song resumes and fades,
"Clap Clap.
My mother told me..."

Retrieved from Volkswagen, Sep 6, 2011, "2012 Beetle High Five: Volkswagen"

Volkswagen has attempted to impart its personality to every car it sells.

The control that German engineering gives the driver leads to a sense of confidence while driving that is greater than the exterior looks of the car.

In this funny story, a dog clearly sings out the words of an R&B song as he is riding inside the Polo. Outside at the butchers', in the bank, and on the street, the dog's tail goes down, his leg is visibly shaking, and the song becomes a muffled whimper. Each time he reunites with his owner in the car, the confidence returns and so does the singing.

Interestingly, his owner takes this all for granted, simply enjoying the dog's company.

VW Polo "Singing Dog"

http://www.youtube.com/watch?v=9beQh1yH5uU

R&B song opens, dog starts singing.

"Oh my pad is very messy, and there's whiskers on chin, and ..."

Music continues, but dog sounds are muffled.

We see the dog is shaking, and nervously humming the song.

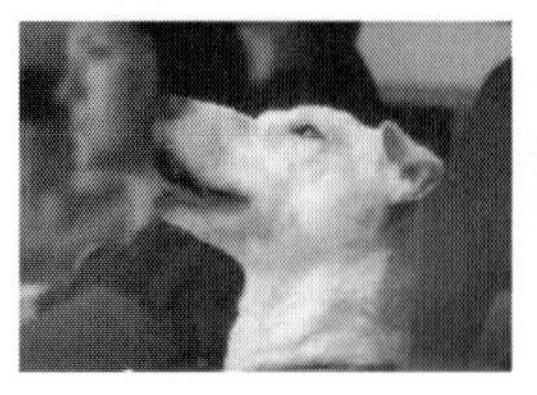

"I ain't got no time for lovin 'cause I'm ..."

Muffled singing and shaking leg.

"Well I'm a man, yes I am,

and I can't help but love you so.

"Well I'm a man and I can't help ... "
song fades as car recedes into distance.

Retrieved from marksautovideos, Mar 3, 2008, "VW Polo Singing Dog ad"

Volkswagen spends a great deal of its commercial time talking about its users' life. This allows VW to tell interesting stories that highlight even the smallest differentiating features of their cars.

The car's features almost become an excuse to talk about their values.

In the following commercial, the future user is born with one oddity—an exceptionally big foot. That big foot is seen as just as perfect as the other by the newborn's parents, regarded as awesome by the kickball buddy, a source of embarrassment in junior high, and managed by using different shoe sizes at the bowling alley. But the "big foot" is in the right place at the right time in the new Jetta, ready and able to elicit a surprising power surge from his VW.

Volkswagen can be urban one moment and suburban the next because its core values are all about humility—a comfortable value set for a car for the masses.

Volkswagen "Big Foot"

http://www.youtube.com/watch?v=tpQWal1lspc&feature=related

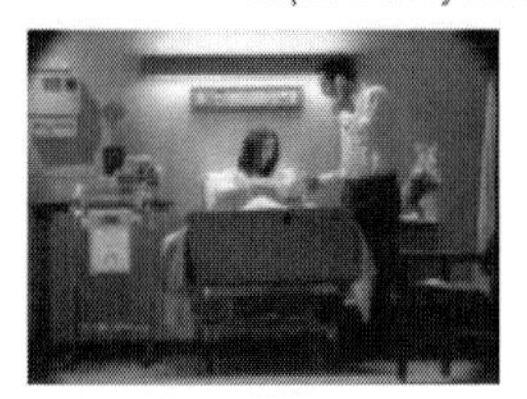

"I'm looking at him just now.

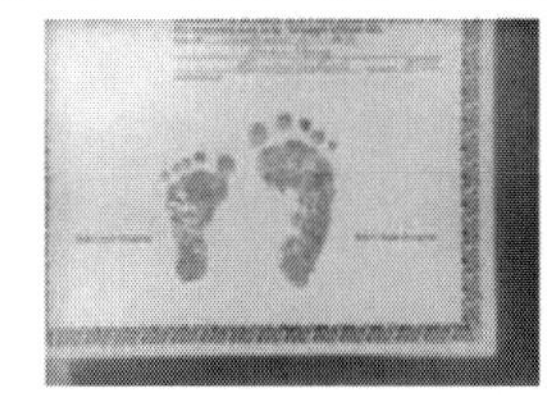

He's perfect."
Shot of birth certificate with one foot imprint much larger.

Boy picks up the kick ball, and sends it out of the playground.

A shy girl and guy exchange glances ...

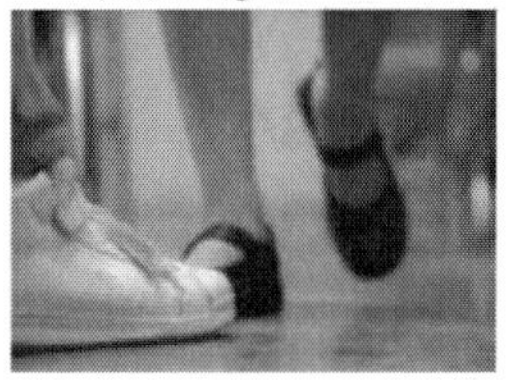

until she trips over his foot.

Guy puts his shoes back after bowling. Size 10 and Size 13.

Same guy gets into his car outside the bowling lanes.

Car sprints away with a skid.

"The new Jetta. For some people, it's a perfect fit.

Retrieved from 682, May 14, 2006, "Jetta – Big Foot Commercial"

This last commercial takes the form of "borrowed format," the *Star Wars* saga.

Here a little boy goes through the house trying to use "the force" to move objects. It doesn't work on the exercise bike, a sleeping dog, the giant washing machine, an obedient doll perched on his bed, or a sandwich that his obliging mom insists he eats. But when his dad comes home, he stands before the Volkswagen Passat, and voilà, the force surprises him by starting the car on command. He couldn't have known that his dad, watching from the kitchen window with his hand on the key fob, remotely started the Jetta at just the right moment for maximum effect.

Perhaps any other car company would have picked a frozen day to remotely start and warm the car, but Volkswagen charms us by showing that it shares the values of its drivers.

Volkswagen “The Force”

http://www.youtube.com/watch?v=mAbGaqSJZrE&feature=related

Star Wars: Darth Vader Theme.

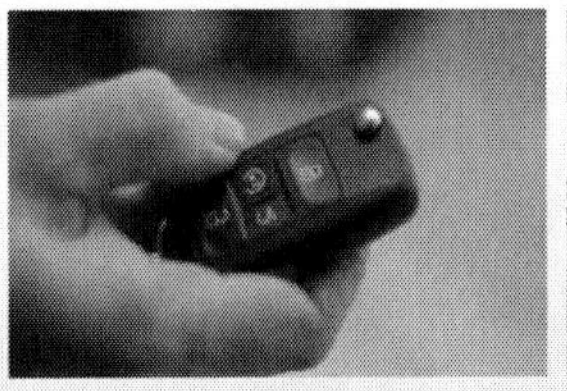

The car switches on, and the young Darth Vader is startled at his power.

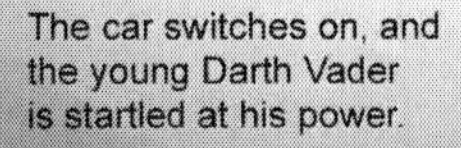

The all-new 2012 Passat.

Retrieved from bettlejuice150, Dec 11, 2006, “Vintage VW: a true story!”

Great Brands with High Trust Reward Their Buyers, Their Shareholders, and the People Who Work for the Company

The bottom line of advertising insights is that they impact the bottom line! Brands that build trust build resilience and can, like Tylenol and Coca-Cola, recover from mistakes. Trusted brands build loyalty, and it is those loyal buyers who provide over 80% of a company's profitable sales.

We've seen that across all the different formats that advertisers use, it's the *insights* connecting brands and people that are the heartbeat of advertising. These insights are the core of why people trust that their brand is and will remain reliable and has the integrity to resonate with their values for the long haul. The brand reputation, which is built on such trust, has the ability to not only span decades but also lifetimes.

INDEX
(commercials)

R

S

T

U

V

W

Y

INDEX
(general)

A

B

C

D

F

G

H

I

K

L

P

S

T

W

Z

Edwards Brothers Malloy
Thorofare, NJ USA
June 5, 2012